Michael Karlberg

D1617103

Constructing Social Reality

An Inquiry into the

Normative Foundations of Social Change

ASSOCIATION FOR
BAHÁ'Í STUDIES
NORTH AMERICA

Constructing Social Reality: An Inquiry into the Normative Foundations of Social Change / Michael Karlberg, author

© 2020 by Association for Bahá'í Studies
34 Copernicus Street
Ottawa, ON
K1N 7K4 Canada
http://bahai-studies.ca

First edition, first printing
Published June 2020
Print ISBN: 978-0-920904-32-9
Ebook ISBN

Cover image: Nautilus shell section by Roberto Atencia Gutierrez
© 123RF.com
Cover design, book design, and typeset by Nilufar Gordon

Constructing Social Reality

An Inquiry into the

Normative Foundations of Social Change

Contents

Table of Figures   vi

Preface   vii

Introduction   1

Chapter 1: Reconciling Truth & Relativity   9

   Reality as Enabling and Constraining Perceptions of Truth   11

   Truths versus Truth Claims   16

   Relative Attunement to Truth   18

   Toward Increasing Attunement   26

   Relative Embodiment of Truth   30

   Toward Increasing Embodiment   40

Chapter 2: Reconciling Knowledge & Power   49

   Conceptualizing Knowledge   50

   Conceptualizing Power   55

   Knowledge, Power, and Justice   61

Chapter 3: Reconciling Science & Religion   65

   The Normative Discourse on Science   69

   The Normative Discourse on Religion   71

Chapter 4: Bahá'í Discourse & Practice   81

   Fostering a Normative Discourse on Religion   82

   Fostering a Culture of Learning   91

   Fostering a Culture of Empowerment   104

Chapter 5: Materialist Frames of Reference   115

   Physicalism   117

   Pragmatism   127

   Proceduralism   136

   Agonism   143

Chapter 6: Looking Forward   153

   Some Ontological Implications   153

   Some Epistemological Implications   174

   Toward a Radical Constructive Program   180

Conclusion   189

Acknowledgements   193

Notes   195

Bibliography   219

Index   237

TABLE OF FIGURES

Figure 1 – Relative perspectives on a complex multifaceted phenomenon   21
Figure 2 – Assessing truth claims about a complex multifaceted phenomenon   22
Figure 3 – Diversifying and deepening insights into a complex multifaceted
                 phenomenon   23
Figure 4 – Integrating diverse insights regarding a complex multifaceted
                 phenomenon   24
Figure 5 – Relative dependence on human agency   36
Figure 6 – Relative embodiment of normative truths in social constructs   37
Figure 7 – Relational and distributive dimensions of power   59
Figure 8 – Expanded analysis of power   60
Figure 9 – Generating oppressive or emancipatory structures of knowledge   105

Preface

Thoughtful observers on all continents are beginning to recognize that the current social order is, in the words of Bahá'u'lláh, "lamentably defective."[1] Humanity cannot continue much longer on its present course. Transformative change has become an existential imperative.

At the 2016 conference of the Association for Bahá'í Studies in Montreal, Farzam Arbab pointed out the need for such change on three levels: the attitudes and behaviors that reflect the interior condition of our hearts and minds, the social structures and institutional arrangements that are external features of our social order, and the systems of knowledge upon which our social order has been constructed and from which many of our attitudes and behaviors derive. Regarding the last of these three levels, Arbab posed the question:

> Is it possible that the intellectual foundations of the present civilization—the ideas, the assumptions, the methods, and the assertions that underpin individual and collective thought—are entirely sound and yet, somehow, give rise to such a defective order? Could it just be that the wrong people have taken hold of sound knowledge and are applying it to create inadequate structures, processes, and behaviors? Should we not also look

for fundamental defects in the knowledge system that defines today's world?[2]

My first book, *Beyond the Culture of Contest*, offers a small contribution toward rethinking the intellectual foundations of Western civilization. In that book, I make a case for rethinking some of the deepest assumptions that have been promulgated in recent centuries regarding human nature, power, and social organization. I demonstrate how the prevailing culture of self-interested competition, which had been built on those assumptions, is unjust, unsustainable, and reflects an impoverished understanding of reality. I examine how the culture of contest is embodied not only in hearts and minds but in social structures and institutions. I look at provisional evidence suggesting humanity is indeed capable of transcending the culture of contest. I explore the paradox of trying to do this through processes of political contestation. What is needed, I argue, are radically non-adversarial approaches to transformative social change.

This current book builds on that earlier work by exploring how we might overcome three deeply ingrained habits of thought that make it difficult to envision such an approach to social change. More specifically, I attempt to reconcile three epistemological tensions that arise in the culture of contest that foster cynicism regarding the possibility of constructing a more peaceful, just, and mutually prosperous social order. These are tensions between truth and relativity, knowledge and power, science and religion. The perennial nature of these long-standing tensions in Western thought suggests there is a problem with the binary way truth and relativity, power and knowledge, science and religion all tend to be conceptualized. I therefore explore ways we can move beyond these binary conceptions to resolve these tensions. In the process, I offer another tentative contribution to the long-term work of laying the intellectual foundations for a new social order.

It should be noted at the outset that this book focuses primarily on overcoming problems and limitations that have arisen within the dominant Western intellectual tradition and that have, to varying degrees, been widely exported through several centuries of Western hegemony. This book does not attempt a global survey of non-Western intellectual traditions, nor of subaltern traditions within the West, and the rich intellectual resources that might be drawn from all such traditions. Nonetheless, this book constitutes an invitation to those who are grounded in myriad non-Western or subaltern intellectual traditions to contribute in these ways.

The one non-Western tradition on which this book does draw extensively is that of the worldwide Bahá'í community, including its foundational texts, emerging intellectual life, and accumulating experience. The book derives, in large part, from my attempts to grasp the profound implications of the vision of Bahá'u'lláh for the transformation of society and to approach this task with academic rigor. In this regard, my thinking has been deeply shaped by the primary texts of the Bahá'í Faith—the writings of Bahá'u'lláh, the interpretations of 'Abdu'l-Bahá and Shoghi Effendi, and the elucidations of the Universal House of Justice—as well as the accumulating practical experience of the Bahá'í community as it learns how to translate the Bahá'í teachings into reality. My thinking has also been shaped by insights found in the written works of Farzam Arbab and Paul Lample, who have helped bring the community's learning into focus.[3] In addition, I have drawn many insights from conversations and collaborations with Todd Smith, whose doctoral work opened new vistas in Bahá'í-inspired epistemology, and from many others too numerous to list here.[4]

The line of reasoning developed in this book attempts to build on these sources of insight while welcoming further inquiry into a set of questions that have significant implications for the future of humanity. Toward this end, a note about the style and approach of the book is in order. This book is not written as a conventional argument attempting to prove a thesis through an exhaustive series of justifications. Rather, it is written as an invitation to begin exploring the fruitfulness of a fresh set of hypotheses. As such, I do not attempt to engage or address every possible criticism. Nor do I frame my line of reasoning by invoking all the classificatory terminology commonly used to describe competing schools of epistemological thought. I touch on that vocabulary and those traditions lightly to illustrate various points as my line of reasoning unfolds. Ultimately, however, I am suggesting the need to transcend the constraints of such vocabulary and the limitations of such traditions. I am trying to clear some of the cobwebs.

This book therefore invites the reader to consider, with an open mind, the intuitive premise that there are foundational normative truths—what some might call moral or spiritual truths—that enable and constrain human agency in complex but important ways. Most people alive today accept some version of this premise.[5] The rejection of this premise by skeptical modern intellectuals, operating within a purely materialist framework, departs from a rational and intuitively compelling view that has probably been held, in one form or another, by most of humanity for millennia. That departure is an understandable response to the ways that many religious leaders and institutions have manipulated these spiritual intuitions for corrupt and self-interested gains. Such religious thinkers have spun cobwebs of another sort—irrational superstitions—that also need to be cleared.

It is time to move beyond irrational superstition as well as cynical materialism. Toward that end, this book articulates a set of rational premises about normative truths, and it invites the reader to envision how we might construct a more peaceful, just, and mutually prosperous social order on those foundations. The social order we inhabit today is an engine of human suffering and ecological ruin. It is time to get on with the work of constructing a new one.

Introduction

Humanity cannot continue its present course much longer. Over the past century, we've transformed the conditions of our existence, but we've not yet adapted to these new conditions. Existential threats such as global warming and nuclear conflict, crippling worldwide pandemics, and a host of acute social injustices and ecological disruptions, are awakening us to the need for profound social change.[6]

The complex, global, interconnected nature of these challenges is without historical precedent. We are entering territory for which we have no map. We don't know how to live together on this contracting planet, and we must learn our way forward. In this sense, *learning* implies the purposeful and systematic generation of knowledge that is partly scientific and technological, but also—perhaps primarily—social. We need to generate knowledge about the new social reality we must construct, including how to construct it.

Knowledge of this kind has an intrinsically *normative* dimension. It is not merely descriptive or explanatory. It is also *prescriptive*. It is about how we *ought* to live together if we hope to adapt successfully to the new conditions of our existence. But what does it mean to generate knowledge with a normative dimension? Upon what foundations can such knowledge rest? Are all normative truth claims mere expressions of our subjective preferences, emotional states, or cultural sensibilities? In other words, are all normative claims merely relative? Or is it rational to speak about foundational normative truths—foundational aspects of reality—upon which we can construct a viable social order? If so, how can knowledge about such truths and their application to the betterment of humanity be generated?

Questions about the normative dimensions of social existence reveal unresolved tensions implicit in how many people understand the relationship between truth and relativity. These questions also disclose unresolved tensions regarding the relationship between knowledge and power. In the latter regard, it is widely understood that power and privilege can shape the categories, concepts, and theories developed across the social sciences, including allegedly objective fields such as economics. Power and privilege can even shape the generation of knowledge in the applied natural sciences in domains such as medical, pharmaceutical, and agricultural research. Indeed, the relationship between knowledge and power has been so extensively interrogated in these and other fields that it has led some to adopt the cynical view that all knowledge—or at least all knowledge about social reality—is a mere function of power, privilege, and social position.[7] And yet, if we accept this cynical view, how can the generation of knowledge illumine a path toward a more peaceful, just, and prosperous social order? How can knowledge contribute to human progress at all if those who dominate its generation and dissemination occupy privileged social positions and are motivated by self-interested biases? Is knowledge merely a function of power? These questions take on profound significance at this historical juncture when we face existential global challenges.

In the face of the preceding questions about truth and relativity, and about knowledge and power, some people have adopted cynical or nihilistic world views that offer no route forward. Against this backdrop, *the central thesis of this book is that foundational normative truths exist and human knowledge can, to some degree, become attuned to them. Moreover, the generation of such knowledge and its application to the betterment of humanity need not be corrupted by power and privilege. It is possible, under the right conditions, to learn our way forward toward a more peaceful, just, and mutually prosperous social order. To do this, we need a framework that reconciles truth and relativity, as well as knowledge and power, in rational and constructive ways. This book suggests a logically coherent and empirically tenable way to do this that enables us to move beyond cynical and nihilistic modes of thought and practice.*

Given that this book is being written for a wide audience, I have tried to minimize philosophical jargon. However, it is not possible to eliminate all specialized terminology without sacrificing efficiency and precision. Therefore, before proceeding, I want to comment on how and why I am using some specific terms that will appear throughout the book.

The first of these is the term *normative*. This term can be used in two ways. It is sometimes used descriptively to signify existing social norms, or *the way things are* within a given social context. For instance, we can make the empirical observation that in contemporary American society, it is still a norm that women tend to be paid less than men for the same work. Yet the term *normative* is also used prescriptively, to signify ideal social norms, or *the way things ought to be* within a given social context. For instance, we can make the normative statement that women *ought* to be paid the same as men for the same work.

Throughout this book, I use the term *normative* in the latter way. I thus use the concept of *normative truths* to denote the existence of objective features or properties or governing principles of reality that underlie and inform *the way things ought to be*. Such truths need not be understood as comprehensive or detailed prescriptions for every aspect of social reality in every context. Rather, they can be understood as indeterminate laws, ideals, or principles that ought to inform the construction of diverse social phenomena in culturally and historically contingent ways—much like the laws or principles of physics inform the construction of diverse technologies. Bahá'ís often refer to such truths as *spiritual principles* and, at some points in this book, I will use the terms *normative truths* and *spiritual principles* in an interchangeable manner.

The existence of normative truths is thus an *ontological* premise in favor of which this book argues. *Ontology* is a branch of philosophy dealing with the nature of reality or the nature of existence. *Ontological premises* are premises about the nature of reality or existence. *Ontological foundationalism* refers to the view that reality is characterized by foundational truths, or laws, or properties, or indelible features of existence that exist independently of whether human minds are aware of them and independently of the degree to which we comprehend them. In this sense, *foundational truths* are sometimes referred to as *transcendent truths* because they transcend human comprehension—they transcend all cultural or linguistic efforts to grasp or signify them. In philosophy, the view that foundational or transcendent truths exist independently of human comprehension is often called *realism*. And the view that normative truths exist independent of human thought is called *normative realism* (or *value realism* or *moral realism*).

Although this book asserts the *ontological* premise that normative truths exist, it asserts the *epistemological* premise that human comprehension of such truths will always be relative, limited, and fallible to some degree. *Epistemology* is a branch of philosophy dealing with the nature of knowledge. *Epistemological premises* are premises about the nature of human knowledge and how it can be generated with any degree of confidence. In relation to ontological truths, *epistemological relativism* refers to the view that diverse truth claims can be oriented toward, or attuned to, different aspects of the truth, which can be understood with varying degrees of clarity. Of course, if one assumes there are no ontological truths, then a more extreme form of epistemological relativism follows in which no truth claim has any meaningful connection to truth because truths do not exist. The argument laid out in this book rests on the former, more moderate, version of epistemological relativism for reasons that will be elaborated in the next chapter.

Finally, the concept of *social construction* enables us to recognize that bodies of human knowledge and the social formations they give rise to are created—or constructed—by groups of people operating within shared systems of meanings and values. In other words, it reminds us that social phenomena are constructed through collective human agency, and they can be constructed in different ways. For instance, systems of taxation can be constructed in progressive or regressive ways, depending on the ideas and values that inform their construction. And that process of construction always depends on human agency.

This broad concept of social construction can, however, be understood in different ways, depending on the underlying ontological assumptions at play. If we assume there are no normative truths underlying and informing social reality, then the concept of social construction leads to an extreme relativism in which there is no way to assess or compare the relative merits of different social constructs. Such relativism would mean there are no truths to which we could appeal in struggles to overcome oppressive social norms, and there is thus no ontological basis for the idea of social progress. On the other hand, if we assume there are normative truths underlying and informing social reality—no matter how limited our understanding of them is—then we open the possibility of striving to construct a social reality that embodies normative truths to greater degrees.

This book is premised on the latter concept of social construction for reasons that will also be elaborated in the next chapter.

This latter conception should not be confused, however, with the concept of *social engineering*. Social engineering implies a reliance on privileged forms of alleged expertise applied to the design of social policies and processes intended to achieve objectives determined by elite social groups. Such formulaic, top-down, and frequently self-interested approaches to social change have proven ineffective at best, oppressive at worst. In contrast to social engineering, the concept of social construction used in this book encompasses the possibility of organic and participatory processes of social change, based on the premises alluded to above: that normative truths exist and that we can construct social phenomena that embody them to varying degrees.

These premises, it must be noted, are not universally accepted. Many people reject the possibility of foundational normative truths. But this latter position leads to an impasse—an inability to agree on normative ideals or commitments—which makes it impossible to address the increasingly acute social and environmental challenges now facing humanity. This is because the generation of knowledge about social reality and corresponding efforts to construct a new social reality have, as mentioned, intrinsic normative dimensions. In the absence of normative foundations, it becomes impossible to agree on what constitutes progress or how to pursue it—which is one of the basic problems facing humanity today. This book explores a route out of this impasse and invites others to contribute to this inquiry.

The route considered in this book derives in part from grounded insights that have been systematically generated from the experience of the worldwide Bahá'í community over the past century and a half. This body of experience offers one form of provisional evidence in support of the line of reasoning laid out in this book—evidence that is significant enough that an entire chapter will be devoted to examining it. But that examination will come after the main line of reasoning is laid out.

To make this line of reasoning clear, its core elements are laid out up front, in the first chapter of the book. In that chapter, for the sake of readability, I have minimized entanglements with other scholarly arguments by engaging with them primarily in footnotes.

After the core of my argument is articulated in chapter 1, subsequent chapters that elaborate and extend my argument will more directly address the most relevant scholarly arguments.

It should also be noted at the outset that the argument in this book and skeptical counter-arguments rest on different ontological and epistemological premises that cannot be empirically verified, at least at this stage in history. Equally rational arguments based on equally plausible premises yield different lines of logic that lead to divergent conclusions. Contrasting arguments must be assessed based on their internal coherence and their consistency with the evidence at hand, no matter how provisional that evidence currently is. Readers are therefore invited to assess the argument in this book by these standards and compare them in this way to the arguments of skeptics.

Normative arguments of this kind must, ultimately, be assessed by their fruitfulness as we test them against reality. Do they support human well-being or human flourishing? Do they contribute to the advancement of civilization? Do they offer a viable path forward toward peace, justice, and shared prosperity? Ultimately, the relative fruitfulness of divergent arguments cannot be fully assessed until significant numbers of people commit to them and translate them into social practices on a large scale so that future generations can offer their verdict with the benefit of hindsight. In the meantime, the initial assessment of such arguments—including the arguments of skeptics—requires an element of rational faith in the underlying premises. Therefore, we would do well to ask ourselves: Which argument appears, in advance, to be the most rational, compelling, coherent, and fruitful? Which argument seems to warrant our allegiance and support as we test it against reality? Which arguments lead to hypotheses worth testing?

With these questions in mind, it is important to recognize not only the role that logic and provisional evidence play in the initial assessment of such arguments, but also the role that intuition plays. When faced with a set of equally rational theses founded on equally plausible premises, supported by equally reasonable interpretations of provisional evidence, intuition becomes our interim guide. There is nothing irrational about this. The systematic generation of knowledge has always depended on it. This is true even in the natural sciences, the history of which is laden with commitments to premises that were, at the outset, intuitively attractive and rationally compelling but unprovable.[8]

Finally, the systematic advancement of knowledge and the assessment of divergent arguments require humility and open-mindedness. Rigid dogmatism and intellectual arrogance have no useful role to play in the generation of knowledge because human logic and intuition are both fallible. Both must be tested against reality. The arguments in this book therefore are offered with a spirit of humility and open-mindedness. The reader is invited to engage with them in the same spirit, born out of genuine concern for the betterment of humanity at this critical juncture in history.

Chapter I

Reconciling Truth & Relativity

The introduction to this book asserts that humanity needs to learn its way forward to adapt to conditions of heightened global inter-dependence, that this learning entails the generation and application of knowledge about emerging social phenomena, and that such knowledge has a normative dimension. Whether these assertions seem rational and compelling hinges, in part, on how we understand the relationship between truth and relativity. To appreciate why this seemingly abstract relationship is so relevant to the exigencies of this age, we can begin by thinking about some of its concrete impli-cations. Two examples should suffice.

Consider, first, the issue of global warming or climate change. As climate science matures, it is becoming evident that the impacts of a warming climate, if the process is not quickly halted and ultimately reversed, will be devastating for many populations who bear the least responsibility for it and who can least afford to cope with it.[9] As sea levels rise, hundreds of millions of people living on low-lying islands and coastal plains in some of the world's poorest and least industrialized countries will be displaced. As glaciers disappear, hun-dreds of millions of small farmers who depend on glacial run-off will also be unable to irrigate their crops. As climate-sensitive ter-restrial species experience drastic population declines or extinctions, millions more will be deprived of traditional foods and livelihoods. And as pH-sensitive aquatic species experience drastic population declines or extinctions, further millions will be deprived of foods and livelihoods. Meanwhile, the world's wealthiest populations from the most industrialized countries who bear the greatest responsibility for global warming will be in the best positions to adapt and survive.

What moral obligations, if any, should fall on the shoulders of privileged populations who are most responsible for these looming humanitarian crises? Are there any normative truths upon which such questions can be decided? Or are the answers to these questions merely relative to the values and interests of diverse stakeholders? If we believe the latter, then all normative questions can be decided only by the exercise of power and privilege. If so, global warming is likely to reduce us to the crude dynamics of social Darwinism—the signs of which we can already see clearly in the world today.

Or consider the issue of human rights. The global discourse on human rights ultimately revolves around the issue of whether diverse cultural or religious traditions, along with assertions of unfettered national sovereignty, can be reconciled with the application of any universal standards of human rights. This issue raises challenging questions. For instance, do all children have the right to be free from exploitation? Do they have the right to an education? Do girls have the same rights as boys to develop their latent capacities through education and access to opportunity? Do all individuals have the right to freedom of conscience and belief so long as their beliefs are not harmful to others? Do peaceful minorities have the right to be free from discrimination or violent persecution? Do populations displaced by civil war or natural disasters have a right to resettle in new lands? Do the poor have a right to health care? Or to food? Or to shelter?

If any of these rights exist, upon what normative foundations do they rest? What obligations might the nations of the world have that require them to safeguard or ensure such rights—within their own borders and beyond? Or are human rights mere social constructs that reflect the relative values and beliefs of specific cultures, religious traditions, nations, or social groups? And are global human rights frameworks merely attempts by powerful social groups or nations to impose their values and beliefs on others? If so, by what justification can marginalized social groups struggle to overcome oppression within the context of their own cultures, religious traditions, and nations? Do oppressed groups even have the right to struggle for change? If so, upon what normative foundation does this right rest?

Questions such as these are not merely academic. They are of profound practical concern. Billions of lives depend on how they are answered. Ultimately, the answers to such questions will depend on whether normative truths are "real" or not. Are some normative principles akin, in any way, to other principles that govern reality, such as the principles of physics? If so, might we learn to explore and apply such normative principles to the betterment of the human condition? Or are all normative truth claims merely relative to our subjective preferences, cultural values, or ideological predilections?

REALITY AS ENABLING AND CONSTRAINING PERCEPTIONS OF TRUTH

As a first step in this inquiry, we need to consider what it means to perceive or "know" anything about "reality." As the introductory chapter mentioned, epistemology is the branch of philosophy that explores this question. Associated with the field of epistemology has been a perennial tension over the basic question of whether we can ever know anything about foundational aspects of reality. Richard Rorty describes this as a tension between *vertical* and *horizontal* approaches to knowledge.[10]

Vertical approaches assume that through the right methods, human minds can come to know aspects of reality that exist independently of our mental and linguistic efforts to represent those aspects of reality. According to this approach, valid truth claims are envisioned, metaphorically, as having a vertical relationship with a foundational reality that underlies them. Viable bodies of knowledge are thus presumed to uncover the hidden workings of, and thus correspond to, basic features of existence.

Horizontal approaches to knowledge, on the other hand, assume that truth claims are nothing more than mental or linguistic constructs with no direct correspondence to foundational reality. Internally coherent sets of truth claims are thus envisioned, metaphorically, as merely hanging together with each other in a horizontal manner, reflecting culturally and historically specific patterns of thought and language use. Such truth claims can serve practical, functional, or even ideological purposes, but they are always social constructs that have no grounding in a reality "out there" that is independent of human minds. Rather, such truth claims are considered "true" only insofar as they are consistent with a network of truth claims deemed viable within a particular tradition of inquiry.

Variations on the vertical and horizontal themes can be seen in epistemological arguments between *objectivism* and *subjectivism*, *foundationalism* and *anti-foundationalism*, *absolutism* and *relativism*, *realism* and *anti-realism*, *essentialism* and *anti-essentialism*, *modernism* and *postmodernism*.[11] A review of the particularities and nuances that characterize each of these opposing traditions of thought would fill an entire volume and distract from the discussion at hand. Rorty's distinction between vertical and horizontal epistemologies will suffice for our purpose.

In a previous publication, Todd Smith and I articulate a set of premises and concepts that reconcile the perennial tension between vertical and horizontal epistemologies.[12] In short, we posit that many phenomena have a real existence that is independent of human thought. Moreover, while human minds can never know the essence of phenomena, we can gain insight into their manifest expressions, such as their observable or measurable attributes, properties, and effects. Even at this manifest level, however, many phenomena are complex and multifaceted. And in relation to this multifaceted complexity, human comprehension is partial, limited, and divergent. This is because human thought and perception are paradigmatically conditioned by the cognitive lenses, or conceptual frameworks, we internalize as we learn languages, are socialized, receive formal education, gain life experiences, and so forth. Such conditioning influences which phenomena, or which aspects of phenomena, we notice, as well as how we interpret them.

These ideas are not new. Variants of some can be found in vertical epistemologies and variants of others can be found in horizontal epistemologies. However, what neither vertical nor horizontal epistemologies take seriously enough is the dynamic relationship between foundational reality and the social construction of knowledge.[13] In our article, Smith and I illustrate how foundational reality both enables and constrains the range of ways we can construct knowledge regarding different phenomena.

One way we explain this is through a simple metaphor that draws on Paul Feyerabend's insight that scientists "are sculptors of reality."[14] Extending this analogy, we point out that sculptors need materials with which to work; otherwise, they cannot sculpt. Materials retain properties; otherwise, they are not materials. Properties involve conditions; otherwise, they are not properties. Conditions impose demands; otherwise, they are not conditions. Demands impose constraints; otherwise, they are not demands. Thus, the social construction of knowledge, like sculpting, is conditioned by the "stuff" with which it works. Or, as Helen Longino puts it, ultimately "there is 'something out there' that imposes limits on what we can say about it."[15]

Even as reality constrains the construction of knowledge about it, it simultaneously enables that same process of construction. One cannot sculpt unless there is something, with properties, to sculpt. By analogy, we explain in the original article, the only reason a sculptor can effectively chisel a piece of marble is because the sculptor is addressing, upon impact, some aspect of "the way marble is"—such as the way it breaks. Using a chisel effectively to chip away marble requires some knowledge, on the part of the sculptor, of various properties of the marble. Thus, the sculptor does not mistake "the way marble is" with "the way water is" in the process of sculpting. Moreover, the reason sculptors have been able to make better chisels over time is because upon repeated encounters with marble, they have become increasingly attuned to its properties and the way it responds to their chisels. In these ways, the marble simultaneously enables and constrains the sculptor while he or she is working.

The enabling and constraining nature of reality affirms that it is foundational. However, some aspects of reality—or some aspects of different phenomena—are more enabling or constraining than others. In other words, different aspects of reality enable or constrain, to different degrees, the extent to which we notice them at all, along with the range of truth claims that can viably be made about them. We refer to this as the relative *tangibility* of different phenomenal aspects. Relative tangibility can be illustrated with the following three examples.

First, tooth decay is a highly tangible phenomenon. The pain caused by a toothache is hard to ignore, and a tooth falling out is even harder to ignore. Both tend, more so than other phenomena, to demand attention regardless of the paradigmatic lenses through which we perceive them. Furthermore, as we begin to empirically investigate the cause of tooth decay, the phenomenon permits a relatively narrow range of viable interpretations of it. We can thus say that tooth decay is highly tangible and that the physiology of a tooth is, compared to other phenomena, a highly tangible object of inquiry.

Second, the subjective experience of human consciousness is a less tangible object of inquiry. Philosophers and scientists debate whether consciousness even "exists" in any meaningful sense or whether it is simply a temporary illusion conjured by biochemical processes in the brain. Even those who accept its independent existence debate the nature and "location" of that existence. The nature of human consciousness thus enables the construction of a wide range of viable truth claims.

Third, the ephemeral images and feelings that flash through many dreams when we sleep are extremely intangible phenomena. The fact that humans dream is not in doubt. But the nature, cause, or meaning of the specific images and feelings we experience in a particular dream—if we remember them at all once we wake—is almost impossible to probe in any rational or empirical manner. Such dreams offer almost no substance with which to construct credible truth claims.

These three examples illustrate relative tangibility. The sculptural metaphor Smith and I invoke in our article provides further insight into this concept: This time, imagine sculptors who work with clay. On one occasion, they come across hardened pieces of clay that have already been through the kiln. The hardness of this clay—its extreme tangibility—prevents the sculptors from molding it in diverse ways. On another occasion, the sculptors come across a tub of water containing scraps of mostly dissolved clay. Now the liquidity of the clay—its extreme intangibility—prevents the sculptors from molding it at all. On a third occasion, the sculptors find a stock of pliant, supple clay. This clay's plasticity—or its semi-tangibility—allows the sculptors to mold it in diverse ways. But the different ways they mold it depends on their respective training and on how their training interacts with specific properties of the kind of clay they are now molding, such as its mineral content.

In our article, Smith and I go on to explore how divergent forms of intellectual training—that is, our paradigmatic conditioning or the conceptual frameworks we internalize—come to bear on efforts to construct knowledge about different phenomena given their varying degrees of tangibility. We discuss how this insight enables us to transcend the debate between vertical and horizontal epistemologies by taking seriously the dynamic relationship between foundational aspects of reality and the social construction of knowledge. We then describe various ways in which different paradigms are, or become, attuned to any given phenomenon or phenomenal aspect, and we conclude by outlining the need for a *consultative epistemology* capable of sifting through and integrating the potentially complementary insights into a given phenomenon that are yielded by diverse cognitive lenses.[16]

For a deeper discussion of these themes, the reader can refer to our original article.[17] The preceding overview is meant only to introduce and clarify some basic premises underlying the argument I articulate in this book. To recap, those basic premises are as follows:

Many phenomena have a real existence that is independent of human thought. Human minds can never know the essences of such phenomena. We can gain insights only into manifest expressions of these phenomena, such as their observable or measurable attributes, properties, and effects. Even at this manifest level, however, many phenomena are complex and multifaceted. In relation to this multifaceted complexity, human comprehension is not only limited and partial; it is often divergent. This divergence is, in part, because much human cognition is paradigmatically conditioned. In addition, different features of reality enable and constrain what we can know of them in different ways due to their relative tangibility. Our cognitive conditioning interacts with this relative tangibility, and this interaction affects what aspects of reality we notice, how we interpret those aspects, the extent to which we can become attuned to them, the ways we can become attuned to them, and thus the range of truth claims we can viably construct about them.

In our initial article, these premises are offered as a way of reconciling truth and relativity and as a rationale for developing a more consultative epistemology. To do this, the article focuses largely on the construction of knowledge regarding already-existing material and social phenomena. The question I now turn to in this book is whether these premises are applicable in the domain of normative truth claims about how we ought to live. Are there foundational aspects of reality that enable and constrain the normative truth claims we can construct about how we ought to live? Is it viable to speak of foundational normative truths that we can investigate through a consultative epistemology? And are there methods by which we can systematically apply such principles to the betterment of the human condition?

TRUTHS VERSUS TRUTH CLAIMS

To advance further along this path of inquiry, it is necessary to clarify how I will be using the word *truth* in this book. In popular discourse, the word *truth* is used in several ways. In some contexts, a *truth* signifies a fundamental feature of reality that exists independently of whether human minds are aware of it or comprehend it to any degree. For instance, the earth revolves on an axis while orbiting the sun. This was true before any humans were alive to observe it and before early humans could comprehend it. It is a truth about our planet that is independent of our comprehension of it. Similarly, the feature of the universe we call gravity causes objects with mass to attract one another. This was true long before humans evolved to observe it, and its truth is independent of the degree to which humans understand how and why it operates—which we still do not fully understand. Let's assume, then, for the sake of this discussion, that there are many features of reality that exist independently of our comprehension of them, and let's refer to these as *truths*—or, more specifically, *foundational truths*—about reality. (This is not to be confused with the problematic idea of "foundational knowledge," which will be discussed later in this book.)

In contrast, the word *truth* can also be used to refer to situational facts that are contingent on circumstantial causes. For instance, it is empirically true that I leave my car keys on my desk every night in a small basket. This is not a *foundational* truth about reality. It is, nonetheless, a circumstantial truth that is contingent on my personal habits. Truths of this kind can therefore be called *contingent truths*, to distinguish them from foundational truths. Contingent truths are not all as trivial as where I leave my car keys. The Holocaust, for example, was also a contingent truth—a tragic historical truth that was contingent on a terrible confluence of socio-political forces. Contingent truths can therefore be very significant. Nevertheless, this book is concerned primarily with questions pertaining to foundational truths. Therefore, when the word *truth* is used throughout this book, it will refer to foundational truths, unless otherwise specified.[18]

With this basic distinction in mind, it is also important to recognize that the word *truth* is sometimes used to signify the *truth claims* (or knowledge claims) people make about what they believe to be foundational or contingent truths. For instance, to explain the effects of gravity, Isaac Newton asserted that two bodies will attract each other with a force that is directly proportional to the product of their masses and inversely proportional to the square of the distance between them. This was a truth claim Newton advanced about a feature of the universe we call gravity. Albert Einstein subsequently advanced another truth claim about gravity, asserting that it is a consequence of the curvature of space-time caused by the uneven distribution of mass and energy. Most physicists today agree that Newton's truth claim and Einstein's truth claim both correspond reasonably well to aspects of reality within different frames of reference. This is because these truth claims have been tested in various ways, and we now have a high degree of confidence in their validity.

However, not all truth claims correspond to reality in equally meaningful ways. For example, despite Aristotle's many profoundly insightful contributions to philosophy, he tried to explain gravity by claiming that all heavy bodies intrinsically seek to find their natural resting place by moving toward the center of the universe. Scientists now agree that the earth is not the center of the universe. Nor is it empirically tenable to say that every material body has a natural resting place in the universe. Therefore, this truth claim offers little insight into the feature of the universe we call gravity.

Likewise, in the domain of contingent truths, most empirical evidence indicates our atmosphere is currently warming due to human activity. This is the clear and overwhelming scientific consensus. Self-interested industries and politicians may deny this truth by asserting the opposite, but such truth claims do not correspond in any meaningful way with the contingent reality of our climate today.

If we limit our discussion of truths to foundational truths, as I will, then the distinction between truths and truth claims is a distinction between *ontological truths* and *epistemological truth claims*. Therefore, throughout this book, I will use the term *truth* to signify that which is ontologically real (like the existence of gravity) and *truth claim* to refer to the epistemological assertions we make about that which is real (like how we try to explain or model the nature and operation of gravity).

This distinction raises important questions that scientists and philosophers have been grappling with for centuries. How can we know, with any degree of confidence, that something has a real ontological existence that is independent of our comprehension? How can we distinguish between a valid truth claim and an invalid truth claim regarding that which is real? Is it even possible to do so? Epistemology is the branch of philosophy that explores these questions. It reveals to us that these questions are not easy to answer with certainty. Even the philosophy of science, which is a branch of epistemology, cannot offer straightforward answers to these questions in relation to the operation of the natural sciences and their exploration of the material world. Such unresolved questions in the field of epistemology have proven especially difficult to resolve in the domain of truth claims about *social* reality.

RELATIVE ATTUNEMENT TO TRUTH

In the preceding discussion, I suggested that some truth claims can be more valid than others based on how well the truth claims correspond to foundational truths. However, the language of "validity" and "correspondence" I invoked is steeped in philosophical debates that will unnecessarily sidetrack the argument at hand if we wade into them. To avoid this, I will generally use the more nuanced concept of *attunement*, which offers a useful way to conceptualize the relationship between truth claims and foundational truths. In our article on consultative epistemology, Smith and I introduce this concept as a means of conceptualizing the *relative*, rather than the absolute, relationship between truth claims and underlying features of reality.[19]

The concept of *attunement*—or *relative attunement*—can be grasped through the analogy of tuning a radio. Radio signals exist independently of any given radio receiver and independently of whether any given radio is tuned to them. If our radio is not tuned to any signal, we will not hear anything on it, even though it has the potential to pick up many such signals. If, however, we start adjusting the tuner on our radio, we can move from a condition of not hearing any signal at all, to a condition of hearing noisy static, to a condition of hearing a relatively clear signal. Attunement can thus be understood as a relative state.

It seems reasonable to assume that the relationship between truths and truth claims has this same general characteristic. Indeed, most natural scientists operate from the premise that features of reality exist independently of our awareness of them. As we do become aware of them, our efforts to comprehend them can move from no comprehension, to very fuzzy comprehension, to relatively attuned comprehension—even if we are never able to reach perfect comprehension. Thus, some truth claims can be more attuned to underlying features of reality than others—just as the truth claims Newton and Einstein made about gravity have proven to be more attuned to reality than Aristotle's were.

It is possible to increase our attunement to reality over time because reality enables and constrains our efforts to understand it, as alluded to earlier in this chapter. Moreover, with relatively tangible aspects of reality, efforts to understand them begin with relatively indisputable observations about reality. In the case of gravity, heavy objects fall to the ground. Repeatedly. Reliably. From this initial observation, efforts to explain the mystery of how and why this occurs have gradually advanced by testing progressively more elaborate explanations against the enabling and constraining properties of reality.

To think through the full implications of this, we need to remind ourselves that many features of reality about which we want to learn are complex. Gravity is a complex phenomenon that we still do not fully understand. Efforts to explain it began with raw observations of heavy objects falling. Newton eventually offered profound insights that enable us to mathematically model and predict the effects of gravity in certain contexts. Einstein offered additional insights into the relationship between gravity, mass, space, and time that are relevant in broader contexts. Physicists continue to explore other aspects of gravity, such as gravitational radiation, yet many questions remain regarding the essential nature of gravity, its precise relationship to other fundamental forces, its relationship to quantum mechanics, and so forth.

It also seems reasonable to assume, then, that many features of reality—or truths—are complex and multifaceted. This conception of truth, alluded to earlier in this chapter, enables us to take another step toward reconciling truth and relativity. Specifically, it enables us to recognize that different perspectives on the same truth can potentially reveal to us different facets, or aspects, of that truth.

Another well-known example that illustrates how different perspectives can illuminate different facets of the same phenomenon is the feature of reality we refer to as *light*. As modern physicists began to investigate the nature of light, some physicists employed observational techniques that appeared to reveal that light had a wave-like nature. Other physicists employed different observational techniques that appeared to reveal light had a particle-like nature. For some time, physicists debated whether light should best be conceptualized as a wave or a particle. The respective observational techniques were repeatedly tested for reliability even as other techniques were sought to triangulate the validity of the observations. Over time, it became apparent that both sets of seemingly contradictory observations were reliable and valid. Many physicists now accept that light is a complex phenomenon that can be conceptualized in a wave-like manner as well as a particle-like manner. Each of these facets is revealed from different observational perspectives. Physicists have also gained insights into many other aspects of light such as its speed, its relationship to mass and gravity, and so forth. Numerous questions about this complex phenomenon remain, such as the following: How does light behave at extreme energy levels and temperatures such as those found in quasars and black holes? How can some forces act at a distance faster than the speed of light? And how do different light frequencies that strike different cone cells in the retina lead to the subjective perception of different colors? Some of these questions may never be explained in meaningful ways. Yet efforts to increase our understanding of light, to some degree at least, are possible because light has properties that enable and constrain the construction of a tentative but useful body of knowledge about it.

From this example, we can better understand how our perspectives on truth are relative to the diverse conceptual frameworks, observational techniques, and so forth that enable different people to glimpse different facets of the same underlying phenomena, as alluded to earlier in this chapter. We can thus begin to see how the distinction between truth and relativity can set up a false dichotomy if we reify that distinction. When we look beyond this dichotomy, we see that diverse people can have relative perspectives on different aspects of the same complex truths—as illustrated by figure 1. As this figure suggests, it is often important to seek out diverse perspectives if we want to increase our attunement to some feature of reality. Hence the need for what Smith and I refer to as a consultative epistemology.[20]

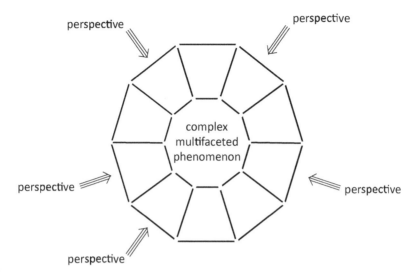

Figure 1. Relative perspectives on a complex multifaceted phenomenon.

This insight regarding *relative perspectives* on the same complex truth is not new. The aforementioned example of light and *the complementarity principle* with which it is associated in physics embody this insight.[21] Indeed, one thing the natural sciences appear to do—cumulatively, over time—is enable people to probe features of the material universe by employing diverse conceptual frameworks and diverse observational techniques that can generate complementary insights into the same objects of inquiry.

Similarly, *standpoint theory* in the social sciences is based on the premise that our social position—our gender, race, economic status, life experiences, education, and so forth—all influence, to some degree at least, which aspects of our social reality we notice or see most clearly and how we interpret them.[22] Diverse perspectives on social reality do not necessarily invalidate each other. Nor does the expression of diverse perspectives and interpretations invalidate the existence of the social phenomena they seek to describe from different vantage points. As in physics, diverse perspectives on complex social phenomena can be complementary.

However, just because diverse truth claims can be complementary does not mean that all truth claims are attuned in a meaningful way to those aspects of reality to which they claim attunement. Some truth claims—such as outright lies and fabrications—have no basis in reality. Other problematic truth claims might be the result of innocent errors of reasoning, observation, and interpretation. Either way, the systematic investigation of reality must include methods for distinguishing truth claims that are relatively attuned to aspects of reality from entirely erroneous or spurious truth claims— as illustrated by figure 2.

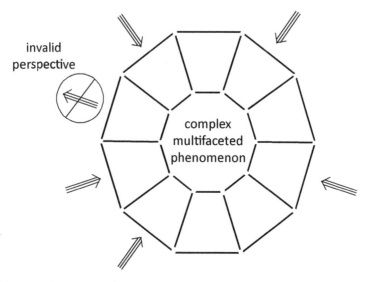

Figure 2. Assessing truth claims about a complex multifaceted phenomenon.

Most people today accept that testing or assessing truth claims about material reality is something science does reasonably well in a cumulative sense over time—even though scientists and philosophers still legitimately debate the best methodologies to do this in specific contexts and even though scientific truth claims always remain tentative and fallible to some degree.

Making and testing truth claims about material reality is, however, a relatively simple process compared to making and testing truth claims about social reality. The latter are much harder to assess, in part because social truths have normative dimensions. For this reason, some people argue that it is not even rational to speak of foundational social truths about which one could make claims (as distinct from contingent truths, such as what social practices or arrangements exist among a given group at a given time and place).

Before we consider whether there might be any normative truths underlying social reality, it will help to stay focused a bit longer on our discussion of attunement to material reality. In this context, let's assume—as most scientists do today—that it is possible, through the application of various scientific methodologies over time, to increase our confidence in the relative attunement of many scientific truth claims to underlying features of reality.

The preceding discussion does not tell us how to do this. It simply helps us visualize this possibility in the abstract, and it provides vocabulary that enables us to advance the argument at hand. To put the argument so far in simple terms, as we seek to increase our attunement to foundational truths about reality, which can entail recognizing the complementarity of diverse perspectives on reality, we also need methods to distinguish erroneous or spurious truth claims from relatively attuned truth claims.

Building on this understanding that diverse perspectives can be complementary but not all perspectives are valid, we can also note that truth claims are often superficial at first, but their depth of insight can increase over time, as can be seen in the historical investigation of phenomena such as gravity. The progression from a pre-Newtonian to a Newtonian understanding of gravity, followed by Einstein's theory of gravity, illustrates a movement toward deeper and richer insight over time. Therefore, the systematic investigation of reality must include methods for deepening our insights into facets of reality that we understand only superficially at first, even as we continue to add new insights into other facets—as illustrated by figure 3.

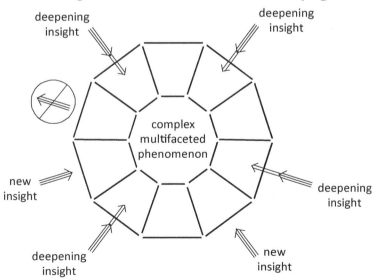

Figure 3. Diversifying and deepening insights into a complex multifaceted phenomenon.

Again, the preceding discussion does not tell us precisely how to diversify and deepen our insights into any given reality over time. It merely helps us envision, in the abstract, that this is something science, at its best, helps us do. The ability to envision this enables us to take another step toward reconciling truth and relativity because we can now think about the *relative depth* of diverse insights into different aspects of the same phenomenon.

As we move beyond superficial conceptions of reality by deepening diverse insights over time, we also need to move beyond fragmented conceptions of reality by understanding how those diverse and deepening insights relate to each other. Therefore, the systematic investigation of reality must also include methods for integrating diverse insights into more comprehensive understandings—as illustrated by figure 4.

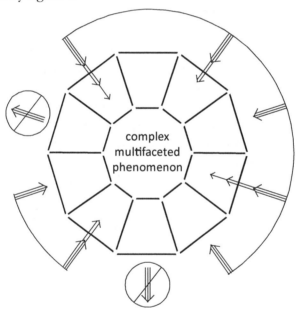

Figure 4. Integrating diverse insights regarding a complex multifaceted phenomenon.

This point enables us to further reconcile truth and relativity because we can now think and talk about the *relative integration* of diverse insights regarding different aspects of a common truth. As we recognize this, we again see the need for a consultative epistemology, exercised over time through processes that are both iterative and integrative, as increasingly complex bodies of knowledge are tested against enabling and constraining properties of complex phenomena.[23]

In the preceding discussion, we have thus seen that attunement to a foundational truth can be relative to (1) *the perspectives* of those who are engaged in its exploration, (2) *the depth of insight* any given perspective generates as it is explored and elaborated over time, and (3) *the degree that diverse insights become integrated into a coherent framework* over time. These are three initial steps we can take to reconcile truth and relativity.

It is not difficult to see that the natural sciences take all these steps in fields such as physics, chemistry, and biology. It is also hard to deny that these fields of research seem to be making progress toward attunement to various truths about reality—even as we acknowledge minor setbacks or major paradigm shifts along the way and even as we recognize ultimate limits to human comprehension. If we did not believe that science was advancing in these ways, we would not trust airplanes to get us from point A to point B, nor would we believe in the voices we hear through our mobile phones. Clearly, most scientists, philosophers, and ordinary people now take these assumptions for granted.

Therefore, let's proceed on the premise that the natural sciences can make relative progress toward attunement to truth in all these ways, in a cumulative manner, over time. It is not obvious, however, that this premise should be adopted in relation to the study of social phenomena that have normative dimensions. Is it rational to speak of normative truths underlying a system of governance, a system of human rights, an economic system, or any other social system? After all, social systems, or structures, are not simply products of nature. They are constructed. So how can the framework we have begun to sketch above apply to the domain of social reality?

To envision this, we would have to accept not only the concept of *foundational material truths* about physical reality, but also the concept of *foundational normative truths* about social reality —or truths that have implications for how social structures *ought* to be constructed. In other words, we would have to posit that principles such as justice, equity, and the dignity or sanctity of human life are foundational normative truths that need to be factored into the construction of social institutions and other social phenomena. But is this a rational, or valid, way to think about constructing social reality? We will return to this question later in this chapter. To answer it, it will help if we first consider more deeply some of the conditions that enable and constrain the generation and application of knowledge in the simpler domain of material truths. Then we can consider what conditions, if any, might enable and constrain the generation and application of knowledge regarding normative truths.

Toward Increasing Attunement

The history and philosophy of science provide insights into many of the conditions that are required for the advancement of science—or for the increasing attunement of scientific truth claims to enabling and constraining features of material reality. In the discussion below, we will examine some of the more widely accepted insights into the operation of science by drawing on the work of Alan Chalmers and Peter Godfrey-Smith, who have distilled and clarified critically informed insights into the nature and operation of science in ways that move us beyond naïve popular conceptions of it.[24]

One basic condition for the advancement of science is rational thought. This includes the capacity to employ various forms of logic such as induction and deduction, to engage in analytical and synthetic modes of reasoning, and to communicate one's thoughts in a coherent and consistent manner. However, efforts to reduce science to the strict application of certain modes of logic, such as the logic of induction, have proven futile. Induction and other modes of rational thought are important tools in the tool box of science. But science is ultimately a more complex enterprise.

As well, the advancement of science requires imagination and intuition. Many of the greatest advances in science required major leaps of imagination combined with an intuitive attraction to the beauty and elegance of compelling ideas. These faculties of the mind played a role in the remarkable contributions to science of people like Galileo, Newton, Curie, Einstein, and others. In this regard, it appears that well-trained faculties of imagination and intuition are capable of some degree of attunement to moderately intangible aspects of reality that enable and constrain human inquiry.[25] Although this process is not well understood, the history of science appears to bear out the importance of these faculties.

Science also depends on the exercise of skepticism, critical thought, and a desire to rigorously test truth claims. In most contexts, this includes an ability to question logical arguments. In many contexts, it also includes methodologies for attempting to falsify empirically testable hypotheses. And in some contexts, it includes a willingness to problematize widely accepted theories, conceptual frameworks, or paradigms.

Science thus advances through a complex interplay of rational, imaginative, intuitive, and critical faculties operating within and among diverse scientific minds over time.

Another characteristic of science is the role empirical observation plays within it. The ability to observe, measure, or detect—whether directly through the human senses or indirectly through specialized equipment—informs our inductive logic, our efforts to falsify hypotheses, and even the exercise of our imaginative and intuitive faculties. In many respects, disciplined and systematic observation is a bedrock of science. It inspires us with ideas about how to explain aspects of reality, even as it enables us to test those ideas against the enabling and constraining features of reality.

Yet it is now widely understood that our observations are conditioned by the categories, concepts, and theories we have previously constructed or internalized, which influence what we notice or fail to notice when we look at the world, how we interpret what we see, and the conclusions we derive—as alluded to early in this chapter. Observation is therefore a far-from-straightforward feature of science that cannot be understood in naïve ways. Our assumptions and concepts about reality and our observations of reality have a dialectical relationship. Nonetheless, the enabling and constraining features of reality make it possible to increase our attunement to some aspects of reality through iterative and integrative epistemological processes.

As the preceding point implies, the progress of science rests on our willingness to make tentative or provisional assumptions about various features of reality and commit to them long enough to test them against reality. Virtually all complex theories rest on some underlying ontological premises, many of which are disputed by skeptics at first. Likewise, the methodologies and techniques we employ to test our theories often rest on additional sets of epistemological and operational assumptions, which are also sometimes disputed.

Indeed, the entire enterprise of science ultimately rests on assumptions that the universe has an underlying material order, that this order is governed by laws or principles of some kind, and that human minds can gain insight into these laws or principles to some degree by applying the right methods over time. When science, as a conscious human endeavor, was first emerging, these latter assumptions would not have been empirically verifiable. These assumptions have been validated over time by their fruitfulness. The fruitfulness is demonstrated by the remarkable accomplishments of the applied sciences—ranging from airplanes to cell phones to the myriad other achievements of science that now surround us. This fruitfulness can be understood, in turn, as a function of the increasing attunement between enabling and constraining features of reality and the bodies of knowledge we construct about those features.

Closely related to the willingness to make provisional assumptions, in the practice of science, is the essential role played by concepts, models, theories, and conceptual frameworks. In this regard, concepts are like lenses that enable us to see aspects of reality that we otherwise might not notice. They are also linguistic devices that help us communicate in reasonably effective ways with others about the aspects of reality we are exploring. Together with assumptions, concepts are essential building blocks of the models, theories, and conceptual frameworks that enable us to explore complex multi-faceted phenomena and probe deeper into certain aspects of those phenomena over time.

Concepts, models, and theories thereby empower us in various ways. But they also limit us. By focusing our attention on some aspects of reality, they divert our attention from others. To use an analogy from physics, concepts operate like lenses that enable us to explore different parts of the electromagnetic spectrum. One lens enables us to explore infrared frequencies. Another enables us to explore ultraviolet frequencies. Other lenses enable us to explore other parts of the spectrum. But as we look through any given lens and see one part of the spectrum, we fail to see the other parts of the spectrum it does not bring into view. Hence the need for a consultative epistemology that can integrate diverse views.[26] Movements in this direction can be discerned today in interdisciplinary research programs and other efforts to integrate diverse theoretical perspectives into more comprehensive understandings. But there is a need for much more effort toward this end.

All the conditions for the advancement of science outlined above are, in turn, contingent on a host of requisite qualities, or virtues, we need to develop to contribute effectively to science. These include curiosity, honesty and integrity, a degree of detachment from preconceived notions, recognition of the ultimate fallibility of human knowledge, a corresponding posture of humility and open-mindedness, and the avoidance of dogmatism. Efforts to foster these qualities rely on processes of socialization and education; on discourses and structures that encourage scientific integrity; and on sanctions against the violation of methodological norms, plagiarism, the fabrication of data, and so forth. Such processes, it should be noted, are all value-laden. The entire enterprise of science thus rests on a set of *normative principles*, or apparent *truths*, about how scientists *ought* to be and do. To the extent that people fall short of these norms—which happens frequently—the advancement of science is impeded.

The need to foster these normative qualities and behaviors speaks to the nature of science as a social enterprise. But the social nature of science extends well beyond the basic norms alluded to above. Science advances as a collective endeavor pursued by communities of scientists. To be effective, scientific communities must strive not only to foster the qualities and behaviors alluded to above, but also to develop shared vocabularies that enable them to communicate effectively, leading to shared understandings. They also need to construct complex forms of social organization for circulating, reviewing, refining, and disseminating their findings. Finally, they need to develop systems of employment, funding, and material support that enable them to pursue their work. In sum, science requires sophisticated forms of cooperation and coordination, including institutional structures, to advance.

Given that science is a social enterprise, it is susceptible to the corrupting influences of various social forces such as expressions of ego and self-interested ambition as well as expressions of power and privilege. To the degree that these forces are expressed, they play out in the complex political economy of mechanisms for scientific funding and recognition. This includes, for instance, partisan pressures that shape the kinds of research funded by government grants or that determine the amount of funding available and who receives it. This also includes reliance on commercial and military sources of funding for scientific research, in contrast to publicly funded research aimed at the promotion of broad public interests or the advancement of knowledge without immediate application. These forces also play out in the ways scholarly journals are funded and peer-reviewed, along with who can afford to access them. And they shape complex systems of review, tenure, and promotion within universities or other research organizations. The advancement of science is thus contingent on ongoing efforts to minimize, regulate, or overcome corrupting social forces in these and other contexts.

In short, science is a remarkably complex enterprise. It can never be reduced to a simplistic formula or a naïve "scientific method." It must always contend with complex social forces. Nonetheless, the enterprise of science has demonstrated its ability to generate profound insights into—or increase our attunement to—innumerable features of reality that enable and constrain the construction of complex bodies of knowledge.

Many features of science that make this possible, outlined briefly above, have been explored in greater depth by Chalmers, Godfrey-Smith, and other historians and philosophers of science on whose insights they draw. It is important to note, however, that these insights tend to derive from studies of the material sciences, which investigate physical and biological aspects of reality. If we consider the possibility that normative truths may underlie our social reality, can we draw any insights from the operation of science that might be relevant in this domain? If so, is it possible to apply any of these insights to constructing a more peaceful, just, and prosperous *social reality*?

RELATIVE EMBODIMENT OF TRUTH

To explore these questions, let's posit, for the moment, that the concept of *foundational normative truths* is ontologically sound. In other words, let's assume normative truths are enabling and constraining features of reality that exist independently of whether we are aware of them or the degree to which we comprehend them. Many skeptics reject this premise. But let's bracket that skepticism off for now and address it later so that we can first explore the implications of the premise. Trying to explore its implications while simultaneously addressing the arguments of skeptics would make the discussion unnecessarily convoluted.

To recap, earlier in this chapter we examined three ways that truth and relativity can be reconciled in the domain of the natural sciences: (1) comprehension of a foundational truth can be relative to the perspectives of those who are engaged in its exploration; (2) comprehension of a foundational truth can be relative to the depth of insight any given perspective generates as it is applied, explored, and elaborated over time; and (3) comprehension of a foundational truth can be relative to the degree that diverse insights become integrated into a coherent framework over time. Together, these three insights help us conceptualize *relative attunement* to foundational truths that enable and constrain our efforts to construct bodies of knowledge about them. To explore the relevance of these insights in the domain of social reality, we now need to clarify our conception of foundational normative truths, along with the relationship between such truths and social reality. This will enable us to consider another way that truth and relativity might be reconciled: (4) the *relative embodiment* of normative truths in the construction of social reality.

Toward this end, it will help to clarify first that foundational normative truths—or truths about how human beings ought to live—tend to be conceptualized in two broadly different ways. On the one hand, they have been conceptualized as comprehensive and detailed prescriptions for right living that should inform individual and collective human affairs. On the other hand, they have been conceptualized as indeterminate principles, or ideals, that align with or underlie the betterment of humanity and that can become expressed in diverse ways within different cultural and historical contexts. To use an analogy from the applied sciences, the former conception would view normative truths as something akin to a comprehensive prescription for constructing a proper airplane. The latter would view normative truths as something akin to a set of physics principles that diverse people could apply in their efforts to construct increasingly safer and more efficient airplanes suited to specific purposes, reflecting various cultural priorities. In the discussion that follows, the latter conception is employed.

To the extent that normative truths can be conceptualized in the latter manner, the logic laid out earlier in this chapter suggests that such truths must have a degree of tangibility that enables and constrains the range of truth claims we can viably make about their expression in social reality. To use the analogy employed previously, if we are sculpting social reality, including bodies of knowledge about social reality, any normative truths underlying this sculptural work must have properties that enable and constrain our efforts. Like pliant clay, we might still mold it in diverse ways depending on how our prior experiences and training interact with its enabling and constraining properties. But there must be something there for us to mold.

With these premises in mind, let's return to the question of how we might generate knowledge about normative truths and apply such knowledge as we construct social reality. Envisioning such a process requires us to consider the fourth expression of relativity alluded to above: the *relative embodiment* of normative truths in the construction of social reality. We will assume for now that the three expressions of *relative attunement*, which we explored in relation to the natural sciences, are also applicable in the social domain. However, they do not provide an adequate framework for reconciling truth and relativity in the latter domain.

To understand why this is the case, we need to distinguish between two kinds of phenomena: (1) phenomena that come into existence independent of human agency and (2) phenomena that come into existence through human agency. For the sake of simplicity, I will refer to the former as *naturally occurring phenomena* and the latter as *socially constructed phenomena* (or social constructs). Examples of naturally occurring phenomena include stars, planets, geological formations, and the myriad forms of biological life that evolved before humans. Examples of socially constructed phenomena include democracies, legal codes, economic systems, and the myriad other things humans have created through collective agency. It should be noted in this regard that science, as a system of knowledge and practice, is itself a socially constructed phenomenon—as are all the concepts, models, and theories scientists employ and the bodies of knowledge these yield. Even so, many of the objects of inquiry scientists study are naturally occurring phenomena that emerged prior to, or independent of, human agency. While bodies of knowledge about such phenomena are constructed, we are assuming these underlying objects of inquiry exist independently of our truth claims about them.

Like all categories, the distinction between *naturally occurring phenomena* and *socially constructed phenomena* should not be reified into a false or overly simplistic dichotomy. The boundaries between these distinctions are not always so clear. For instance, material technologies, such as cell phones, are socially constructed from naturally occurring phenomena such as silica and various metals. Likewise, genetic engineering has enabled humans to socially construct entirely new species with a biological existence that can carry on independent of further human agency. Naturally occurring phenomena can thus interact with, or become entangled with, processes of social construction in complex ways. Even the human genome co-evolved with expressions of human agency in complex ways that were mutually constitutive. A simple example is the development, at a genetic level, of bovine lactose tolerance within populations that domesticated cattle. More complex examples might include the co-evolution of language and the physiological mechanisms that enable us to use it—along with many other socio-biological traits that co-evolved during the early emergence of our species or during its subsequent spread across the planet.

Acknowledging these complexities enables us to move beyond a simple binary conception of *naturally occurring phenomena* and *socially constructed phenomena*. Rather, we can conceptualize them on a continuum, with relatively pure examples on each end of the continuum and areas of overlap, or entanglement, in the middle. Despite the areas of overlap and entanglement, the distinction has value because it enables us to recognize another way that truth and relativity can be reconciled. In much of the natural sciences, the generation of knowledge requires methods to increase attunement to already existing objects of inquiry. But in the social domain, the generation of knowledge about an object of inquiry cannot be separated from the construction of that object of inquiry.

For instance, an educational system can be an object of inquiry. That is, it can be something we try to learn about systematically, presumably to improve it. But all educational systems are constructed, and any given system reflects some prior state of knowledge that, at least in part, informed its construction. The subsequent generation of knowledge about that system will, if it is not ignored, inform the ongoing construction or reconstruction of the system. The same is true for all objects of inquiry in the social domain. In this domain, the generation of knowledge about an object of inquiry and the construction of that object are inseparably intertwined. The two processes are mutually informing, or mutually constitutive. This mutually constitutive relationship is, in part, the way we bring social phenomena into existence and the way such phenomena develop or evolve over time. But what role, if any, might foundational normative truths play in this mutually constitutive process?

The concept of *relative embodiment* offers a way to begin conceptualizing the role of normative truths in this mutually constitutive relationship. The term *embodiment*, in this context, refers to the expression of abstract laws, ideals, or principles in manifest material or social forms. In this regard, one can say that specific material technologies, such as airplanes or cell phones, must embody various principles of physics if they are to function properly in ways that contribute to the betterment of humanity on a material level. Likewise, one can say that various social constructs, such as legal codes or institutional structures, must embody various normative principles if they are to function in ways that contribute to the betterment of humanity on a social level.

To further grasp the relative embodiment of normative truths, it will help to consider the concept of *latency*. Latency is most easily illustrated by the analogy of a tree that is latent in the seed. When the tree matures, one could say that it embodies a form that was latent in the seed. No matter how closely we examine the seed, we cannot see the tree that will emerge from it. However, if the seed is cultivated under the right conditions, it will eventually grow into a tree. Furthermore, even if we know, in advance, what species of tree a given seed will yield, we cannot predict the exact size and shape of the mature tree that will grow from it. Under different growing conditions, the same seed will grow into somewhat different mature shapes. But any of its potential shapes would still be the same species of tree. We can thus say that the tree is *latent* in the seed, even though the final shape of the tree is indeterminate. We can also say that the purpose of the seed is to give rise to the tree so that the tree can bear its fruit.

With this concept of latency in mind, we can posit that all natural and social phenomena must, in some respect, have been latent "in the seeds of existence," so to speak, even if they only became manifest over time. This does not mean that every latent possibility will become a manifest reality—any more than every seed in a large field will germinate. Nonetheless, many latent phenomena have become manifest, or have come to fruition, in the diverse physical and biological entities that emerged in the phenomenal universe prior to, and independent of, human agency. It is important to note, in this regard, that the nature and range of latent physical and biological phenomena derive from foundational *material truths* about reality.

Likewise, we can posit that other kinds of foundational truths—*normative truths*—make other kinds of latent phenomena possible. They make possible social phenomena that can become manifest, or come to fruition, only through human agency. For instance, all human societies require systems that enable some degree of collective decision-making and mutual coordination. We can refer to these as systems of governance. Systems of governance come into existence only as the result of human agency, and they can take diverse forms. But can systems of governance manifest underlying normative truths to different degrees?

With the distinction between *material truths* and *normative truths* in mind, we can conceive of two different expressions of latency. On the one hand, we can conceive of (A) latent material phenomena, such as planets or species, that become manifest as expressions of foundational material truths, such as the laws of physics and biology. Those latent expressions come to fruition in the universe *independent of human agency*. On the other hand, we can conceive of (B) latent social phenomena, such as social practices or institutions, that become manifest as expressions of foundational normative truths, or truths about how we ought to live. The latter phenomena *depend on human agency* to come to fruition. While the formation of diverse planets and stars, or the evolution of diverse biological life forms, are examples of A, the formation of governments, economies, and systems of education are examples of B. Furthermore, both A and B are characterized by a degree of indeterminacy regarding the precise forms they manifest, depending on environmental and historical contingencies.

In addition, as alluded to above, some phenomena, such as material technologies, could be situated on a continuum between (A) that which is entirely independent of human agency and (B) that which

is almost entirely dependent on human agency. Material technologies—from ploughs to mobile phones—clearly incorporate physical
elements that came into existence independent of human agency,
but human agency is then exercised to transform those elements
into new, partly constructed, phenomena. Social institutions, on the
other hand—from markets to parliaments—are almost entirely socially constructed. Granted, there are certain physical and biological
factors that enable and constrain, to some degree, how markets or
parliaments can be constructed. But within those parameters, social
institutions are almost entirely constructed through human agency
(as distinct from the physical architecture that houses some kinds
of social institutions, such as the parliament building that houses a
parliament).

We can thus recognize that different phenomena can be located
on a continuum. On one side are phenomena that come into existence through processes that are entirely independent from human
agency. On the other side are phenomena that come into existence
through processes that are almost entirely dependent on human
agency. This relationship is illustrated in figure 5, which carries forward, from the previous figures in this chapter, the metaphor of a
complex multifaceted object of inquiry.

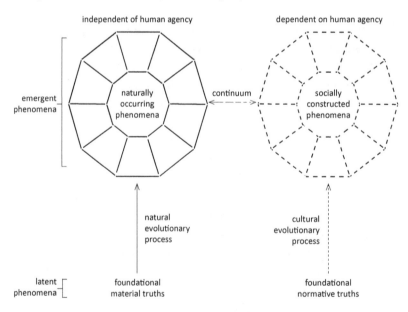

Figure 5. Relative dependence on human agency.

The distinction between naturally occurring and socially constructed phenomena has, of course, been widely recognized for a long
time. But the way this distinction becomes illuminated through the
concept of latency has not been adequately explored or articulated.
Moreover, the way this relationship is conceptualized in figure 5
enables us to consider the *relative embodiment* of normative truths in
social constructs. This is a form of relativity that does not apply to
naturally occurring phenomena, and it is a key to reconciling truth
and relativity in the social domain.

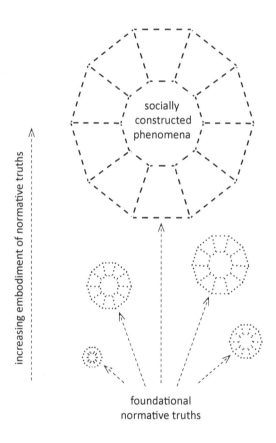

Figure 6. Relative embodiment of normative truths in social constructs.

To understand this, it is helpful to discuss an example. Consider various systems of rights that have been constructed throughout history. Among them are systems that accorded some people the rights to enslave and others the virtually non-existent rights associated with being enslaved. Most people today would agree that slavery, as a socially constructed institution, failed to embody normative truths such as justice, equity, and the inherent dignity of every human being. Caste systems, feudal systems, democratically constructed bills of rights, or the Universal Declaration of Human Rights would all appear to embody these truths to varying degrees. By extension, one can imagine the future construction of even more mature frameworks of human rights that represent an even fuller expression or fruition of these normative truths. (And, of course, one can also imagine the construction of increasingly mature systems of moral obligation, or social responsibilities, since the concept of "rights" does not exhaust the ways relationships are understood or organized.)

Thus, it is possible to speak of the relative embodiment of normative truths in social constructs—as illustrated in figure 6 above. In this figure, the progressively larger constructs represent increasing embodiment of normative truths.

As another example, consider the prevailing global system of food production and distribution as a socially constructed system that can be assessed in terms of its relative embodiment of normative truths. In this example, those truths might again include justice, equity, and the inherent dignity of every human being. They might also include a normative truth associated with responsible stewardship of our natural environment or living in harmony with nature. As Lample explains:

> One might imagine a reasonable aim for such systems would be to provide all the world's people with a sufficient and healthy diet produced by sustainable methods and efficient delivery systems in harmony with the ecosystem. What we witness, instead, is a bizarre arrangement centered on control and extraction of wealth for a few at the expense of the masses; the prostitution of science in service to food engineering, which makes harmful products addictive and ushers in a self-inflicted health crisis; the perpetuation of hunger among more than ten percent of the world's population, including some one hundred million

children; and systems of production and distribution at war with the environment.[27]

It is not difficult to imagine the construction of a modern food system that represents a more mature expression of normative truths. Moreover, it should be possible to find intersubjective methods by which communities of people can begin to assess a wide range of social constructs, such as food systems, in terms of their relative embodiment of various normative truths. This logic applies to systems of governance, education, mass communication, and so on.

In the domain of social constructs, we can therefore speak of the *relative embodiment* of underlying normative truths. This concept enables us to more fully reconcile truth and relativity in the social domain. It is worth noting, in this regard, that the relative embodiment of truth in social constructs can also be understood in relation to the normative demands placed on societies in changing historical conditions. In other words, the relative embodiment of truth can be understood in historically contextual ways.

For instance, if we consider systems of food production and distribution again, the normative demands placed on a small hunting and gathering community on a sparsely populated planet may not be the same as the normative demands placed on an interdependent global community of seven billion people armed with biologically disruptive and planet-altering agricultural technologies. Likewise, when considering the opportunity structures within different societies, the normative demands placed on a relatively small, isolated, homogenous tribe may not be the same as the normative demands placed on a large, heterogenous, modern state dealing with the legacy of colonial genocide, slavery, and entrenched forms of systemic discrimination that cannot be addressed without processes of restorative or reparative justice.

In addition, the concept of relative embodiment should not be confused with ethnocentric distinctions such as "uncivilized" versus "civilized" or "primitive" versus "advanced." Processes of normative development are far more complex, contextual, non-linear, and uneven than such ethnocentric notions suggest. Consider, in this regard, the oppressive conditions in which many people lived in early modern Europe, along with the brutality that characterized much European colonialism. On some measures at least, societies that were colonized or enslaved by Europeans undoubtedly embodied some normative truths to higher degrees than their colonial over-lords. Yet we also need to avoid romanticizing "pre-modern" societies. Inequity, oppression, social exclusion, violence, and other social maladies are not modern inventions. Although they have grown in scale and complexity in recent centuries, all human societies have struggled with such problems in different ways.

Toward Increasing Embodiment

If social constructs can embody normative truths to varying degrees, then there may be strategies or approaches by which the relative embodiment of normative truths can be more purposefully increased over time. In other words, it may be possible that processes of social change can consciously and systematically apply foundational normative principles to the betterment of the human condition. But how might this be possible? What approaches might be needed? To what extent are such approaches already employed by groups of people working—or struggling—for social change? And are there ways to refine such approaches?

Given the preceding discussion about how processes of attunement to material truths advance in the domain of the natural sciences, it seems reasonable to assume that efforts to increase our attunement to and our embodiment of normative truths would share at least some of the same features. For example, since efforts in both the material and social domains involve the systematic generation of knowledge, it seems reasonable to assume that if we want to apply foundational normative principles to the betterment of the human condition, our efforts need to be characterized by the exercise of rational thought, imagination and intuition, as well as skepticism and critical thinking. We would also need to rely on disciplined and systematic observations and articulate provisional assumptions as well as concepts, models, theories, or conceptual frameworks that could be tested over time. We would need to cultivate qualities such as curiosity, honesty and integrity, a degree of detachment from pre-conceived notions, recognition of the ultimate fallibility of human knowledge, a corresponding posture of humility and open-mindedness, and the avoidance of dogmatism or fanaticism. In short, the systematic generation of knowledge about processes of social change should be understood as a complex but recognizable enterprise that has much in common with the natural sciences and cannot be reduced to simplistic or naïve formulas.

In addition, efforts to increase the embodiment of normative truths in the construction of social reality would clearly have to be understood, like science, as a social enterprise—a collective endeavor pursued by communities of people. Protagonists of social change need to develop shared vocabularies and use language in ways that enable them to communicate effectively. They need to develop complex forms of social organization that enable them to share and refine insights at the frontiers of learning. They require sophisticated forms of cooperation and coordination, including institutional capacities that enable them to advance. And, as with endeavors in the natural sciences, they must contend with a variety of social forces, including self-interested expressions of power and privilege.

In other ways, however, efforts to increase the embodiment of normative truths in the construction of social reality will be distinct from the endeavor of science. Whereas science generates knowledge about naturally occurring phenomena that emerge prior to and independent of human agency, it is quite another thing to generate knowledge about social phenomena that are being brought into existence at the same time we are trying to learn about them. Granted, the applied sciences generate knowledge about the construction of new technologies as we bring them into existence. But generating knowledge as we learn about the construction of purely social phenomena is an order of magnitude more complex. This is because the construction of social reality is characterized by dynamic processes, patterns, and systems that are all brought into existence and then unfold almost entirely through collective agency.

Moreover, as cautioned in the introduction to this book, such approaches cannot be understood in terms of social engineering. Social engineering implies a reliance on privileged forms of alleged expertise applied to the design of social policies and processes intended to achieve instrumental objectives determined by elite social groups. Such approaches have been ineffective at their best, oppressive at their worst.

In contrast to social engineering, efforts to increase the embodiment of normative truths through processes of social construction require reflective modes of collective learning through action. If the objects of our learning are the products of human agency, we need to be consciously exerting collective agency in processes of social construction to learn from such processes. It also follows logically that the exercise of agency in this way needs to be accompanied by ongoing processes of reflection on action. Otherwise, we could not learn from our actions. Therefore, the capacity to pursue social change through collective action, as well as the capacity to reflect collectively on such efforts, are indispensable features of the generation of knowledge in this domain.

Another indispensable feature is the conscious and intentional application of normative principles—such as the principles of justice, equity, and human dignity—to processes of collective decision-making, action, and reflection. If our goal is to increase the embodiment of underlying normative truths in the social phenomena we are constructing, then we must make efforts to apply relevant normative principles at every stage within this process. But where is the starting point for such processes? How do we initially come to recognize the existence of normative truths?

If we accept the premise that foundational normative truths exist, a compelling case can be made that human intuition, when it is not clouded by ego or perverted in other ways, is capable of some initial, rudimentary recognition of, and attunement to, such truths. Many religious systems are based on this premise, broadly construed; otherwise, people could never recognize and respond to "revealed" truths. Many moral philosophers, past and present, have also posited secular variations on this theme.[28] And a body of empirical evidence seems to point toward the existence, in our species, of some kind of normative intuition or an innate moral sense.[29]

However, even if we accept the existence of some rudimentary form of normative intuition, initial intuitions would still need to be repeatedly tested against reality—not merely individually, but collectively—in an iterative manner over time, to increase our intersubjective attunement to normative truths. This speaks to the need for deliberative processes, or consultative processes, that involve planning for the kinds of constructive action alluded to above and that also involve reflecting on such action. These processes would need to be characterized by conscious attention to the application of normative principles and conscious reflection on what is learned through such efforts. The capacity for principled deliberation and reflection at this level is thus another requisite of systematic learning in the domain of social reality.

The application of normative principles in a consultative mode is, of course, no simple matter. Although efforts to apply the principles of physics to the construction of an airplane can be assessed in an objective manner, the application of normative principles to the construction of a social practice or institution requires a subjective—or intersubjective—mode of assessment, as alluded to above. This further underscores the need for a consultative approach, because consulting about the application of normative principles involves subjective interpretations supported by the faculty of intuition. If we are concerned about the role of subjective interpretation and intuition in this process, we should recall from the previous discussion of science that subjective interpretations and intuition already play an invaluable role in the advancement of the natural sciences. Therefore, we should not be inherently skeptical of these human faculties. At the same time, we must recognize that in the domain of social change, they take on elevated importance.

The challenge, in this regard, is that subjective interpretation and intuition are not infallible faculties of discernment. But neither are the faculties of logic and reason, as the histories of science and philosophy amply demonstrate. Furthermore, most forms of logical reasoning rely on a degree of underlying interpretation and intuition. In science and philosophy, the limitations of subjective and intuitive understanding are addressed by striving for intersubjective agreement—that is, consensus among the subjective understanding of many people. Higher degrees of intersubjective agreement, when they are consistent with all available evidence and become stable over time, increase our confidence in conclusions. The same might be said for intersubjective agreement regarding the application of normative principles in the social domain. Under the right conditions, public deliberation can lead to relatively high levels of confidence in intersubjective conclusions based, in part, on the exercise of intuitive faculties of discernment. This is one of the reasons so many people today can confidently assert that slavery is a violation of basic normative truths—moral or spiritual truths—while assertions to the contrary no longer have any credibility in most contemporary public discourse.

As the movement from slavery to emancipation to ongoing struggles for civil rights illustrates, intersubjective agreement becomes meaningful only to the extent that marginalized and oppressed populations are included as full participants in the deliberative processes, or consultative processes, alluded to above. If intersubjective agreement is reached only among the most powerful and privileged segments of society, who have internalized narrowly self-interested conceptions of reality, this would not advance efforts to increase normative truths in social constructs. Processes of collective learning about the application of normative principles to social reality are rendered meaningful only when previously excluded groups become full protagonists. How else can we assess and increase the embodiment of principles such as justice in social structures that are emerging through human agency? The subjective experiences and interpretations of the oppressed are essential to these processes.

This is one of the ways that such efforts can contend with the social forces alluded to earlier in this chapter, such as the exercise of power, privilege, ego, and self-interested interpretations of reality. And we cannot be naïve about these social forces. This is an important theme we will return to in the next chapter when we discuss the relationship between knowledge and power. In the meantime, we can recognize that the inclusion of diverse and historically marginalized segments of society is essential to constructing a new social reality that embodies normative truths such as justice to greater degrees. We can also recognize that many movements for social change—such as movements to abolish slavery, movements to achieve women's suffrage, and movements to improve labor conditions—have done precisely this.

With these insights in mind, we can begin to see the relationship between relative attunement and relative embodiment even more clearly. Our approach to the embodiment of normative truths must encompass many of the same features as our approach to attunement to material truths. But relative embodiment has additional requirements because it necessitates simultaneously generating knowledge about the products and processes of human agency within normatively guided struggles for social change.

As with attunement to material truths, attunement to normative truths can be relative to the perspectives of those who are engaged in their exploration. Attunement to normative truths can also be relative to the depth of insight any given perspective generates over time. Attunement to normative truths can also be relative to the degree that diverse insights become integrated into a coherent framework over time.

With those similarities noted, some differences must also be considered. Aspects of some material truths can be modelled mathematically, and those models can be applied with a high degree of precision within certain frames of reference—such as the laws of Newtonian physics and the calculations that follow from them. It is unlikely that we will ever be able to model normative truths in these ways. One reason for this, it seems, is that normative truths interact in exceedingly complex ways that are context-dependent and defy modelling. Consider, for example, the normative principles of justice and mercy. It seems plausible that different individuals can develop different degrees of attunement to, or understanding of, these principles. But even for an individual who has developed a relatively high degree of such understanding, the application of these principles will always remain situational. There is no mathematical formula for reconciling justice and mercy in every context. Rather, it seems that a quality of normative discernment often referred to as *wisdom* is required. In this sense, a normative truth cannot be conceptualized or modelled as a context-independent law.

Also, unlike material truths, in the domain of normative truths the concept of relative attunement needs to be supplemented by the concept of relative embodiment, for the reasons discussed earlier in this chapter. Relative embodiment is a much richer concept that enables us to recognize the constitutive, as well as the context-dependent, expression of normative truths in the phenomena we construct through human agency. With this recognition, we can reconcile truth and relativity on yet another level. We can see that "truth versus relativity" is a false dichotomy even in the domain of social reality and normative truths.

Furthermore, if we return to the question of material technologies alluded to earlier in this chapter, we can recognize that normative truth and relativity are also inseparable in material constructs. As the previous discussion pointed out, material technologies can be situated on the continuum between that which is entirely independent of human agency and that which is entirely dependent on human agency. Material technologies embody elements that came into existence independent of us, but we incorporate those elements into the construction of new material phenomena. Moreover, it is important to note that material technologies, like all social constructs, simultaneously embody and shape human values.[30] In other words, all technologies have a normative dimension.

For instance, the invention of guns has exerted a profound influence on our social reality, as did the invention of cars. And the invention of smart phones and social media apps is now exerting an equally profound influence. Clearly, the things we choose to forge from iron or silicon have normative dimensions. In this regard, it is possible to conceive of the relative embodiment of normative truths in material technologies. Computerized axial tomography scans (CAT scans) and atomic bombs both apply the physics of radiation in an instrumental manner. But one is an instrument used to prolong human life; the other is an instrument used to end human life on a massive scale. These are profound normative distinctions.

If it is possible to conceive of the relative embodiment of normative truths in material technologies, then it is also possible to consider the conscious and intentional application of normative principles in processes of technological development and adoption. This implies another learning process. Specifically, it implies the need to systematically generate knowledge about the normative implications of different paths of technological innovation and diffusion.

In the domain of technological innovation, as in the domain of social change, many efforts have already been made to apply normative truths in conscious and intentional ways. The development of many medical technologies, some communication technologies, and many other beneficial forms of technology have, at least in part, been motivated in this way—even as other technologies have been driven purely by profit motives or military objectives or other narrowly self-interested agendas. However, even when technological innovations are well intentioned, their normative implications are still difficult to predict due to unintended consequences. For instance, who could have predicted that the introduction of snowmobiles as a labor-saving technology for reindeer herding would have had such a destabilizing effect on the social and ecological integrity of the Skolt Lapps, as the classic study by Pertti Pelto demonstrates?[31]

We clearly have much to learn about how paths of technological innovation and adoption can be guided by deliberative processes of collective action and reflection. Toward this end, it will again be important to include all relevant segments of society in these processes, especially marginalized and vulnerable groups who often have little say regarding the nature and direction of technological development. Today, even the most altruistically motivated processes of technological innovation tend to be undertaken by privileged segments of society who are relatively disconnected from the alleged beneficiaries of their work and thus tend to be blind to unintended negative consequences. The transfer of technology through international development projects is replete with examples of this, from the disruption of women's support networks via the introduction of technologies that isolate them socially, to the dispossession of peasant farmers through the introduction of technologies that increase their debt burdens to unsustainable levels.[32]

Ultimately, most technological innovation today is driven by the logic of the market and is motivated by profit. It thus tends to be indifferent to social and environmental externalities that do not factor into the market calculus. Even when efforts are made to factor in such externalities, they are hard to anticipate or address without the input of all relevant segments of society. But as the stakes of technological innovation continue to rise, we clearly need to develop more thoughtful, knowledge-driven, participatory, deliberative, and normatively sound approaches. The normatively indifferent market-driven approaches of the past are, like so many other inherited social patterns, proving deeply maladaptive in an age of heightened social and ecological interdependence.

As difficult as such approaches are in the construction and refinement of new technologies, they are even more challenging in the construction and refinement of new social norms, relationships, and institutions, because they are less palpable. Nonetheless, we can identify countless efforts to increase the embodiment of normative truths in social constructs, past and present. Every social movement animated by commitments to justice and equity, or motivated by altruistic and mutualistic values, constitutes such an effort, as does every social policy deliberation animated by similar commitments and values. The question we need to ask is not whether people exert agency in efforts to apply normative truths to processes of social construction. What we need to ask is how effective are different strategies, methods, and approaches that people pursue in this regard? How can these become more effective? What capacities do we need to develop—at the level of individuals, institutions, and communities—to increase our efficacy? And by what standards can we assess our progress?

The discussion throughout this chapter has suggested, in outline form, what many of these capacities and standards might be. Some of these have already been explored in great depth by others. For instance, Jürgen Habermas has devoted a remarkable career to exploring communicative norms that play an essential role in these processes. His work, along with the wider dialogues and critiques surrounding it, are rich with relevant insights.[33] Likewise, the works of John Rawls, Amartya Sen, Christine Korsgaard, Hilary Putnam, Charles Taylor, Kwame Appiah, Alasdair MacIntyre, Thomas Nagel, and many others have contributed profound insights and raised equally profound questions regarding the nature of normative principles and values as well as the processes by which they can be translated into a new social reality.[34]

Throughout all this work, however, an unresolved tension between truth and relativity limits our ability to address the most pressing exigencies of the age in which we live. This chapter provides a rational and coherent framework for reconciling this tension—one that rests on a set of clearly stated premises that not everyone will accept. But rejection of this framework requires the acceptance of other premises that are no more empirically verifiable than the premises articulated above, as will become clear later in this book. In the meantime, suffice it to say that the choice is not between a rational and proven set of premises and an irrational and disproven or extraneous set of premises. Rather, the choice is between two sets of equally rational premises with profoundly different social implications.

Before we can have that discussion, we need to examine another unresolved tension—the tension between *knowledge* and *power*. This tension is closely associated with the tension between truth and relativity, and it further limits our ability to address the exigencies of the age in a rational and coherent manner.

Chapter 2

Reconciling Knowledge & Power

Twentieth-century scholarship exposed a deeply problematic relationship between knowledge and power. In short, it became increasingly apparent that the generation of knowledge is highly susceptible to the corrupting influences of power. Indeed, Foucault argued that all knowledge is shaped by power, and this line of thinking has been influential in the humanities and social sciences.[35]

To better understand this relationship between knowledge and power, consider knowledge about history. Histories are often written by members of dominant social groups who, consciously or unconsciously, articulate narratives that reinforce their positions of power and privilege. For instance, even in this post-colonial era, generations of young people still grow up reading historical narratives from perspectives that obscure or ignore genocides against indigenous peoples, slavery, and other forms of organized violence and exploitation against colonized, oppressed populations. Such narratives also tend to neglect the agency and accomplishments of marginalized groups before, during, and after colonization.

Similar patterns can be found in the social and behavioral sciences. Obvious examples of this can be found in the field of economics, which has been dominated by a neoliberal framework that serves the short-term interests of narrow segments of society. This framework has normalized self-interested behavior at the expense of community well-being, promoted massive disparities of wealth and poverty, encouraged the liquidation of ecological capital for short-term gain, and destabilized the climate for delusionary notions of economic growth.[36] The generation of knowledge in other disciplines has also been corrupted by power and privilege, as with the application of social and behavioral research methodologies to refine techniques for the mass manipulation of consumers and voters.

Nor is this relationship between knowledge and power limited to the production of knowledge in the humanities and social sciences. It is even present in the applied natural sciences. Eugenics and other expressions of social Darwinism in the natural sciences were among the most troubling twentieth-century examples. As well, medical research has for decades been biased toward the study of male physiology, disease, and health.[37] Likewise, systemic biases in pharmaceutical and nutritional research have been driven more by the profit motives of powerful industries than the well-being of vulnerable populations.[38] The same is true for systemic biases in agricultural research, which tend to promote concentrations of agro-industrial wealth rather than socially equitable and ecologically sustainable practices.[39] And, of course, the development of military science and the exorbitant spending on military research by the world's wealthiest nations is perhaps the most egregious ongoing example of the troubling relationship between knowledge and power in the applied natural sciences.

Therefore, as with the relationship between truth and relativity, the relationship between knowledge and power is not merely an abstract academic concern. It directly impacts billions of lives. This concern becomes ever more acute in an age characterized by explosive growth in the generation and diffusion of knowledge. With this concern in mind, we would do well to ask: How can the generation of knowledge be shielded from the corrupting influence of power? Or can it? And if it can, how can the generation of knowledge be more fully informed and guided by normative principles such as justice?[40]

CONCEPTUALIZING KNOWLEDGE

Answering these questions requires us first to clarify what we mean by *knowledge* and to consider its role in the construction of social realties. The generation, application, and intergenerational transmission of knowledge is a defining characteristic of our species. Other species engage in various forms of learning, and some species even transmit some learned behaviors from one generation to another.[41]

But humans engage in the systematic generation and transmission of knowledge on a scale that is many orders of magnitude more complex and sophisticated than any other species, as demonstrated by collective enterprises such as science. Indeed, the human capacity to generate knowledge is a primary driver of our social evolution.

Remarkably, in the modern era, many people have lost sight of this. Many have come to view economic activity as the primary driver of progress. This view has characterized the ideologies of capitalism and communism. It informed most efforts to reconstruct Europe and Asia after the devastation of World War II. It has shaped dominant approaches to international development in nations emerging from the devastation of Western colonialism. And it continues to dominate public policy discourses and popular news discourses that project measures such as Gross Domestic Product as indicators of progress.

Likewise, a closely related modern narrative views technological innovation as the primary driver of progress. This narrative tends to be associated with the logic of technological determinism, which suggests that technological innovation drives and shapes the development of social norms, structures, and values.[42] Extreme versions of this view assert that the steady advancement of the natural sciences leads us down inevitable paths of technological development that drive social progress in deterministic ways. Technological determinism also fosters a narrowly instrumental rationality by which technology is understood as a means to an end that is not clarified, resulting in little reflection about the nature of the ends that should guide our technological choices. Furthermore, technological determinism is often coupled with a capitalist ideology that assumes the free market will, through its mythical invisible hand, stimulate and coordinate paths of technological innovation that maximize human well-being in ways that are little short of magical. According to this view, technological determinism is a corollary of economic determinism.

On closer inspection, however, economic growth and technological innovation are both functions of the underlying generation of knowledge. Economics, as well as every technological field, are domains within a much larger and ever-expanding field of human knowledge. This larger field includes all disciplines within the natural sciences, social sciences, and humanities—which contribute to the advancement of civilization in diverse ways. In addition, this includes knowledge regarding education, training, and the development of human capacity at the individual, institutional, and community levels. And as the previous chapter in this book suggests, it may also include knowledge regarding the application of normative principles to the betterment of humanity—a domain that enables us to transcend consciously the dangerous logic of economic or technological determinism. We can thus recognize the centrality of knowledge to human existence, its fundamental role in processes of social evolution, and the diverse forms of knowledge that humans can generate.

In this context, it is important to consider how the concept of *knowledge* relates to the concept of *truth* discussed in the previous chapter. Toward this end, consider a simple form of human knowledge: knowledge regarding how to make stone tools by striking stones together in purposeful ways. This was knowledge that our early ancestors presumably did not possess at one time. At some point, this knowledge must have been generated in an experiential manner, and it must have subsequently been passed on from one generation to the next as it also began to diffuse, or emerge independently, across regions and then continents. Over time, this emergent knowledge regarding how to make stone tools was refined and expanded into an increasingly sophisticated body of knowledge, producing increasingly complex and diversified tools.

For such bodies of knowledge to advance in a fruitful manner, there must have been some relationship between (a) the experiential learning process that contributed to the generation of knowledge and (b) underlying material truths about the nature of stones and the mechanical forces required to fashion them into tools. Therefore, there is undoubtedly a relationship between knowledge and foundational truths about reality. But this relationship is complicated.

For one thing, inherited bodies of knowledge are not always well attuned to foundational aspects of reality. For instance, people lived for centuries with misplaced confidence in the apparent knowledge that the sun, along with many other objects in the night sky, revolved around the earth. Science has since demonstrated that, excepting the moon, this is not the case. Therefore, knowledge, like truth claims, has a relative relationship to truth. Truth claims, as I use the term, are discrete statements, models, or theories about reality, but knowledge, as I use the term, signifies a broader concept encompassing not only discrete truth claims but also experientially learned ways of doing things that can be transmitted through simple imitation or instruction—such as the construction of stone tools. We did not need formal theories of physics and chemistry to generate and share practical knowledge regarding how to fashion stone tools. Nor did we need a formal theory of biology to develop basic agricultural practices.

Aristotle distinguished the two types of knowledge alluded to above with the terms *episteme* and *techné*.[43] The former is associated with universal forms of knowledge derived from analytical rationality—such as scientific truth claims about aspects of reality. The latter is associated with the practical knowledge of trades, crafts, and arts, and it is derived from a more technical rationality. Aristotle also recognized a third type of knowledge, *phronesis*, associated with practical reason, wisdom, and ethics. Phronesis involves the rational application of values in context-dependent ways.

Still, Aristotle's three categories do not exhaust the concept of knowledge. For instance, some knowledge is purely subjective. Someone can know with certainty that chocolate is their favorite flavor of ice cream. This purely subjective knowledge is valid and real, but it is not an example of episteme, techné, or phronesis. Likewise, the discussion in chapter 2 about the relative embodiment of truth in social constructs implies a way of thinking about knowledge that is not adequately captured in Aristotle's typology.

The point of this discussion is not to outline a new or exhaustive typology of knowledge. Rather, it is to reinforce the points made above about the centrality of knowledge to human existence, its fundamental role in processes of social evolution, and the diverse forms of knowledge that humans can generate—while distinguishing the broad concept of knowledge from the narrower concept of truth claims. The two concepts are related and overlap, but they are also distinct. Both are needed to advance the discussion at hand.

The concept of knowledge enables us to discuss the relationship between bodies of knowledge and power. Bodies of knowledge can be shaped, consciously or unconsciously, by self-interested expressions of power, as the opening paragraphs of this chapter illustrate. Hence it is possible to talk about oppressive bodies of knowledge, or oppressive structures of knowledge, that are not attuned to or built upon foundational normative truths. These structures of knowledge can, in turn, influence the form of other social structures. For instance, the structures of knowledge that have characterized neoliberal economics in recent decades have exerted a profound influence on economic policies, trade agreements, market structures, and business models across the planet. The same structures of knowledge have also influenced policies, practices, and social structures across a wide range of other fields, from politics to education to health care.

This broad conception of knowledge, and bodies of knowledge, also informs the ways we think about learning. It is common to think about learning as something people without knowledge receive from people with knowledge. In this sense, learning is about the transmission and reception of existing bodies of knowledge. Learning processes of this kind have clearly played an essential role in human societies since we began fashioning stone tools, and probably much earlier. However, another form of learning entails the conscious generation of new knowledge. Science is, in this sense, a learning enterprise. The natural sciences are focused on learning about diverse aspects of reality that emerged independent of human agency. Likewise, it is possible to engage in processes of systematic and collective learning about aspects of reality that emerge only through human agency, as discussed in the previous chapter.

In this regard, if we consider the exigencies of the age in which we live, the most important questions that must ultimately frame our learning include the following: How can we construct more mature systems of governance capable of coordinating human affairs in more peaceful, just, and sustainable ways? How can we create economic systems that support these same normative values? How can we develop educational systems that raise human capacity to participate in more mature and responsible ways within such political and economic systems? How can we construct other social systems, such as systems of media and communication, that more effectively support and enhance these same values and capacities? And how can we begin to do all of this in ways that recognize the increasing interdependence of diverse individuals, communities, and institutions across the planet?

In short, as the introduction to the book asserts, humanity has not yet learned how to live in a peaceful, just, and mutually prosperous manner on an increasingly crowded planet. We therefore need to consciously, purposefully, and systematically learn our way forward in these ways. These are the most important forms of knowledge we now need to generate and diffuse across the planet. This process encompasses the formulation and testing of specific truth claims, but the generation and application of knowledge is a larger enterprise.

Such aspirations will, however, be dismissed as naïve unless we can address concerns regarding the relationship between power and the generation of knowledge. If these concerns cannot be addressed, it is reasonable to assume that a more peaceful, just, and prosperous social order is beyond our capacity to construct. The reason for that conclusion would be simple. If power inevitably corrupts the generation and application of knowledge, then conflict, injustice, and unsustainable patterns of existence will be inevitable features dominating social reality since, according to this cynical premise, social phenomena can be constructed only with self-interested and oppressive structures of knowledge.

CONCEPTUALIZING POWER

The way we conceptualize power and its operation in human affairs can lead to either optimism or cynicism about humanity's ability to address the exigencies of this age in a learning mode, through the generation of knowledge. In previous publications, I have examined the limitations of prevailing conceptions of power and made an argument for an expanded conception.[44] The discussion that follows distills my previous arguments and then adapts and expands them for the discussion at hand.

In the latter half of the twentieth century, theorists of power began to invoke what has become a widely used distinction between two broad ways of thinking and talking about power. This distinction is made by contrasting the expression "power to" with the expression "power over."[45] As Thomas Wartenberg explains, "The expressions *power-to* and *power-over* are a shorthand way of making a distinction between two fundamentally different ordinary-language locutions

within which the term 'power' occurs. Depending upon which locution one takes as the basis of one's theory of power, one will arrive
at a very different model of the role of power in the social world."[46]

Contemporary social theory tends to invoke the "power over"
model. This Machiavellian understanding of power can be traced
through the work of influential thinkers ranging from Thomas
Hobbes to Karl Marx to Max Weber.[47] As Anthony Giddens points
out, this conflictual model of power underlies virtually all major
traditions of Western social theory.[48] Sophisticated versions of this
model recognize that power over others is not merely exercised
through force and coercion; it can also be exercised through the
inculcation of oppressive values and beliefs, the shaping of oppressive perceptions and desires, the construction of oppressive bodies
of knowledge, and the propagation of other oppressive forms of
cultural hegemony.[49]

Although "power to" models are acknowledged by some social
theorists, those models are often dismissed as irrelevant to social
theory.[50] As Steven Lukes asserts, such models "are out of line with
the central meanings of 'power' as traditionally understood and
with the concerns that have always centrally preoccupied students
of power."[51]

Even Foucault, in his effort to radically rethink the nature and
function of power, ends up reinforcing the "power over" model.
Foucault understands power as a relational property or force that
permeates society, connecting all social groups in a web of mutual influence, while constituting social organization and hierarchy through
the production of discourses, the imposition of discipline and order,
and the shaping of human desires and subjectivities. In this context,
Foucault sees power as simultaneously productive and oppressive.
Society cannot function without it, despite its perennially oppressive
manifestations. By recognizing the productive and enabling function
of power, Foucault seems to embrace a "power to" model. However,
Foucault situates his analyses within the "power over" tradition, and
his overarching project is one of resistance to such power. Furthermore, he calls others to do the same. "We should direct our research-
es on the nature of power," he writes, "towards domination and
material operators of power," and we should "base our analyses of
power on the study of the techniques and tactics of domination."[52]

There are, however, notable exceptions to this "power over" bias.

For instance, Giddens defines *power* as "transformative capacity" or "the capacity to achieve outcomes"—a definition that is consistent with the "power to" locution introduced above.[53] Although Giddens recognizes the importance of studying "power over" relations in some contexts, he asserts that power is not intrinsically linked with conflict, nor is it inherently oppressive.

Likewise, some feminist social theorists have articulated variations of the "power to" theme, along with critiques of the narrow focus on "power over." According to these critiques, the "power over" model normalizes conflictual and competitive expressions of power in ways that buttress male privilege. When struggles for domination are viewed as inevitable expressions of human nature, many women are put at a physical disadvantage to men. When political and economic systems are based on competitive power relations, those systems tend to reward men over women. Even when women adopt aggressive and competitive behaviors, they often encounter double standards that punish them for behavior that is not considered appropriate to women.[54] Furthermore, beyond the relative disadvantages that women experience within these structures of male privilege, such structures promote the domination of certain qualities over others—regardless of whether these qualities are displayed by women or men. In this regard, a culture that privileges aggressive and competitive qualities is a culture that devalues caring and mutualistic qualities.[55]

With such critiques in mind, Jean Baker Miller advocates for a broad reconceptualization of power as the capacity to produce change, which includes nurturing and empowering others or enhancing rather than diminishing the power of others.[56] Along these same lines, Nancy Hartsock argues that a feminist theory of power should view power not as domination but as capacity, often expressed at the level of the community, rooted in experiences of connection and mutual relationship.[57]

Kenneth Boulding, a peace studies scholar, echoes these ideas in his integrative theory of power. He associates power with the capacity to build social structures and organizations, to inspire loyalty, and to bind people together. For him, power operates through ties of cooperation and reciprocity, friendship and collective identity, the growth of a sense of community, the ability to create and pursue constructive images of the future together, and the belief that one's own well-being is linked to the well-being of others. Peaceful and just social systems can be constructed only on the normative basis of these integrative "power to" relations. Although Boulding acknowledges the existence of "power over" relations, he argues that the conditions in the contemporary world demand a much wider recognition and promotion of integrative power in human affairs.[58]

As these arguments suggest, the concept of "power over" does not provide an adequate basis for analyzing existing social reality. Nor does it provide an adequate normative basis for constructing a new social reality. On both counts, the concept obscures as much as it reveals. "Power over" relations exist, and they warrant sustained critical attention. What is needed, however, is a more comprehensive schema that recognizes the full spectrum of power relations and provides an adequate basis for critical as well as normative social theory.

To develop a more comprehensive schema, we first need to recognize that the distinction between "power to" and "power over" does not set up equivalent categories. "Power to" denotes power as *capacity*. "Power over" is a special case of this overarching concept. If we say that we have "power over" someone, this is simply another way of saying that we have the capacity to exercise some form of control over that person.

Moreover, "power over" is not the only subcategory of power as capacity. People who are acting in a cooperative or mutualistic manner in the pursuit of a common goal are exercising "power with" one another, which is yet another expression of power.[59] But "power over" and "power with" are still not equivalent subcategories of "power to." In this regard, consider two equal adversaries exercising "power against" one another in a manner that results in mutual frustration. Neither adversary is exercising "power over" the other. Yet they are clearly not exercising "power with" one another. We can thus see that people either exercise "power with" one another in a mutualistic manner or they exercise "power against" one another in an adversarial manner.[60] These are equivalent subcategories of "power to." This distinction between what can be called *mutualistic power relations* and *adversarial power relations* constitutes the broadest relational categories within the more general concept of power as capacity.

Where does "power over" fit into this schema? Mutualistic power relations and adversarial power relations can each be divided into two further subcategories, and it is at this level that the concept of "power over" can be located. Exercising power over others is one subcategory of adversarial power relations. The other subcategory of adversarial relations is the "balance of power" relations alluded to above. What distinguishes "balance of power" relationships from "power over" relationships is the relative equality or inequality of the adversaries. In a "balance of power" relationship, power is distributed equally such that neither adversary can dominate the other.[61] In a "power over" relationship, power is distributed unequally such that one adversary can dominate the other.

The distinction between *power equality* and *power inequality* has a mirror counterpart in mutualistic power relations because two or more agents acting cooperatively can also be characterized by equal or unequal distributions of power. In this context, power equality results in the "mutual empowerment" of all cooperating agents. Examples include two spouses in a healthy relationship or a group of workers forming a profit-sharing cooperative. On the other hand, power inequality within a mutualistic relationship results in the "assisted empowerment" of the less powerful agents by the more powerful agents. Examples include a nurturing relationship between a parent and child or the mentoring relationship between a caring teacher and a motivated student.

This schema offers a more coherent and more comprehensive way to conceptualize power relations than schemas that focus primarily or exclusively on power as domination. By representing the schema as a two-dimensional diagram, we can map various power relations relative to the axes *adversarialism* ↔ *mutualism* and *equality* ↔ *inequality*, as figure 7 illustrates.

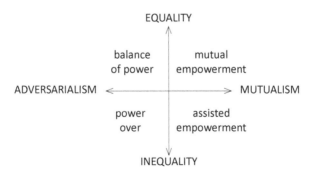

Figure 7. Relational and distributive dimensions of power.

On this conceptual map, "power over" relations—as important as they are to recognize and address—constitute only one of four possible expressions of power, situated in the lower-left quadrant of the diagram. Compromise, gridlock, and other "balance of power" relations are situated in the upper-left quadrant. Nurturing, educating, and other assisted empowerment relations are situated in the lower-right quadrant. Cooperation, reciprocation, coordination, and other mutual empowerment relations are situated in the upper-right quadrant.

This conceptual map brings into focus the relative nature of adversarial and mutualistic relations of power, along with the relative nature of power equality and inequality. It thereby reminds us that movement is possible along both axes. A nurturing relationship may begin with a high degree of inequality and steadily progress toward a state of relative equality, as is the goal in healthy parental and educational relationships. Conversely, a relationship may become more adversarial or more mutualistic over time, as in oscillations toward or away from partisanship and non-partisanship.

This schema also helps us see beyond the problematic distinction power theorists often draw between "power over" and "power to." The former is situated in the lower-left quadrant. The latter constitutes the entire plane on which both axes exist. The schema thus enables us to critically analyze oppressive power relations while expanding our field of vision to recognize normatively desirable expressions of power, as illustrated in figure 8.

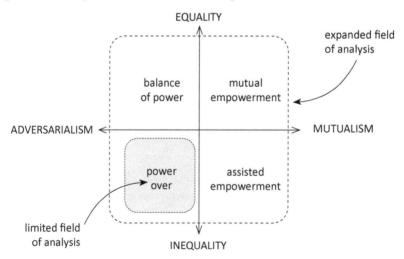

Figure 8. Expanded analysis of power.

This conceptual schema also enables us to think more clearly about the relationship between power and knowledge. When the generation of knowledge is characterized by the "power over" dynamics in the lower-left quadrant, the result will be oppressive structures of knowledge—as history has all too frequently demonstrated. But the generation of knowledge need not occur within this quadrant. It is also possible to pursue the generation of knowledge within the quadrants on the right side of this schema, which are characterized by mutualistic relations of power.

History provides many examples demonstrating this. The development of the polio vaccine by Jonas Salk and his decision not to patent it to ensure its universal affordability and availability is a well-known example. Recent trends toward open-source software developments, the crowd-sourcing of knowledge, open-access scholarly journals, and other innovations at the intersection of the knowledge economy and the sharing economy also illustrate this. Furthermore, it would be absurd to categorize the contributions of individuals like Newton and Einstein to the field of physics as oppressive forms of knowledge embodying "power over" relations—even though those contributions have occasionally been applied by others in such ways. Clearly, the generation of knowledge can be driven by disinterested or even altruistic motives within a mutualistic framework, even if this is not always the case.

The question we need to ask, then, in this regard, is how can the systematic generation and application of knowledge be more consistently pursued in mutualistic and universally empowering, rather than oppressive, ways? Or stated another way, how can the structures and practices that foster the generation and application of knowledge more fully embody the principle of justice?

KNOWLEDGE, POWER, AND JUSTICE

Generating and applying knowledge in universally empowering ways that embody the principle of justice is not a simple or easy matter. Such efforts will, it seems, need to be characterized by all the conditions for pursuing attunement to truth and embodiment of truth outlined in the previous chapter.

To some skeptics, the latter conditions associated with the relative embodiment of truth might seem hopelessly naïve. Yet it is equally plausible to argue that these conditions have become exigencies of the age in which we live that require our urgent and sustained attention. For the sake of argument, let us assume that the achievement of these conditions is a difficult yet urgent need of the twenty-first century that will test our collective capacities to the limits. Are we certain we can achieve these conditions? Perhaps not. Do we need to try? Yes. The stakes are too high not to do so. Do we have anything to lose by trying? No. If we are unsuccessful, we will simply return to the oppressive conditions that frequently characterize the generation and application of knowledge today—and at least we will have learned something about the outer limits of our collective capacity. We currently do not know where those limits lie.

If we accept that we need to learn how to generate knowledge in universally empowering ways that embody the principle of justice, we can begin thinking about how to do this by reasoning backwards from the conditions—or ideals—outlined in the previous chapter. As we recall, those ideals include the capacity to analyze dynamic social processes, patterns, and systems while they unfold as a result of our own agency; the capacity to operate in modes of collective learning characterized by constructive action and ongoing processes of reflection on action; the capacity to consciously identify and apply relevant normative principles in systematic and deliberative, or consultative, ways within these collective and inclusive learning processes; and the capacity to strive for intersubjective agreement regarding the application of normative principles within a collective and consultative learning mode.

In this context, let's remember that normative principles refer to principles such as justice, equity, compassion, and the inherent dignity of every human being. As the discussion in the previous chapter acknowledged, such principles are relatively inscrutable, and our understanding of them therefore relies, in part at least, on the faculty of human intuition. One question we need to ask in this regard is whether the faculty of intuition can be trained in ways that increase its attunement to foundational normative truths? Let's assume, for the moment, that it can. After all, the material sciences rest on the premise that the faculty of reason can be trained in ways that increase its attunement to foundational material truths. It is not unreasonable to assume that other faculties of the human mind can be trained as well.

If intuition is a faculty that can be trained to increase its attunement to foundational normative truths, what would such training entail? One thing that seems clear is that it must involve the ability to transcend narrowly self-interested—or egoistic—interpretations of reality. In relation to normative intuition, egoism can be understood as a form of ignorance, or irrationalism, characteristic of the untrained mind. Egoism may be a survival imperative of the newborn child. Yet within healthy families and healthy communities, children growing toward maturity as social beings can be trained to overcome their egoistic tendencies by increasing their sense of mutualism and interdependence with others. Egoistic tendencies, it seems, can be transcended through the development of altruistic qualities. It can thus be argued that efforts to quiet the ego through the development of altruistic qualities helps attune the faculty of intuition with foundational normative truths. Let us refer to this outcome as the development of the capacity for *normative discernment*.

Normative discernment is not simply intuitive. Logic, or reason, can also play an important role. Immanuel Kant's "categorical imperative" and Rawls's "original position" both illustrate the role that logic can play in the exploration of normative truths.[62] Thus, logic and intuition can both contribute to normative discernment. Such discernment will always be fallible, since logic and intuition are both fallible human faculties. Therefore, intersubjective agreement is an essential condition for increasing confidence in our normative discernment. Moreover, intersubjective agreement in the domain of normative truth claims is meaningful only when it is pursued through deliberative, or consultative, processes that encompass the views of all relevant segments of society—especially the most marginalized and oppressed. Otherwise, normative agreement can easily degrade into self-interested interpretations of reality by privileged segments of society exercising power over marginalized others who have been denied a voice. Therefore, justice requires broad and inclusive participation in the generation of knowledge about social transformation.

Skeptics might once again find this line of reasoning to be naïve or unrealistic. However, if we are committed to constructing a more peaceful, just, and prosperous social order, it seems important to test this line of reasoning. Unless we can foster more systematic and purposeful processes of collective learning and social transformation along the lines suggested, it is unlikely that we can address the most basic existential challenges now facing us. This might well prove to be the new realism arising from the conditions of the age in which we live.

Chapter 3

Reconciling Science & Religion

In chapter 1, we examined how the operation of the natural sciences enables us to recognize three ways that *truth* and *relativity* can be reconciled: (1) comprehension of a foundational truth can be relative to the perspectives of those who are engaged in its exploration; (2) comprehension of a foundational truth can be relative to the depth of insight any given perspective generates as it is applied, explored, and elaborated over time; and (3) comprehension of a foundational truth can be relative to the degree that diverse insights become integrated into a coherent framework over time. Together, these three insights help us conceptualize *relative attunement to foundational material truths*. Although the concept of relative attunement also applies in the social realm, it does not adequately account for the normative dimensions of social reality and the fact that social phenomena are constructed through human agency. To address these latter considerations, another concept was proposed and explored: (4) the *relative embodiment of foundational normative truths* in the construction of social reality.

In chapter 2, we then examined the relationship between *knowledge* and *power* and how this relationship shapes the processes discussed in chapter 1. To consider the complexity of this relationship, an expanded conception of power was proposed and discussed. The chapter concluded by exploring how this expanded conception of power might help us approach the generation and application of knowledge in universally empowering ways that embody the principle of justice—especially in the construction of a new social reality.

We now turn to the relationship between science and religion in the construction of social reality.

When religious communities strive to apply "spiritual principles" to the betterment of humanity, they are contributing to the embodiment of normative truths in the construction of social reality.[63] When they do this in a learning mode, they begin to resemble the processes of knowledge generation described in chapter 1. Consider, for instance, the religious communities—especially Black churches in the southern United States—that advanced the struggle for racial justice during the civil rights movement in the 1950s, 1960s, and 1970s. There was a learning dimension to that socially transformative work. Actions were taken, insights were gained, approaches were adjusted, and victories were eventually won. Likewise, more than a century earlier, the Quakers and other justice-oriented religious communities who led struggles to abolish slavery engaged in somewhat similar processes.

Moreover, if we accept the premise (from chapter 2) that justice requires broad and inclusive participation in the generation of knowledge about social transformation, then it is difficult to imagine how broad and inclusive participation can be achieved without engaging religion. Most people across the planet continue to identify as religious.[64] Religion has been the central domain of normative inquiry in the lives of most people for millennia. Religion reaches to the depths of human motivation, and it has the capacity to organize and guide collective expressions of human agency on large scales. Of course, materialist ideologies such as Marxism and Nazism have also motivated collective agency on large scales, and some people continue to argue that human progress lies in materialist ideologies such as Marxism. No materialist ideology, however, has demonstrated the universal reach or transhistorical presence that religion has demonstrated in human affairs.

It thus seems reasonable to ask how, and to what degree, has religion historically supported transformative learning regarding normatively guided processes of social construction? At the same time, we need to ask the following questions: How has religion failed or distorted these processes at various times? And how might religion contribute more effectively to these processes in the future?

With these questions in mind, we can conceptualize both science and religion, at their best, as complementary systems of knowledge and practice concerned with the betterment of humanity, as Arbab and Lample have done.[65] Science, we have seen, can be understood as a system of knowledge and practice focused largely on the exploration and application of material truths. Similarly, religion can be understood as a system of knowledge and practice, but one focused largely on the exploration and application of normative truths—or spiritual truths. Science and religion thus generate complementary forms of knowledge about the betterment of the human condition.

The complementarity of these systems need not, however, be understood in a binary, mutually exclusive, or radically independent manner. Science and religion, conceived in the ways alluded to above, overlap in significant ways. Both are concerned with the systematic generation of knowledge about reality, and reality is, ultimately, one. Both are concerned with the betterment of the human condition, which entails generating and applying knowledge about enabling and constraining features of reality. Toward this end, both can be characterized by the exercise of rational thought, imagination and intuition, as well as skepticism and critical thinking. Both can rely on disciplined and systematic observations. Both can articulate provisional assumptions as well as concepts, models, theories, or conceptual frameworks that can be tested over time. Both require virtues such curiosity, honesty and integrity, cooperation, a degree of detachment from preconceived notions, recognition of the ultimate fallibility of human knowledge, a corresponding posture of humility and open-mindedness, and the avoidance of dogmatism or fanaticism. Both are social enterprises pursued by communities of people that need to develop shared vocabularies and complex forms of social organization. And both must contend with a variety of social forces that can distort or pervert them. For reasons such as these, we can avoid the trap of false dichotomies when conceptualizing science and religion. Rather, they can be understood as complementary and overlapping systems of knowledge and practice.

This, of course, is not the only way to conceptualize science and religion. Nor, in the case of religion, is this a dominant conception in contemporary discourse. Nor is the preceding conception of religion incompatible with more personal or mystical understandings of religion that focus on spiritual development, communion with God or meditation on Truth, love and grace, salvation, or spiritual enlightenment. Rather, the preceding conception of religion is intended to bring into focus a significant but often overlooked and arguably underdeveloped dimension of religion: its role in the systematic generation and application of knowledge for the advancement of civilization. In this sense, it offers a developmental conception of religion as a collective enterprise that does not preclude personal relationship with, or growth toward, a Divine Creator or Great Spirit. Indeed, if we understand human nature in terms of a twofold spiritual purpose—developing our spiritual potentialities on individual and collective levels in a mutually enabling manner—then the personal and social dimension of religion can easily be reconciled.

Moreover, this understanding of religion is broadly compatible with past traditions of thought that view religion as a developmental phenomenon—that is, conceptions that religious knowledge and practice evolve through gradual or epochal transformations across history—which is one of the ways that religion is understood today. Many traditions of thought in Judaism, Christianity, and Islam embody developmental narratives of various kinds. And as Benjamin Schewel demonstrates, even among modern philosophers and historians of religion, developmental conceptions rank among the major ways that religion is commonly understood.[66] Moreover, based on the discussion in the earlier chapters of this book, conceptualizing religion (at least in part) as an evolving system of knowledge and practice focused on the exploration and application of spiritual truths would be a constructive and fruitful way to understand and enact religion in the modern world.

Regrettably, at this critical juncture in history, when humanity needs to harness the highest potential of both science and religion, they are each, as Arbab points out, in a state of relative crisis.[67] To most thoughtful observers, the crisis of religion is abundantly clear. One sign of this is the fragmentation of religious thought into competing factions that claim to be the exclusive or final arbiters of truth. A related sign is the spread of religious intolerance, fanaticism, and violence, as ancient religious traditions encounter emerging social phenomena and competing truth claims they are ill-equipped to engage. Another sign of the crisis of religion is the gap that is often revealed between professed normative ideals and actual behaviors and practices. Yet another sign of the crisis is the frequent rejection of scientific knowledge by religious leaders and the degradation of religion into irrational superstition and unthinking imitation of the past. Given the degraded conditions that such religious practices signify, it is no surprise that religion is viewed with indifference or hostility by many people today.

The crisis of science is less apparent to many observers. The fruits of science are so visible today that it is easy to overlook the way that science has alienated or disempowered large segments of humanity who have been taught to view the generation of knowledge as something that can be done only by elites in specialized research laboratories or institutions of higher learning. It is also easy to overlook the way that concentrations of power and wealth have bent the direction of so much scientific inquiry in ways that disproportionately serve the interests of privileged segments of society. Likewise, it is easy to overlook the fragmentation that has occurred within science as competing disciplines and research programs view the world through increasingly reductionist lenses while rarely learning from one another. Finally, it is easy to overlook the dogmatic materialism that is associated with some scientific thought today, which obscures the normative—or spiritual—dimensions of reality, breeds prejudice against even the most thoughtful and mature expressions of religion, and gives rise to misguided applications of science ranging from increasingly sophisticated techniques for mass manipulation to increasingly lethal weapons of mass annihilation. Dogmatic materialism is every bit as harmful as the superstition and unthinking imitation that characterizes the crisis of religion.

As this discussion points out, science and religion both have yet to realize their full potential to contribute to the betterment of humanity. How, then, can we foster the ongoing development of each? One way we can do this is to advance the normative discourse on each—or the discourse on how each system ought to function and the normative standards by which it ought to be assessed.

THE NORMATIVE DISCOURSE ON SCIENCE

A normative discourse on science, as a system of knowledge and practice, has already been unfolding for several centuries. This discourse, advanced initially by scientists and philosophers, has focused on efforts to prescribe how science ought to be practiced. In the process, the discourse has articulated various normative standards to which scientific practice is held publicly accountable.[68]

Of primary concern, in the past century, have been standards pertaining to methodological questions. At times, efforts have been made to articulate a central method that should characterize the entire enterprise of science and clearly demarcate it from that which is not science. In other words, such efforts have attempted to clarify an overarching standard for "*the* scientific method." One of the most influential of all such efforts was undertaken by Karl Popper, who prescribed *falsification* as the overarching method for all science.[69] Many philosophers of science now regard such efforts to articulate "*the* scientific method" as naïve, given the complex and multifaceted nature of the scientific enterprise, as discussed in chapter 1 of this book. Furthermore, in practice, methodological pluralism is now generally accepted across diverse fields of scientific inquiry because different kinds of research questions require different kinds of approaches. But normative discussions about methodology continue to prove fruitful within distinct disciplines and research programs in relation to distinct objects of inquiry.

Another concern in the normative discourse on science pertains to the ethics of the research process. Such concerns are often focused on academic honesty, the integrity of data, plagiarism, and the like. Processes of scientific training, along with systems of review, reward, and punishment, have been set up to apply and enforce normative standards in this regard. Such concerns also, increasingly, focus on the reduction or elimination of harm to human or animal research subjects. This development arose from growing public awareness of unethical research practices undertaken in the name of science, ranging from lethal experimentation on Jews during the Holocaust to lethal experimentation on African Americans in the United States.[70] Today, most publicly funded research that is potentially harmful to human subjects and much research on animal subjects must be approved in advance by ethical review boards at universities and, in some cases, other institutions hosting the research. Although many ethical issues still arise in scientific research, the increasing attention paid to them is a direct consequence of this normative discourse.

In the latter part of the twentieth century, the normative discourse on science also began to encompass broader sociological concerns regarding the operation of power and privilege in science. This work can be traced in part to the work of Thomas Kuhn, who was among the first scholars to look critically at the social nature of science and its historical operation. Since Kuhn, much work has been done to examine the political economy of science, gender, and racial biases in science, the commercialization or militarization of science, and other related concerns—all of which raise significant normative questions about the ongoing operation of science that are now being critically examined.

Even though some of these questions are still debated and actual scientific practice often falls short of even the most widely accepted normative standards, this discourse has been a major factor propelling the advancement, refinement, and maturation of science in recent centuries. The history of science includes many spurious truth claims, self-interested corruptions, and political abuses. At this moment in history, however, we clearly benefit from an ongoing public discourse about what constitutes valid science, along with an evolving set of standards and rules of conduct that are applied, however imperfectly at times, to all who claim to be engaged in science. Based on these standards and requirements, we are increasingly able to distinguish valid science from pseudoscience or junk science.

What is still needed, however, is much deeper attention to concerns that arise from the systemic operation and corruption of science through its militarization, its crass commercialization, and its elitism. How can science, as a system of knowledge and practice, become increasingly focused on the betterment of humanity? How can its resources be more effectively organized and channelled according to the principle of justice? And how can a culture of scientific learning be extended to the masses of humanity so that all people can more fully develop their capacities as protagonists in the generation and application of knowledge? The further maturation of science will depend on sustained attention to these and other normative issues.

THE NORMATIVE DISCOURSE ON RELIGION

If we view religion in a parallel manner, as a system of knowledge and practice through which people strive to understand and apply *normative* truths to the advancement of civilization, then we can see the urgent need for a similarly robust discourse seeking to clarify legitimate standards of religious practice and holding religious practice to public account in this regard. For the past two centuries, such a discourse has been eclipsed by secularization theory, which has assumed that the proper role of religion in the modern world is to gradually disappear so that it can be entirely replaced by scientific rationality. Yet it is now becoming apparent to many observers that this theory's predictions have not been realized.[71] On the contrary, religion remains a significant force in the lives of many people on the planet, even in Europe and North America, where secularization theory emerged and is most entrenched. Humanity must now come to terms with the role of religion in modernity. If religion is here to stay, it makes sense to envision and work toward an increasingly constructive role for it.

Although religion is not disappearing, the record of religion is complex. On the one hand, religious concepts, ideals, commitments, and organizational capacities have been major drivers of many progressive social movements. These include abolition movements, suffrage movements, labor movements, independence movements, civil rights movements, anti-apartheid movements, peace movements, humanitarian assistance movements, solidarity movements, and truth and reconciliation movements spanning the nineteenth and twentieth centuries and into the present century.[72] Religious communities are also increasingly aligning themselves with environmental causes.[73] And for many centuries, religions have been a primary source of non-violent strategies to overcome injustice and oppression.[74]

On the other hand, religion has all too frequently been corrupted and abused by political and economic interests that pervert its accomplishments and distort its ends, foster superstition and unthinking imitation, set religion at odds with science and reason, and breed sectarian conflict and violence in its name. In addition, religious belief and practice has often been characterized by the uncritical transmission of inherited cultural prejudices and oppressive social norms. All these debased expressions of religion are, understandably, what has led many modern thinkers to view religion as an anachronistic social construct that should be replaced by a purely scientific rationality and entirely secular belief systems.

Against this complex backdrop, an emerging body of "post-secular" scholarship is beginning to take a more nuanced look at the ongoing role of religion in the modern world and to explore its potentially constructive contributions.[75] Also, in response to resurgent religious fanaticism, public discourse is being fostered by many moderate voices from within the world's dominant faith traditions who are seeking to steer religious communities away from such fanaticism. Likewise, a renewed ecumenical discourse is emerging across these communities in interfaith forums such as the Parliament of the World's Religions, and it includes a focus on religious reform. In these trends, we find the seeds of a normative public discourse on religion that, if cultivated more actively and widely, could parallel the normative discourse on science alluded to above.

Religion, like every social institution, will need to continue to evolve or mature if it is to make an ongoing contribution to peace, justice, and shared prosperity. The discussion in this chapter enables us to conceptualize, however dimly at present, a maturing expression of religion that complements and overlaps science.

If a normative discourse on religion can contribute to this process of maturation, it seems especially important that it focus on how religion can be reconciled to conditions of increasing global interdependence. Transcending conflict and violence committed in the name of religion has become a global imperative. Even though this will not be easy, the stakes have become too high to ignore this. But this will require a deep rethinking of the concept of religion and its normative dimensions, along with a corresponding change in the way we invoke the term "religion."

If we begin to understand religion as a system of knowledge and practice through which we can increase the embodiment of normative truths in social reality, then practices that undermine principles such as unity and justice may not qualify as religion. In other words, if actions committed in the name of a belief system are not conducive to peace, justice, and collective prosperity, then why refer to such a belief system as religion? Why not reject the validity of such claims to religion? Why not deny the label "religion" to belief systems that do not meet some minimal normative standards established through thoughtful public discourse? Simply because some people claim to be doing something in the name of religion does not mean their claims should be publicly validated. Why not validate them only if they meet accepted normative standards of religious practice—as we do with science?

Consider, in this regard, the way scientific practice is increasingly held to normative standards. A classic case study, in this regard, is the Tuskegee Study of Untreated Syphilis in the Negro Male.[76] From 1932 to 1972, the United States Public Health service conducted a study to understand the natural course of untreated syphilis. Six hundred impoverished African-American men were recruited for the study. They were told the study would last six months and that they would receive free health care, meals, and burial insurance for their participation in the study. The study lasted forty years. None of the men were told that they had syphilis, and none were treated with penicillin, even after the drug was proven in the 1940s to treat syphilis effectively. Many of the men died of syphilis, many of their sexual partners contracted it, and a substantial number of children were born with it as a result. The gross ethical failures of this study led to the widespread establishment of institutional review boards for the protection of human subjects at universities and other research institutes, and such review boards are now considered essential to the scientific enterprise. The Tuskegee case study is also widely used to teach research ethics to students today so that generations of aspiring scientists understand there is a normative dimension to the proper practice of science.

Similarly, at the same time the Tuskegee Study was initiated, eugenics programs were being pursued in the name of science across the Western world, leading to forced sterilization programs in North America and the Holocaust in Europe. Today, if scientists wedded to the ideology of social Darwinism tried to assert that eugenics is a valid scientific program that justifies racial or ethnic genocide, this assertion would be quickly and widely rejected as a spurious claim that fails to meet the most basic normative standards of scientific practice.

As these examples illustrate, the normative discourse on science extends beyond rational and empirical standards of scientific practice. Although the normative discourse on science began with those concerns, it has expanded to include ethical standards of scientific practice, along with the institutional mechanisms needed to train scientists in those standards and enforce them. While such training and enforcement is far from perfect and ethical violations still can be found, these normative standards are increasingly regarded as essential to the proper practice of science.

Why can we not hold the practice of religions to account in parallel ways? Why do we uncritically apply the label "religious" to groups of ideological extremists who commit acts of terrorism in the name of religion? Is this not because no widely accepted normative standards currently apply to the practice of religion? Labels such as "religious terrorism" thus continue to circulate freely in public discourse, as though they must be mutually compatible concepts.

In contrast, imagine if the concept of "scientific genocide" circulated freely today, as if *science* and *genocide* were mutually compatible concepts. Sadly, the history of the eugenics movement and the experience of the Holocaust in the mid-twentieth century demonstrate that such concepts were considered mutually compatible only a few generations ago. Thankfully, the normative discourse on science has evolved significantly since that time. A parallel evolution in the discourse on religion is now urgently needed. Is it not possible that we could, over time, through such a process, begin to distinguish ideologically motivated practices that are violent, oppressive, and divisive from legitimate religious practices that embody some minimal normative criteria?

This is not a sectarian argument in favor of one existing religion, or religious denomination, over another. Rather, it is an argument that we need to move beyond sectarianism altogether in our understanding of religion. It is an argument that we need to move from a plural conception of *religions* to a singular conception of *religion*—the same way we have developed a singular conception of science over recent centuries. There are, of course, many branches of science. Within each of them, diverse conceptual frameworks can emerge and generate distinct research programs that test different hypotheses about reality. Some of those programs advance over time, and some decline, depending on their relative attunement to reality. But all this diversity is encompassed within the modern conception of *science* as a singular global enterprise—or even as a faculty of human nature. Of course, science is also an imperfect enterprise, susceptible to the corrupting influences discussed above, so we need a realistic understanding of it. In addition, contemporary science is still fragmented and lacks adequate mechanisms for interdisciplinary or inter-paradigmatic collaboration and integration in ways that continue to limit it. But reality is ultimately one, so science is ultimately a single enterprise in which we engage to investigate different aspects of the same reality. Might we not begin to conceptualize religion in a similar way?

Another core concern in any normative discourse on religion might be the relationship between knowledge and power. In the normative discourse on science, considerable attention has recently been paid to the ways that power can corrupt the generation of knowledge—as it did in the example of the eugenics program. Science, in that case, became an instrument by which dominant social groups exercised power over other social groups. In such cases, scientific practice has been situated in the lower-left quadrant (i.e., the domain of *power over*) of the schema represented by figure 8 in the previous chapter. Increasingly, however, science secures its public legitimacy only when it is seen to be universally empowering—or when it advances the well-being of all, as represented by the quadrants on the right side of that same schema (i.e., *mutualistic expressions of power*). Even though the practice of science continues to fall short of this standard in many cases, it is increasingly called to account in this regard.

Consider, for example, the growing chorus of public criticism aimed at industry-funded scientists who, for financial or ideological reasons, use their positions to confuse the public regarding the detrimental public health impacts of tobacco smoking or refined sugar consumption, or who try to obfuscate the role of fossil fuel consumption and other human activity in global warming. Likewise, consider the widespread condemnation of scientists who continue to invoke spurious data in support of white supremacy, male superiority, and other demonstrably false and oppressive truth claims—condemnation that has helped root out such practices from publicly funded science in many countries. Scientific practice has clearly become an object of growing public scrutiny in recent years, and normative assessments of the practice are regular themes in contemporary public discourse.

What would it mean for religion to be held to a parallel set of normative standards, including peaceful coexistence, justice, and universal empowerment? Clearly this would eliminate terrorism, violence, persecution, and oppression as valid forms of religious practice. Whenever religion is invoked to justify such practices, those claims could be publicly rejected as spurious. Such practices could be understood, instead, as ideologically and politically motivated—not as religious. This may seem like mere semantics. But systems of meaning, and language, matter in the pursuit of social justice. Today, few people would say the Holocaust was motivated by science. We are more likely to say it was motivated by a fascist ideology that perverted science to advance its self-interested aims. Likewise, few people would say global warming has been motivated by science, even though we can recognize it has been caused, in part, by the perversion of various applied sciences in service to the self-interested motives of industrial profiteering and unsustainable consumer lifestyles.

Therefore, if we conceptualize religion as a system that generates knowledge regarding the embodiment of normative truths in social reality, then violence and superstition have no role to play in this enterprise—any more than they do in the scientific enterprise. Rather, religion would begin to be viewed and practiced as a capacity-building enterprise concerned with universal inclusion, participation, and empowerment in the process of learning how to improve the human condition. These are standards to which all claims to religion might one day be held.

Of course, standards such as this do not reflect dominant conceptions of religion today. But the concept of *religion* is, itself, an evolving concept that has relatively recent historical origins.[77] Pre-modern societies were characterized by diverse sacred practices and beliefs that were woven throughout the entire cultural matrix. The concept of religion, as we generally understand it today, emerged as a modern Western construct that appears to have served at least two initial functions. On the one hand, it was employed for comparative studies that differentiated Christian practices and beliefs from the presumably inferior practices and beliefs of diverse others in the context of global voyages of discovery, colonization, and missionary work. On the other hand, it was employed to bracket off sacred practices and beliefs from other social domains such as politics, commerce, labor, art, and science, in service to the modern project of secularization.

The first of these functions, the comparative study of religious practices and beliefs, followed in the tradition of prior work by Islamic scholars such as Al-Shahrastani, who pursued comparative studies of diverse religious traditions in the twelfth century. The modern Western conception of religion added to this comparative dimension by bracketing off religion from emerging secular

domains. This modern Western conception was thus linked simultaneously to two sets of normative commitments—global Christian-
ization and Western secularization. Although some tension existed
between these two normative commitments, the broad conception
of religion that crystallized in the modern era was flexible enough
to serve both.

The first of these normative commitments has since been widely
rejected within academic discourse and much public discourse due
to its Christian-centric bias. More recently, the second of these commitments is also being problematized by post-secular scholars and
non-Western scholars who are beginning to question the strict reli-
gious/secular dichotomy as another hegemonic Western construct.[78]
The purpose of this all-too-brief genealogy is not, however, to dismiss
the concept of religion as a pure fabrication in service of hegemonic
agendas. All concepts are socially constructed. Yet according to the
framework sketched in chapter 1, some concepts can still be relatively
attuned to aspects of reality, and the attunement of such concepts can
increase over time as they are refined. As Schewel explains:

> Every concept was constructed at some point in history. Un-
> less we embrace the most aggressive forms or relativism and
> subjectivism, we all already accept the idea that a concept can
> be constructed and true. Articulating a concept's genealogy
> therefore does not suffice to undermine its validity. Addition-
> ally, a concept need not be perfect from the outset in order to
> constitute a discovery . . . . We can now see that early modern
> thinkers conceptualized religion in problematic ways. Howev-
> er, without their initial insights, our knowledge of the religious
> dimensions of human history and culture would be much less
> advanced. Thus, even though our understanding of religion has
> evolved, and must continue to evolve . . . our development of
> this concept has helped us radically extend our understanding
> of social reality.[79]

Schewel also goes on to suggest that an evolving concept of religion
cannot remain purely descriptive: "Religion is an irreducibly normative phenomenon; it seeks to tell us how things are and how we
ought to live. Nevertheless, contemporary academics endeavor to
use the term 'religion' in a descriptive way."[80] He continues:

To get a sense of the difficulties involved in this dynamic, imagine using the term "science" to describe all efforts to learn about and control the natural world. This would mean that modern science is no more "scientific" than shamanistic healing or mediaeval alchemy. We do not normally wrestle with such absurdities when discussing science, as most people think about science in a normative way, which is to say as a phenomenon that must be evaluated by its nearness to or distance from certain ideals. This means that there is such a thing as good science and bad science, and that research is scientific only to the extent that it embodies scientific ideals. Most scholars therefore have no problem saying that shamanistic healing and medieval alchemy are less scientific than particle physics or evolutionary biology, though they do appreciate how these endeavors presaged more mature forms of scientific endeavor.[81]

Schewel argues, as I have, that the same logic should apply to our understanding of religion. At the same time, he acknowledges that "a great deal of constructive work remains to be done if we are to ever develop a normative concept of religion that can be confidently deployed in our increasingly global and interconnected age."

The purpose of this discussion is to illustrate the desirability—indeed, the urgency—of a renewed discourse regarding the concept of religion and its normative underpinnings. Toward this end, we can draw yet another insightful parallel between the discourse on science and the discourse on religion. The concept of *science* is also a relatively modern concept. And the enterprise of modern science is distinct in many ways from anything that existed in the pre-modern world. Yet practices associated with the generation, application, and transmission of knowledge about material reality were also woven into the fabric of all pre-modern cultures. Those practices were not formalized, organized, and systematized in the ways we understand science today. Some pre-modern civilizations—such as the Egyptian, Chinese, Greek, and Islamic civilizations—made significant strides in these directions and laid the foundations for modern science. And all pre-modern societies were generating knowledge in some ways because this is a universal faculty of human consciousness. Even the pre-modern shamanistic practices that Schewel refers to above often embodied profound forms of knowledge that were valuable and effective to varying degrees. The modern discourse on science has emerged from this universal historical experience, augmenting it in ways that have fostered the further advancement and increasing maturation of science. Why should a parallel process not characterize religion, which also reflects a universal faculty of human consciousness that was manifest in pre-modern forms and continues to evolve in modern forms?

Chapter 4

Bahá'í Discourse & Practice

The preceding chapter proposes that science and religion can be understood as complementary and overlapping systems of knowledge and practice, that a normative discourse on science helped propel the maturation of science, and that a parallel discourse on religion is now needed. The normative discourse on science has advanced efforts to increase our attunement to foundational material truths that both enable and constrain our efforts to construct bodies of knowledge about material reality. A parallel discourse on religion can advance efforts to increase our attunement to and relative embodiment of foundational normative truths that enable and constrain our efforts to construct social reality.

Beyond the logical coherence of these propositions, as outlined in the previous chapter, another reason we might take them seriously is because the experience of the worldwide Bahá'í community offers some provisional support for them. The Bahá'í Faith is among the most diverse and geographically widespread religions on the planet.[83] It constitutes a steadily growing microcosm of humanity. And it embodies an emerging conception of religion that has taken root among people from virtually every culture, nationality, and religious background in existence.

In the discussion that follows, I examine the discourse and practice of the worldwide Bahá'í community as a form of provisional evidence in support of the propositions laid out above. I first examine the normative discourse on religion that is unfolding within the Bahá'í community, as well as the nature of its contributions to the discourse on religion in the wider society. I then examine how this discourse both fosters and reflects the emergence of a universal and participatory culture of learning within the Bahá'í community and among those who collaborate with Bahá'ís. Finally, I examine the way power is being reconceptualized in the Bahá'í community and how this is being translated into empowering forms of practice.

Before examining these aspects of the Bahá'í community, it is important to note that any community can be studied from either of two vantage points: from an *emic* (internal) or an *etic* (external) perspective.[84] When modern social sciences emerged, many social scientists adopted etic perspectives in their study of "the other"—as when anthropologists from the West began studying diverse cultural communities from around the world. By the latter half of the twentieth century, it became clear that etic perspectives had limitations, and emic perspectives were also needed. Therefore, the study of indigenous cultures by indigenous people, for example, is now valued. Similarly, no one would deny the legitimacy of feminist scholars studying feminist organizations and movements. Having turned this corner on analytical perspective, emic and etic analyses are now widely understood as complementary and mutually informing rather than contradictory and mutually exclusive. With that said, the following analysis proceeds from an emic perspective and is based on several decades of experience as a participant-observer within diverse Bahá'í communities on four continents.

FOSTERING A NORMATIVE DISCOURSE ON RELIGION

Bahá'í discourse has been shaped by four primary sources. First, there are the writings of Bahá'u'lláh, the founder of the Bahá'í Faith, which are considered scriptural. Second, there are the writings and recorded talks of 'Abdu'l-Bahá, whom Bahá'u'lláh appointed as the Center of his Covenant after his passing. Third, there are the writings of Shoghi Effendi, whom 'Abdu'l-Bahá appointed the Guardian of the Bahá'í community after his passing. Fourth, there is the written guidance of the Universal House of Justice, which is the globally elected body governing the Bahá'í community that was formed shortly after the passing of Shoghi Effendi in accordance with clear provisions established by Bahá'u'lláh and 'Abdu'l-Bahá. Together, these four bodies of texts constitute the authoritative sources of guidance that inform the work of the Bahá'í community. These texts are therefore at the center of the community's internal discourse. But Bahá'í discourse also includes the evolving ways Bahá'ís think and talk together about Bahá'í practice—or about the evolving ways they are learning to collectively apply the principles articulated in their primary texts.

At the center of Bahá'í discourse is a set of normative statements about religion from those four primary sources. An examination of these statements will begin to illustrate an emerging discourse on religion that has become global in scope. These statements are all closely related to the core Bahá'í principle: the oneness of humanity. The oneness of humanity is understood by Bahá'ís as a spiritual truth that must be increasingly embodied in human consciousness and in social reality for humanity to realize its latent social and spiritual potential. Expounding on this core principle, Bahá'u'lláh states that God cherishes "the desire of beholding the entire human race as one soul and one body."[85] 'Abdu'l-Bahá thus exhorts every person to "regard humanity as a single individual, and one's own self as a member of that corporeal form."[86] As Shoghi Effendi elaborates:

> The principle of the Oneness of Mankind—the pivot round which all the teachings of Bahá'u'lláh revolve—is no mere outburst of ignorant emotionalism or an expression of vague and pious hope. Its appeal is not to be merely identified with a reawakening of the spirit of brotherhood and good-will among men, nor does it aim solely at the fostering of harmonious cooperation among individual peoples and nations. Its implications are deeper . . . . Its message is applicable not only to the individual, but concerns itself primarily with the nature of those essential relationships that must bind all the states and nations as members of one human family . . . . It implies an organic change in the structure of present-day society, a change such as the world has not yet experienced . . . . It represents the consummation of human evolution.[87]

It is within the context of this core Bahá'í teaching that all normative statements on religion from the primary Bahá'í writings assume their full meaning. These normative statements can be organized into a number of key themes. One theme is the underlying unity of all the world's major religions. As 'Abdu'l-Bahá states, "The gift of God to this enlightened age is the knowledge of the oneness of mankind and the fundamental oneness of religion."[88]

Elaborating on this theme, 'Abdu'l-Bahá explains that "the foundation underlying all the divine precepts is one reality . . . . Therefore the foundation of the divine religions is one . . . . If we set aside all superstitions and see the reality of the foundation we shall all agree, because religion is one and not multiple."[89] And again: "Religions are many, but the reality of religion is one. The days are many, but the sun is one . . . . The branches are many, but the tree is one."[90] And again: "The different religions have one truth underlying them; therefore, their reality is one."[91] Thus can we understand Bahá'u'lláh's statement: "This is the changeless Faith of God, eternal in the past, eternal in the future."[92] Similarly, we can grasp his statement:

> There can be no doubt whatever that the peoples of the world, of whatever race or religion, derive their inspiration from one heavenly Source, and are the subjects of one God. The difference between the ordinances under which they abide should be attributed to the varying requirements and exigencies of the age in which they were revealed. All of them, except a few which are the outcome of human perversity, were ordained of God, and are a reflection of His Will and Purpose. Arise and, armed with the power of faith, shatter to pieces the gods of your vain imaginings, the sowers of dissension amongst you. Cleave unto that which draweth you together and uniteth you.[93]

In Bahá'í discourse, another theme closely related to the oneness of religion is that the fundamental purpose of religion is to promote the oneness of humanity and that this purpose is a standard for assessing the validity of all religious truth claims and practices. As Bahá'u'lláh writes, "The fundamental purpose animating the Faith of God and His Religion is to safeguard the interests and promote the unity of the human race, and to foster the spirit of love and fellowship amongst men. Suffer it not to become a source of dissension and discord, of hate and enmity. This is the straight Path, the fixed and immovable foundation."[94] And again: "The religion of God is for love and unity; make it not the cause of enmity or dissension."[95] Also: "Consort with the followers of all religions in a spirit of friendliness and fellowship."[96]

Yet another closely related theme in Bahá'í discourse is that if religion becomes a source of division, it is better to be without religion. 'Abdu'l-Bahá expresses this unambiguously when he states, "If a religion become the cause of hatred and disharmony, it would be better that it should not exist."[97] And again: "If it rouses hatred and strife, it is evident that absence of religion is preferable and an irreligious man better than one who professes it."[98] Also: "Religion must be conducive to love and unity among mankind; for if it be the cause of enmity and strife, the absence of religion is preferable."[99]

The final theme in Bahá'í discourse relevant to the discussion at hand is the need for religion to be in complete harmony and agreement with science. 'Abdu'l-Bahá states:

> There is no contradiction between true religion and science. When a religion is opposed to science it becomes mere superstition: that which is contrary to knowledge is ignorance. How can a man believe to be a fact that which science has proved to be impossible? If he believes in spite of his reason, it is rather ignorant superstition than faith. The true principles of all religions are in conformity with the teachings of science.[100]

Elaborating on this theme, 'Abdu'l-Bahá says, "If we say religion is opposed to science, we lack knowledge of either true science or true religion, for both are founded upon the premises and conclusions of reason, and both must bear its test."[101] And again: "Any religion that contradicts science or that is opposed to it, is only ignorance—for ignorance is the opposite of knowledge."[102] Bahá'ís are thus exhorted to "put all your beliefs into harmony with science; there can be no opposition, for truth is one."[103]

For Bahá'ís, this normative principle—the harmony of science and religion—has implications that go beyond the need to respect science and to reconcile religious beliefs with scientific insights. It also has implications for the practice of religion itself. In this regard, Shoghi Effendi explains that the Bahá'í Faith is "scientific in its method."[104] The meaning of this statement will be explored in the next section of this chapter when the culture of learning in the Bahá'í community is examined. At this point, suffice it to say that for a community that understands science and religion as complementary systems for the generation and application of knowledge, it follows that there would be some overlap at the level of method.

All these normative statements—and the conceptions of religion they embody—constitute core elements of Bahá'í discourse. Bahá'í children hear these statements and learn these concepts from an early age. Bahá'í youth study the implications of these concepts for their conduct and pursuits. Those who enter the Bahá'í community as adults do so in part because they find these concepts compelling and attractive. These concepts are, in turn, translated into myriad forms of Bahá'í practice that include seeking fellowship with people of all religions, eschewing religious argumentation and conflict, pursuing scientifically sound education, contributing to the frontiers of science, and approaching the generation and application of religious knowledge in systematic, rational, and empirically informed ways.

These practices illustrate key conceptual propositions explored earlier in this book. For instance, an expanding global community that seeks fellowship with people of all religions and eschews religious argumentation and conflict illustrates a growing body of grounded experience learning how a consultative epistemology might begin to reconcile truth and relativism in interfaith discourse based on the understanding that people from diverse religious traditions can have complementary perspectives on different aspects of the same complex truths. Likewise, a community that is committed to scientifically sound education, that is actively contributing to the frontiers of science, and that is also approaching the generation and application of religious knowledge in systematic, rational, and empirically informed ways illustrates a grounded effort to contribute simultaneously to humanity's increased attunement to material truths as well as humanity's increased embodiment of normative truths.

Of course, even within the Bahá'í community, these ideals are achieved with varying degrees of consistency or success. The Bahá'í community comprises a cross-section of humanity. Every Bahá'í bears the traces of their cultural conditioning and their complex lived experiences, and every Bahá'í advances along the development path alluded to above at different paces. But few fair-minded observers would deny that the Bahá'í community, as a whole, is beginning to manifest these ideals and commitments in ever-increasing measure.

Even so, it must also be acknowledged that the experience of the Bahá'í community does not constitute conclusive proof that all of humanity will one day embrace similar ideals and practices. Rather, it constitutes provisional evidence that striving toward these ideals and practices is within human capacity. After all, if a microcosm of humanity—representing every ethnic, religious, national, and economic background on the planet and characterized by an extraordinarily wide range of views, interests, and habits of mind—has already demonstrated significant advancement along the path alluded to above, then the path may well be open to all of humanity. In this regard, one could say the Bahá'í community is like a group of scouts who are beginning to report back their experiences exploring a path that has not yet been widely travelled.

Toward this end, Bahá'ís are increasingly contributing to the normative discourse on religion in the wider society. Bahá'ís have been participating in interfaith and ecumenical discourse at local, national, and international levels since the inception of the modern interfaith movement. They have also been contributing to the discourse on religion within the United Nations system since its creation. Building on these experiences, in 2002, the Universal House of Justice published an open letter to the world's religious leaders in which they invited a more robust dialogue on the role and responsibilities of religion in the modern world.[105] This letter, written in the aftermath of the September 11, 2001, terrorist event in New York City and the heightened tensions that followed, was delivered by local and national Bahá'í communities to thousands of religious leaders around the world, resulting in many opportunities for constructive dialogue. Since this letter illustrates so clearly the nature of Bahá'í contributions to the wider discourse on religion, its contents merit close examination.

The letter begins by illustrating the many ways that humanity has, since the dawn of the twentieth century, been advancing toward a recognition of our underlying oneness as members of a single global community. At the level of global discourse, these include a growing recognition of the principles of racial equality and gender equality, along with a growing recognition of the need to transcend unfettered nationalism and militarism by constructing a more secure and mutually prosperous global order. While acknowledging ongoing conflicts and injustices on all these fronts, the letter asserts that "fundamental principles have been identified, articulated, accorded broad publicity and are becoming progressively incarnated in institutions capable of imposing them" and, in the process, "a threshold has been crossed from which there is no credible possibility of return."[106]

The letter goes on to warn, however, that such a threshold has not yet been crossed on another imperative front: the need to transcend religious conflict, which threatens to engulf growing numbers of innocent people in violence, suffering, and dislocation. "Other segments of society," the letter explains, "embrace the implications of the oneness of humankind, not only as the inevitable next step in the advancement of civilization, but as the fulfilment of lesser identities of every kind that our race brings to this critical moment in our collective history. Yet, the greater part of organized religion stands paralyzed at the threshold of the future, gripped in those very dogmas and claims of privileged access to truth that have been responsible for creating some of the most bitter conflicts dividing the earth's inhabitants."[107] The letter continues:

> To this accounting must be added a betrayal of the life of the mind which, more than any other factor, has robbed religion of the capacity it inherently possesses to play a decisive role in the shaping of world affairs. Locked into preoccupation with agendas that disperse and vitiate human energies, religious institutions have too often been the chief agents in discouraging exploration of reality and the exercise of those intellectual faculties that distinguish humankind. Denunciations of materialism or terrorism are of no real assistance in coping with the contemporary moral crisis if they do not begin by addressing candidly the failure of responsibility that has left believing masses exposed and vulnerable to these influences.[108]

These statements, the letter explains, are made not as an indictment of organized religion, but as a reminder of its constructive powers—its ability to reach to the roots of human motivation and awaken in entire populations the capacity to love, forgive, overcome divisions, sacrifice for the common good, and create a new social reality. The statements also serve as a reminder of the profound and ongoing influence of religion in human affairs. The letter thus does not call for the abandonment of faith in foundational religious truths. But it urges "renunciation of all those claims to exclusivity or finality that, in winding their roots around the life of the spirit, have been the greatest single factor in suffocating impulses to unity and in promoting hatred and violence."[109]

> It is to this historic challenge that we believe leaders of religion must respond if religious leadership is to have meaning in the global society emerging from the transformative experiences of the twentieth century. It is evident that growing numbers of people are coming to realize that the truth underlying all religions is in its essence one. This recognition arises not through a resolution of theological disputes, but as an intuitive awareness born from the ever widening experience of others and from a dawning acceptance of the oneness of the human family itself. Out of the welter of religious doctrines, rituals and legal codes inherited from vanished worlds, there is emerging a sense that spiritual life, like the oneness manifest in diverse nationalities, races and cultures, constitutes one unbounded reality equally accessible to everyone. In order for this diffuse and still tentative perception to consolidate itself and contribute effectively to the building of a peaceful world, it must have the whole-hearted confirmation of those to whom, even at this late hour, masses of the earth's population look for guidance.[110]

The letter goes on to note that "the scriptures of all religions have always taught the believer to see in service to others not only a moral duty, but an avenue for the soul's own approach to God."[111] Elaborating on this theme, the letter states that "Today, the progressive restructuring of society gives this familiar teaching new dimensions of meaning. As the age-old promise of a world animated by principles of justice slowly takes on the character of a realistic goal, meeting the needs of the soul and those of society will increasingly be seen as reciprocal aspects of a mature spiritual life."[112]

"If religious leadership is to rise to the challenge that this latter perception represents," the letter continues,

> such response must begin by acknowledging that religion and science are the two indispensable knowledge systems through

which the potentialities of consciousness develop. Far from being in conflict with one another, these fundamental modes of the mind's exploration of reality are mutually dependent . . . . The insights and skills generated by scientific advance will have always to look to the guidance of spiritual and moral commitment to ensure their appropriate application; religious convictions, no matter how cherished they may be, must submit, willingly and gratefully, to impartial testing by scientific methods.[113]

Finally, the letter makes explicit its conviction that "interfaith discourse, if it is to contribute meaningfully to healing the ills that afflict a desperate humanity, must now address honestly and without further evasion the implications of the overarching truth that called the movement into being: that God is one and that, beyond all diversity of cultural expression and human interpretation, religion is likewise one."[114] It then points out the perils of ignoring these truths at the outset of the twenty-first century:

With every day that passes, danger grows that the rising fires of religious prejudice will ignite a worldwide conflagration the consequences of which are unthinkable. Such a danger civil government, unaided, cannot overcome. Nor should we delude ourselves that appeals for mutual tolerance can alone hope to extinguish animosities that claim to possess Divine sanction. The crisis calls on religious leadership for a break with the past as decisive as those that opened the way for society to address equally corrosive prejudices of race, gender and nation. Whatever justification exists for exercising influence in matters of conscience lies in serving the well-being of humankind. At this greatest turning point in the history of civilization, the demands of such service could not be more clear. "The well-being of mankind, its peace and security, are unattainable", Bahá'u'lláh urges, "unless and until its unity is firmly established."[115]

This letter has been cited at length because it conveys in such clear language the way Bahá'ís are learning to think and talk about religion and the nature of their ongoing contributions to the wider public discourse on the role of religion in the modern world. This learning process is a noteworthy illustration of how a normative discourse on religion might be advanced today, as discussed in chapter 3. Baháʼís are, of course, not the only people attempting to advance such a discourse, as the discussion in that chapter makes clear. But the Baháʼí community's efforts illustrate some of the substance of this evolving discourse, as well as the tone and posture that can be adopted within it. On this latter point, Baháʼís have learned how to adopt an invitational rather than argumentative tone and posture that values diversity and is characterized by appeals to both reason and moral intuition—reflecting once again the consultative epistemology discussed in chapter 1.

FOSTERING A CULTURE OF LEARNING

The consultative epistemology discussed above is increasingly characterizing the Baháʼí community's approach to learning—or its approach to the systematic generation and application of knowledge—on all fronts. In the discussion that follows, salient features of this culture of learning will be examined to further illustrate the possibility that a religious community can translate the conceptual propositions outlined in chapter 1 into collective practice.

Since the passing of ʻAbduʼl-Bahá, which ushered in the formative age of the Baháʼí Faith, Shoghi Effendi and the Universal House of Justice have successively operated in a learning mode that draws insight from the accumulating experience of the community. This theme is examined at length by Lample in *Revelation and Social Reality*.[116] As Lample demonstrates, much of this learning initially grew out of the early growth and internal development of the Baháʼí community, including raising up the earliest structures of its global administrative order. Systematic learning processes have subsequently been expanding to other domains. These include, for instance, relations with governmental agencies and human rights organizations regarding the defense of persecuted Baháʼís, contributions to the social and economic development of wider communities of which Baháʼís were a part, and participation in public discourses on the exigencies of the age.

For most of the twentieth century, although these learning processes were being guided by Shoghi Effendi and then the Universal House of Justice, the number of Baháʼí individuals and agencies that consciously understood the nature and implications of these processes and had the capacity to systematically contribute to them was relatively small. However, by the dawn of the twenty-first century, the House of Justice observed that a conscious and systematic "culture of learning" was taking root across the entire global Bahá'í community.[117]

One of the key factors that fostered this culture of learning was the establishment throughout the Bahá'í world of a network of training institutes, a process that began in earnest in the 1990s. This development arose, in part, from insights that had accrued through the experience of the Ruhi Training Institute, which began to emerge in Colombia in the 1970s. The story of how the Ruhi Institute emerged, and the systematic learning process it adopted, are documented in a publication titled *Learning About Growth*.[118] The insights documented there include a recognition that the movement of a population on a path of spiritual development is an organic process that begins with the transformation of hearts and minds but must soon manifest itself in the transformation of social structures and relationships; that systematic approaches to education and capacity building are needed to support this process; that the concept of "paths of service" provides a valuable way to organize these processes; that diverse individuals within a population will move along distinct paths of service at different rates; that the advancement of a population must be propelled by unifying and constructive forces generated from within; and that ongoing processes of study, action, reflection, and consultation that are open to all—and are participatory, coordinated, systematic, and free from the trappings of ego—are needed to generate knowledge on all of these fronts.

Drawing on these insights and others that had accrued from experiences throughout the Bahá'í world, the Universal House of Justice, in 1996, called upon Bahá'í communities in every country to establish training institutes to raise up human resources and build capacities to accelerate the ongoing growth and development of communities.[119] This worldwide network of training institutes was soon operating, with varying degrees of efficacy, in a learning mode characterized by action, reflection, and consultation at the grassroots in every country. Each training institute, in proportion to its developing capacities, began contributing to, as well as drawing from, a global process of systematic learning that has been advancing steadily since that time. There are now over 300 national and regional training institutes established around the world, reaching tens of thousands of localities through a decentralized approach.[120]

By 2005, the House of Justice announced that the insights into community building that had accrued through these global learning processes had "crystallized into a framework for action" that could be pursued throughout the Bahá'í world with confidence.[121] Growing numbers of individuals and communities across the planet began learning how to take initiative within this framework, becoming protagonists in a global enterprise that is continually advancing the frontiers of knowledge about community growth and development.[122] At the heart of this process is an effort to learn how to translate spiritual principles into social practice—or how to increase the embodiment of normative truths in social reality—by constructing new patterns of community life. Toward this end, humility and initiative are cultivated by the training institute based on a recognition that the Bahá'í community is not an all-knowing creed with answers to every question. On the contrary, it is a community that is continually generating new questions, which it pursues in a posture of learning.

This culture of learning includes the ongoing development of institutional structures and capacities needed to systematize and coordinate the generation and dissemination of knowledge among local and national communities across the planet. Just as modern scientific communities need institutional structures and capacities to support and advance the generation and dissemination of knowledge on a global scale, as discussed in chapter 1, the Bahá'í community has been developing in a similar manner.

These institutional capacities are developing within and across multiple levels. The training institutes, alluded to above, are organized through an evolving system of coordination at various geographic levels, from the local to the global. Those who serve in the training institutes' evolving scheme of coordination collaborate closely with another institution, the Continental Board of Counsellors, and their Auxiliary Board members, which in turn function under the guidance of the International Teaching Center. The International Teaching Center, established in 1973, plays a central role in fostering global processes of learning about community growth, including processes of learning about the advancement of training institutes.[123] The International Teaching Center is a unique institution. It has no legislative, executive, or judicial authority. In conjunction with the Continental Board of Counsellors, their Auxiliary Board members, and a wide network of assistants to the Auxiliary Board members that reaches to the grassroots of local communities around the planet, its responsibilities include fostering a culture of growth and development throughout the Bahá'í world; providing, toward this end, relevant advice, information, analysis, and support to the community's elected institutions; stimulating the spiritual, intellectual, and social aspects of community life; and enhancing the capacity of the community to devise and carry out systematic plans of action, and to learn systematically from their experience in executing these plans.

Building upon these capacities that have been developing in the domain of community growth and development, the Bahá'í community has also been adapting this culture of systematic learning to other domains of activity. Most notably, as the Bahá'í community grows, it is naturally drawn ever more deeply into the life of the wider society. In the process, it has been developing systematic approaches to learning about social action and participation in the discourses of society. Bahá'í social action contributes to the social and economic development of the wider communities in which Bahá'ís reside. Bahá'í participation in the discourses of society contributes to the evolution of thought on matters of broad public concern. On both these fronts, Bahá'ís are increasingly collaborating with all like-minded people, learning their way forward with others in unifying and constructive ways.

As in the domain of community growth and development, Bahá'ís have been developing institutional structures and capacities to foster and coordinate the respective learning processes in the domains of social action and social discourse. In the domain of social action, an international Office of Social and Economic Development was established at the Bahá'í World Center in 1983 to help systematize and support these learning processes—processes that primarily emerge through grassroots initiatives when conditions are propitious. By 2018, the work of that Office had expanded to the point that it was reconstituted as the Bahá'í International Development Agency, which is overseen by a board of directors from multiple continents.[124]

Bahá'í involvement in social action dates back over a century when, for example, Bahá'í communities began to establish schools for girls where none existed and to contribute to other developmental processes in the societies of which they were part.[125] By 1983, such initiatives had become sufficiently widespread, and some had become sufficiently complex, that it was timely to foster more systematic global learning processes. Since that time, the Office of Social and Economic Development, and more recently the Bahá'í International Development Agency, has been fostering evolving systems of coordination in distinct areas of global learning, as those areas reach a sufficient level of complexity to warrant such support. This includes, for instance, a system of coordination for learning about the Junior Youth Spiritual Empowerment Program and another system for learning about Community Schools.[126] In addition, in recent decades, some grassroots initiatives have reached such levels of complexity and sustained accomplishment that they have developed their own institutional capacities and learning processes, which also enable them to contribute more effectively to wider global learning processes. This can be seen, for instance, in the experience of The Foundation for the Application and Teaching of the Sciences (FUNDAEC), which originated as a social and economic development project in rural Colombia and has since made significant contributions to learning processes across the Bahá'í world.[127]

Likewise, Bahá'ís have been increasing their capacity to make substantive contributions to public discourse for many decades and have been developing institutional structures to support this work and the learning processes associated with it.[128] On a global level, they have been contributing to discourse within the United Nations system since its inception, along with discourses in other international spaces, coordinated by Bahá'í International Community offices in New York, Geneva, Brussels, Jakarta, and Addis Ababa. For instance, the Bahá'í International Community offices have long been engaged with discourses on gender equity, peace, and the environment. In such work, Bahá'ís collaborate with like-minded organizations in meaningful dialogue focused on identifying constructive paths forward.

At the national level, by 2013, the capacity of many Bahá'í communities to contribute to public discourses in their respective countries had grown to the point that an international Office of Public

Discourse was established to support processes of systematic learning across countries. In some countries, national offices of external affairs had already been established and were already engaged in this work, but since 2013, the number of such offices has continued to grow, and they now benefit from and contribute to a global learning process. Such offices are learning to contribute in increasingly effective ways to matters of national concern such as race relations, gender equality, and social cohesion.

Many Bahá'ís have also historically contributed in substantive ways to their respective professional and academic discourses. In 1975, an Association for Bahá'í Studies formed in North America to support such efforts, and it was replicated in some other parts of the world where conditions warranted. This Association is becoming increasingly systematic in its learning and capacity-building processes in recent years through the organization of large annual conferences, smaller seminars, publications, and other means of contributing to the evolution of thought in academic and professional disciplines.

Likewise, in 1999, the Institute for Studies in Global Prosperity was founded to build capacity in individuals, groups, and institutions to contribute to prevalent discourses concerned with the betterment of society. Among its endeavors, this institute has raised up a global network of seminars focused on capacity building among undergraduate students, graduate students, and young professionals.

The examples alluded to above in the domains of community building, social action, and public discourse do not exhaust the learning processes and their corresponding institutional structures unfolding across the worldwide Bahá'í community today. But they illustrate the institutional forms being developed to support the systematic generation, diffusion, and application of knowledge by a religious community in a manner that parallels the institutional forms developed by scientific communities, as discussed in chapter 1.

One more feature of this culture of learning warrants attention, beyond the posture of learning adopted by its participants and the institutional structures that support their efforts. This other feature is the increasing coherence of the learning processes unfolding across the domains discussed above, which is made possible by a shared conceptual framework that guides and informs all these processes. Again, just as scientific research programs advance within shared but evolving conceptual frameworks, as discussed in chapter 1, the learning processes of the Bahá'í community are similarly developing.

At the center of the Bahá'í conceptual framework is a set of core assumptions, concepts, principles, approaches, and methods that derive directly from the writings of Bahá'u'lláh and inform all Bahá'í practice. These core elements have proven to be enduring, compelling, and suggestive of inter-related lines of learning. These elements include foundational assumptions about reality, basic conceptions of human nature and the social order, guiding spiritual principles or normative ideals, consultative approaches that draw diverse insights into the learning process, and an action-orientation that continually tests ideas and interpretations against reality. Operating together, these core elements foster a logic of discovery that drives the generation and application of knowledge in the Bahá'í community. This logic of discovery suggests relevant questions and guides systematic inquiry along relevant lines in different domains of learning—such as the expansion and consolidation of the community, its engagement in diverse forms of social action, and its participation in the discourses of society.

Deriving from this core logic of discovery is an evolving but secondary set of tentative insights, concepts, methods, and applications associated with the frontiers of learning within the framework. As specific lines of learning are pursued, these secondary elements emerge, are continually tested against reality, and are variously discarded, adopted, or refined over time in the light of accumulated knowledge and experience. This process, in turn, further deepens and enhances the Bahá'í community's understanding of the core elements themselves.

For instance, spiritual and intellectual capacity building are core elements of the Bahá'í conceptual framework, as is the need to apply one's developing capacities to the betterment of the society in which one lives. As the Bahá'í community began to learn how to foster these processes more systematically and effectively, the secondary concept of a training institute emerged. Over time, through accumulated experience, the application of this concept is being continually refined. Likewise, community building is a core element of the Bahá'í framework. As the Bahá'í community began to learn how to approach this process more systematically and effectively, the secondary concept of a geographic cluster emerged as a scale on which community-building efforts could be stimulated, organized, and coordinated. In addition, within this context, the Bahá'í community identified a set of core activities that have proven central to the success of all community-building efforts. These include regular devotional gatherings that are open to people from all religious backgrounds in a village or neighborhood, regular classes for the spiritual education of children in a village or neighborhood, a program for the spiritual empowerment of adolescents or "junior youth" in the same local context, and study circles for the training of youth and adults to initiate the other core activities and take on other essential responsibilities. This way of schematizing "core activities" cannot be found in the writings of Bahá'u'lláh. It is a secondary element of the framework guiding the work of the Bahá'í community that emerged through a systematic process of learning in action driven by an underlying logic of discovery. Today, Bahá'ís around the planet are in turn learning how to multiply the number of these activities systematically so that steadily expanding numbers of people have access to them, as well as how to increase simultaneously the quality or efficacy of these activities. Many other lines of learning also are being pursued within the domain of community building. Likewise, in the domains of social action and public discourse, parallel lines of learning are advancing systematically within the same overarching conceptual framework, lending coherence to the entire enterprise.

Within this framework, a common vocabulary is also emerging that enables growing numbers of people to build on collective advances, to share emerging insights more widely, and to construct systems that can aggregate, distill, and disseminate the most universally valid insights. Some of these systems were alluded to above in the discussion of institutional structures that support learning processes. And within each domain of learning, Bahá'ís are developing the capacity to apply the same general methods of action, reflection, consultation, and study in contextually appropriate ways. Through this approach, tentative ideas are tested continuously against reality as concepts and practices are refined progressively over time. The insights that accrue are distilled into study materials (such as the evolving curricula of the training institutes) that form the basis for the learning of each successive generation and its subsequent contributions to the growing body of knowledge—just as they would be within a scientific community, as discussed in chapter 1.

Another feature of this culture of systematic learning within the Bahá'í community, which mirrors an important feature of scientific communities, is the capacity to distinguish context-specific insights from universally applicable insights. Many insights generated by Bahá'ís acting and learning at the grassroots are localized or context-dependent. But when the myriad insights emerging at the grassroots are aggregated and compared with insights generated in other contexts, a more limited number of universal patterns can be identified.

For instance, developing the capacity to initiate and sustain any of the core activities alluded to above is not easy. And the process by which people are invited to participate in those activities will vary in different contexts, as will the way the activities are conducted depending on cultural sensitivities, social and economic conditions, the personalities involved, and other factors. Success thus requires the ability to learn about and account for diverse local considerations. But what has become clear everywhere is that individuals who are trying to initiate core activities for the first time will be more successful if they are accompanied by someone with more experience. Therefore, *accompaniment* is a universally relevant practice that the Bahá'í world has come to appreciate, and it is one that people everywhere can be trained to understand and engage in. Likewise, when individuals develop the capacity to accompany others in these ways, there is always a hazard that their sense of self-importance can become inflated. When this happens, it undermines the community-building process. Experience has shown this to be a universally applicable truth. Therefore, Bahá'í training institutes have developed ways to help people everywhere reflect on this possibility and resist the promptings of their own egos.

Bahá'ís are increasingly learning to distinguish context-specific knowledge from universally applicable knowledge in these ways. The former pertains to particular conditions of a given people at a particular place and time. Many significant forms of knowledge are of this localized type. This is true even in applied fields of scientific practice such as agriculture, because even though many biological truths are universal, specific ecological conditions vary in ways that require local knowledge as well. Any robust global system of applied knowledge and practice thus needs to generate both local and universal forms of knowledge.

In all the ways described above, we can see in the experience of the Bahá'í community an example of a religious community that is striving to develop the capacity to be "scientific in its method."[129] Many of the features of science discussed in chapter 1 can be seen in this emerging culture of learning. This includes the disciplined exercise of rational thought, imagination and intuition, skepticism and critical thinking. It includes systematic modes of observation. It includes the articulation of assumptions and concepts within a coherent conceptual framework that can be tested over time. It includes the cultivation of qualities such curiosity, honesty and integrity, a degree of detachment from preconceived notions, recognition of the ultimate fallibility of human knowledge, a corresponding posture of humility and open-mindedness, and the avoidance of dogmatism or fanaticism.

As with science, the generation of knowledge within the Bahá'í community is also a social enterprise, with many of the same social characteristics described in chapter 1. The Bahá'í community is developing a shared vocabulary that supports a global process of knowledge generation. And it is developing complex forms of social organization, cooperation, and coordination that enable a growing diversity of people to participate in and contribute to the generation of knowledge.

Yet, in other ways, the generation of knowledge by the Bahá'í community is distinct from science. As discussed in chapter 1, science aims to advance knowledge primarily about naturally occurring phenomena that emerge prior to and independent of human agency. It is quite another thing to advance knowledge about social phenomena that a community is bringing into existence at the same time it is trying to learn about them. This is because, as chapter 1 clarifies, the construction of social reality is characterized by dynamic processes, patterns, and systems that unfold entirely through human agency. Within the Bahá'í community, such agency is motivated by the desire to increase the embodiment of normative truths in social constructs. This entails the conscious and intentional application of normative principles in processes of social construction.

While natural scientists assume that truths about the material world can be discovered by studying nature, Bahá'ís assume that normative truths—or spiritual principles—can be discovered by studying the revelations that have given birth to the world's great religious systems. Revelation, in this sense, can be understood as a mystical process by which human consciousness becomes informed of latent spiritual potentialities—from the potentialities of the human soul to the potentialities of human civilization. The founders of the world's great religious systems all intimated these truths to varying degrees through a process often referred to as revelation. As history amply demonstrates, these intimations of spiritual truth have been so compelling that they have inspired entire populations to construct new social realities in response. These responses have always been acts of faith because at the outset, people can never prove potentialities that have not yet become manifest through human agency. People need to exert such agency to test these articles of faith.

Collective expressions of agency based on faith can be understood in part by revisiting the concept of latency discussed in chapter 1. The analogy that was used to convey this concept was the analogy of the fruit that is latent in the seed of the fruit tree. We can cut open the seed and see no sign of the tree and its fruit. But the tree and its fruit are latent phenomena within the seed.

With this analogy in mind, we can imagine a time before agriculture when humans did not fully grasp the concept of a seed. Only with the subsequent understanding of this concept did agriculture become possible. We can thus imagine a person from a pre-agricultural society picking up a seed and, thinking it worthless, tossing it away. But a second person, who understood the concept of a seed, might explain to the first person that if the seed were planted in the right soil and carefully tended for many years, it would develop into a tree that would yield a wonderful fruit. This second person could not, in the moment, prove this proposition. The first person would have to accept such advice as an article of faith. Only by cultivating the seed over a span of many years could the proposition be tested and the fruit become manifest.

Revelation can, in this sense, be understood as the process by which humanity learns about its latent spiritual reality. In this regard, Bahá'ís believe that the seeds of existence, so to speak, contain spiritual truths that, when cultivated, will ultimately give rise to a peaceful, just, and mutually prosperous social order that reflects the organic oneness of humanity. This future civilization is thus understood as a latent reality—an expression of "potentialities as yet unrealized."[130]

The collective commitment to act on this article of faith—striving to cultivate or construct this latent reality through collective agency—does not mean that Bahá'ís can envision the exact form that this future civilization will take, any more than an orchardist can envision the exact size and shape of the tree into which a seed will grow. As the orchardist knows, a given genotype can yield trees with a range of phenotypical expressions, but they will all bear the same type of fruit. However, this will occur only if the seeds are actively cultivated.

'Abdu'l-Bahá makes numerous references to this concept of latency by employing the analogy of the seeds and the fruit, so this concept is a familiar element of Bahá'í discourse.[131] He also alludes to this concept in more philosophical terms when he articulates the proposition that

> existence and non-existence are both relative. If it be said that a certain thing was brought forth from non-existence, the intent is not absolute non-existence; rather, it is meant that the former condition was non-existence in relation to the present one. For absolute non-existence cannot become existence, as it lacks the very capacity to exist.[132]

This proposition speaks to the relativity of existence itself. Or stated another way, it speaks to the relative embodiment of foundational truths in manifest phenomena, as discussed in chapter 1. Some truths, such as the laws of physics, become manifest only in naturally occurring phenomena over time in the form of physical entities, through processes that are independent of human agency. Other truths, such as normative truths, become manifest over time only in the form of social entities, through processes that depend on human agency. But in both cases, even before the respective phenomena became manifest, they "existed," so to speak, as latent phenomena that were made possible, or probable, because of foundational features of reality. Thus, Bahá'ís find in their primary texts many allusions to the relative embodiment of normative or spiritual truths in social constructs.

However, having faith in revealed spiritual truths and committing to act on them is not the same as knowing how to construct new social phenomena that embody such truths. The latter necessitates a process of learning—or the generation of knowledge. Bahá'u'lláh thus writes that "it is incumbent upon every man of insight and understanding to strive to translate that which hath been written into reality."[133]

The culture of learning that has been developing throughout the worldwide Bahá'í community is focused on this task. But the application of normative principles in a systematic learning mode is still no simple matter. Learning about the application of normative principles involves subjective interpretations supported by the faculty of intuition. As the discussion in chapter 1 pointed out, subjective interpretation and intuition play a crucial role in the advancement of the natural sciences. In the construction of social reality, they take on elevated importance.

In the natural sciences, the limitations of subjective and intuitive understanding are addressed by striving for intersubjective agreement. Higher degrees of intersubjective agreement, when they are consistent with all available evidence and when they become stable over time, increase our confidence in conclusions. The same can be said for intersubjective agreement regarding the application of normative principles in the social domain.

In this latter context, however, intersubjective agreement becomes meaningful only when marginalized and oppressed populations are included as full participants in deliberative, or consultative, processes of collective learning—as discussed in chapters 1 and 2. In this regard, the global Bahá'í community has, from its inception, been constituted by large numbers of marginalized people, beginning with the most oppressed segments of Iranian society. Since that time, an increasingly diverse body of historically marginalized people from every background across the planet have become leading protagonists at the frontiers of learning in the community. As the contributions of such people expand in range and depth, the community as a whole is coming to understand why "justice demands universal participation" in the generation of knowledge about the construction of a new social reality.[134]

FOSTERING A CULTURE OF EMPOWERMENT

Even if religion can be understood as a system of knowledge and practice that complements and partially overlaps science, and even if the Bahá'í community illustrates this possibility, the relationship between knowledge and power still needs to be taken seriously and critically examined in this context. As the discussion in chapter 2 demonstrated, twentieth-century scholarship exposed a deeply problematic relationship between knowledge and power. The generation of knowledge is highly susceptible to the corrupting influences of power, and for this reason structures of knowledge often become oppressive. History is replete with examples of this, a few of which were discussed in chapter 2. Yet the discussion in that chapter demonstrated that it is possible to pursue the generation and application of knowledge in mutually empowering, emancipatory ways, and examples of this were also discussed.

This raises practical, but crucial, questions. How can the generation and application of knowledge by a religious community be shielded from the corrupting influence of power? And how, in this context, can the generation and application of knowledge be more fully informed and guided by the principle of justice? To explore this, it will help to recall first the expanded conception of power articulated in chapter 2. This conception was captured in figure 8, which is reproduced below.

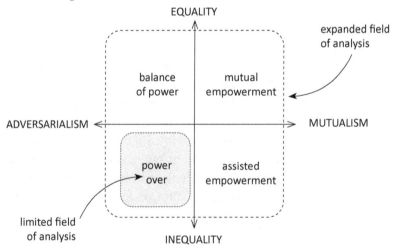

Figure 8. Expanded analysis of power.

The schema above enables us to think holistically about the relationship between power and knowledge. When the generation of
knowledge is characterized by adversarial power relations—especially the "power over" dynamics in the lower-left quadrant—the result
will be oppressive structures of knowledge. But it is also possible to
pursue the generation of knowledge through mutualistic relations
of power, represented on the right side of this schema. The result,
in the latter case, will be emancipatory structures of knowledge.
Figure 9, below, illustrates this distinction.

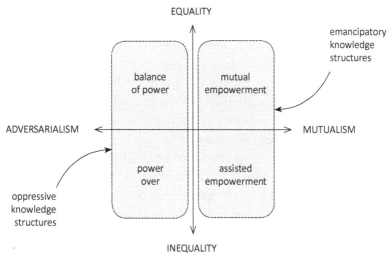

Figure 9. Generating oppressive or emancipatory structures of knowledge.

Even though the culture of learning in the Bahá'í community is
still in a relatively nascent stage of development, Bahá'í discourse
and practice attempts to shift the generation and application of
knowledge toward the quadrants on the right side of this schema.
This does not mean that Bahá'ís are asked to ignore the oppressive
forces acting in the world today. On the contrary, the primary texts
of the Bahá'í Faith contain powerful critiques of a wide range of
oppressive forces, and Bahá'í training institutes actively foster the
capacities of young people to analyze the social forces acting on
their communities. These critically informed perspectives should
motivate and guide all Bahá'í efforts. But the primary focus of those
efforts is generating and applying knowledge about the construction
of a more just social order. This occurs in many ways, the most
salient of which are discussed below.

One way this occurs is through a growing discourse within the Bahá'í community about the nature and function of power in human affairs—coupled with learning processes that are enabling the Bahá'í community to gradually transcend narrow conceptions of power. As the Universal House of Justice explains,

At the heart of the learning process is inquiry into the nature of the relationships that bind the individual, the community, and the institutions of society—actors on the stage of history who have been locked in a struggle for power throughout time. In this context, the assumption that relations among them will inevitably conform to the dictates of competition, a notion that ignores the extraordinary potential of the human spirit, has been set aside in favour of the more likely premise that their harmonious interactions can foster a civilization befitting a mature humanity. Animating the Bahá'í effort to discover the nature of a new set of relationships among these three protagonists is a vision of a future society that derives inspiration from the analogy drawn by Bahá'u'lláh, in a Tablet penned nearly a century and a half ago, which compares the world to the human body. Cooperation is the principle that governs the functioning of that system. Just as the appearance of the rational soul in this realm of existence is made possible through the complex association of countless cells, whose organization in tissues and organs allows for the realization of distinctive capacities, so can civilization be seen as the outcome of a set of interactions among closely integrated, diverse components which have transcended the narrow purpose of tending to their own existence. And just as the viability of every cell and every organ is contingent upon the health of the body as a whole, so should the prosperity of every individual, every family, every people be sought in the well-being of the entire human race. In keeping with such a vision, institutions, appreciating the need for coordinated action channeled toward fruitful ends, aim not to control but to nurture and guide the individual, who, in turn, willingly receives guidance, not in blind obedience, but with faith founded on conscious knowledge. The community, meanwhile, takes on the challenge of sustaining an environment where the powers of individuals, who wish to exercise self-expression responsibly in accordance with the common weal and the plans of institutions, multiply in unified action.[135]

In this context, the House of Justice further elaborates:

> If the web of relationships alluded to above is to take shape and give rise to a pattern of life distinguished by adherence to the principle of the oneness of humankind, certain foundational concepts must be carefully examined. Most notable among them is the conception of power. Clearly the concept of power as a means of domination, with the accompanying notions of contest, contention, division and superiority, must be left behind. This is not to deny the operation of power; after all, even in cases where institutions of society have received their mandates through the consent of the people, power is involved in the exercise of authority. But political processes, like other processes of life, should not remain unaffected by the powers of the human spirit that the Bahá'í Faith—for that matter, every great religious tradition that has appeared throughout the ages—hopes to tap: the power of unity, of love, of humble service, of pure deeds. Associated with power in this sense are words such as "release", "encourage", "channel", "guide" and "enable". Power is not a finite entity which is to be "seized" and "jealously guarded"; it constitutes a limitless capacity to transform that resides in the human race as a body.[136]

The writings of Bahá'u'lláh—on which Bahá'ís meditate at the start and end of every day—are replete with references to these latter expressions of power. Bahá'í training institutes, alluded to above, have also created opportunities across the planet for Bahá'ís and other like-minded people to collectively study these expressions of power (along with many other concepts), learn how to translate them into forms of social practice, reflect together on the insights generated, and contribute these insights to a global process of learning. This process is playing a significant role in the empowerment of previously marginalized social groups across the planet.

For instance, Bahá'í training institutes organize their training processes through decentralized study circles led by a facilitator (a "tutor") who has previously completed the core sequence of training courses and then volunteers to take others through the courses. In many countries, youth have been at the forefront of these processes. This includes female youth, who tend to be among the most marginalized of social groups on the planet. In villages and neighborhoods throughout the world, we can now find girls in their late teens or young women in their early twenties facilitating study circles that include older male participants—a dynamic that would otherwise be very rare in many cultures. Moreover, in countries with inherited caste systems, we can find girls and women from lower castes facilitating study circles whose participants include male elders from upper castes—a dynamic that reflects an extraordinary form of empowerment in which oppressive hierarchies of gender, age, and caste are all simultaneously dissolving. Similar dynamics are playing out in countries with histories of racial discrimination and other forms of oppression. The protagonists of these processes on every continent are contributing to the systematic generation of new insights that are distilled and incorporated into the Ruhi Institute's global process of learning.

On another front, the Institute for Studies in Global Prosperity has been creating a steadily growing number of spaces on every continent in which university students and young professionals further explore the implications of this expanded conception of power (along with many other concepts) for their professional and academic fields. These seminars are increasingly facilitated by graduates of the program who are empowered then to serve the program as volunteer facilitators. At these seminars, young adults are learning how to approach their higher education in more thoughtful, reflective, and critically informed ways; are striving for greater coherence between their spiritual values, their studies, their career aspirations, and their service to the wider community; and are developing the capacity to contribute in meaningful ways to the professional or academic discourses into which they will be entering. And the Institute itself has been systematically learning, through the accumulated experience at all these seminars, how to approach these processes in increasingly effective ways.

Since the Bahá'í Faith has no clergy, the work of Bahá'í training institutes, the Institute for Studies in Global Prosperity, and other collective learning processes unfolding along parallel lines are all fostered and coordinated by a steadily multiplying number of collaborators, from every background on the planet, most of whom volunteer their time and energy toward these ends, within evolving schemes of coordination. In the training they receive to perform these services, they are learning to pay special attention to the quality of their relationships and interactions with the steadily expanding numbers of people who participate in these learning processes. As alluded to earlier in this chapter, this training seeks to quiet the ego and foster a posture of humility while promoting habits of encouragement and mutual accompaniment. Calling Bahá'ís to this high standard, the House of Justice explains that

> in such a state souls labour together ceaselessly, delighting not so much in their own accomplishments but in the progress and services of others. So it is that their thoughts are centred at all times on helping one another scale the heights of service to His Cause and soar in the heaven of His knowledge. This is what we see in the present pattern of activity unfolding across the globe, propagated by young and old, by veteran and newly enrolled, working side by side.[137]

A good illustration of this is the aforementioned Junior Youth Spiritual Empowerment Program, which has taken root across the planet. This program emerged through a recognition that the period of adolescence is a formative age in which attitudes, values, and ideas about the individual and society are shaped in ways that can carry forward through the rest of one's life. At this age, a young person experiences rapid physical, intellectual, and emotional changes. They begin to explore newfound talents and capacities. Their vision of social reality expands, and they begin to grapple with profound questions about the meaning and purpose of life. At this age, they also become more acutely aware of injustice and hypocrisy.

The Empowerment Program seeks to foster a sense of constructive agency in adolescents as they move through this period of life so that they become oriented toward a life of selfless service to humanity. It fosters their powers of expression, their ability to analyze social forces in the world around them, and their capacity to consult together about forms of social action in which they can engage to contribute to the betterment of their communities. These ends are pursued through the formation of groups of peers who, with the accompaniment of one or two older youth, commit to a process of collective learning and capacity building within a mutually support- ive environment. The program is structured around study of a se- ries of short texts that have, themselves, been developed and refined through a global process of learning through action. And the older youth who accompany—or "animate"—the junior youth are trained for this service role through a parallel process. Increasingly, those older youth are graduates of the junior youth program themselves.

As the experience of the Bahá'í community has shown, however, we should have no illusions about how challenging it is to introduce and sustain this program. Nor should we have any illusions about how difficult the path is that many junior youth groups find them- selves on. But in communities where this program has taken root, the results are promising.[138] It should also be pointed out that this program, although sponsored by the Bahá'í community, is open to everyone. It is neither a program of religious instruction nor in- doctrination. At the same time, it is transparent about its focus on universally applicable spiritual principles and concepts such as the principles of unity and justice or the concept that humans have a twofold moral purpose, which is to develop their latent individu- al capacities in the process of contributing to the development of their latent collective potentialities. Through this open, inclusive, and transparent approach, Bahá'ís seek to erase boundaries of oth- erness and foster universal participation.

Relating this back to the power schema outlined above, junior youth who participate in this program learn how to engage in meaningful forms of mutual empowerment. In the process, they develop an experiential understanding of, and relationship to, a ma- ture conception of power that they can further refine and apply throughout their lives. Likewise, the youth who accompany a junior youth group learn how to engage in a meaningful form of assisted empowerment that is neither patronizing nor self-serving. The aim is to help raise up the next generation of equals who will become full protagonists in the generation and application of knowledge regarding the construction of a new social reality. Similarly, as youth animators are developing these capacities, they are accompanied by slightly older coordinators who have prior experience animating ju- nior youth groups and have subsequently arisen to accompany new animators and coordinate the multiplication of junior youth groups within the program. What we see at this level is a self-replicating system, already established in virtually every country on earth, in which growing numbers of young protagonists labor together in mutually empowering ways.

A related logic of empowerment plays out through the formal institutions that the Bahá'í world has been constructing for many generations. In the absence of a clergy, the affairs of the Bahá'í community at local and national levels are ultimately guided by elected local or national assemblies. These institutions are elected through processes that are entirely free of competition and the contest for power. In short, every adult Bahá'í is eligible to vote and to be voted for. Elections are held without any reference to individuals, through secret ballots. Following a process of prayerful reflection, voters identify the requisite number of individuals they deem most worthy to serve the common good based on their qualities of character, their demonstrated abilities, and their record of selfless service within the community. Before they fill out their ballots, voters are also explicitly encouraged to pay attention to the diversity of those whom they elect so that assemblies can benefit from a maximum diversity of perspectives. There are no campaigns, no electioneering, no competition of any kind. In thirty years of participating in and observing Bahá'í elections in several countries, at the local, national, and international level, I have never seen anyone seeking to be elected or soliciting votes. Rather, those who are elected through a plurality vote take on the unsolicited responsibility of serving the respective institution, which inevitably entails a sacrifice of time, energy, and prior aspirations.

Once an assembly has been elected, it strives to employ a consultative process in which diverse views are sought, including relevant views from outside the assembly, to inform its decision-making. On mature assemblies, views are offered, from a disinterested and humble posture of collective inquiry, as resources that the assembly is free to examine, adopt, or reject as it seeks to understand the multifaceted nature of a complex issue and choose the wisest course of action. In this consultative process, participants also seek to consciously apply spiritual principles—or agreed upon normative standards—to their decision-making process. Once decisions are made, the entire community is encouraged to implement those decisions in a unified manner so that mistakes can be identified and decisions modified as experience accrues. To the extent this is achieved, elected institutions and the communities they serve are empowered to operate in a true learning mode.

Together, these electoral and decision-making processes shift the exercise of institutional power away from the competitive or adversarial dynamics that characterize so much contemporary politics and toward the domain of mutualistic empowerment. In other words, they shift the exercise of institutional power from the left side to the right side of figures 8 and 9 above.

Moreover, such institutions have proven viable in every culture on the planet, as they have been elected in over 10,000 localities and over 180 nations or territories worldwide.[139] Furthermore, by operating as integrated parts of a single global community, under the guidance of an internationally elected Universal House of Justice, this entire administrative order functions in a globally coordinated manner, characterized by a collective learning mode on a global scale. Every institution can thus contribute to and benefit from mutualistic processes of learning and capacity building that are unfolding across the planet. All these processes are focused on constructing a new social reality that embodies spiritual principles to increasing degrees.

The examples of Bahá'í practice discussed above illustrate only a few of the many ways that Bahá'ís are learning to engage mutualistic expressions of power in the generation and application of knowledge. Stepping back from these examples, we can see a coherent approach to social change premised entirely on a positive relationship between knowledge and power. This approach is not naïve about oppressive relations of power. On the contrary, the approach has emerged as a means of transcending those oppressive relations.

Bahá'ís recognize oppression as a condition that takes myriad forms. As Bahá'u'lláh wrote a century and a half ago, "Justice is, in this day, bewailing its plight, and Equity groaneth beneath the yoke of oppression. The thick clouds of tyranny have darkened the face of the earth, and enveloped its peoples."[140] And as he wrote elsewhere, "On every side the flame of oppression and tyranny can be discerned."[141] As the Universal House of Justice has asserted more recently, humanity continues to be "battered by forces of oppression, whether generated from the depths of religious prejudice or the pinnacles of rampant materialism."[142] In this context, the Bahá'í response to oppression can be described as a program of "universal reconstruction"[143] founded on the conceptions of knowledge and power discussed above.

It is also important to note, in this regard, that what Bahá'ís seek to construct, in collaboration with like-minded people from all backgrounds, is not a social order characterized by uniformity. Rather, it is an order characterized by unity in diversity; an order characterized by a rich, expansive, inclusive vision of "the good"; an order characterized by myriad creative and culturally distinct expressions across the planet.

The Bahá'í community is thus increasingly illustrating the claim made in chapter 3 that religion can function as a system of knowledge and practice focused on the application of normative principles to the advancement of civilization. Moreover, it is striving to do this in a way that addresses the concerns raised in chapter 2 regarding the relationship between knowledge and power. Of course, the experience of the Bahá'í community is not proof that religion will universally evolve along the lines suggested in chapters 2 and 3. But the Bahá'í experience offers provisional evidence that religion can function this way.

If humanity has been able to conceptualize science in increasingly coherent and fruitful ways and articulate normative standards by which practitioners of science can increasingly be held to account, then we should be able to do the same with religion. Indeed, given the exigencies of the twenty-first century—the interdependence of all human beings in a context of mounting existential threats—holding religion to account in this way may prove to be an essential means of securing our future. Superstition, fanaticism, conflict, and violence in the name of religion are threats to human well-being on a global scale. Why shouldn't religion, like every other socially constructed system, continue to evolve and be held accountable to standards that promote human well-being? Why should the security and prosperity of our species be sacrificed at the altar of obsolescent modes of social thought and practice that no longer support human well-being?

Chapter 5

Materialist Frames of Reference

In this book, I have argued that human knowledge can, to some degree, become attuned to foundational normative truths, that the generation of such knowledge need not be corrupted by power and privilege, and that it is possible, under the right conditions, to learn our way forward toward a more peaceful, just, and mutually prosperous social order. To do these things, we need a framework that reconciles truth and relativity, as well as knowledge and power, in rational and constructive ways. I suggested a way to do this by reconciling ontological foundationalism and epistemological relativism within a moderate social constructionist framework. I then explored the implications of this framework for reconciling science and religion as complementary and overlapping systems of knowledge and practice, and I examined the experience of the Bahá'í community to illustrate this possibility.

This line of reasoning runs against the grain of influential traditions of thought that all share a materialist conception of reality. In the following discussion, I examine four of these traditions in relation to my argument: first, the broad tradition of physicalism, which is roughly synonymous with materialism itself; second, within physicalism, the current of thought known as pragmatism, which arose, in part, to address the normative relativism that physicalism gave birth to; third, proceduralism, a current of thought within pragmatism that seeks procedural solutions to the problem of relativism; and fourth, agonism, a current of thought within proceduralism that seeks to address the problem of power.

In discussing each of these traditions, it is not my purpose to dismiss them as baseless. Rather, it is to show how each offers some valid insights from within their own frames of reference, or in relation to the material dimensions of social reality that they seek to explain and navigate. Moreover, some of these traditions, such as pragmatism and proceduralism, share areas of common ground with the line of reasoning outlined in previous chapters of this book. Yet the frames of reference that characterize and delimit each of these traditions do not encompass all aspects of social reality—including latent social phenomena with normative dimensions—that we need to factor into the generation of knowledge. And there is some urgency to this. To address the mounting challenges of the twenty-first century and to learn our way forward toward the construction of a more peaceful and just social reality, we need an expanded frame of reference. And this requires some understanding of the limitations of materialist frames of reference.

Before examining some of these limitations—by looking at the examples of physicalism, pragmatism, proceduralism, and agonism—I want to reiterate a point that was alluded to in the preface to this book. This book focuses primarily on overcoming problems and limitations that have arisen within the dominant Western intellectual tradition and that have, to varying degrees, been widely exported through several centuries of Western hegemony. One way to attempt this would be through a global survey of non-Western intellectual traditions, as well as subaltern traditions within the West, that offer many implicit or explicit arguments for moving beyond purely materialist frames of reference. This is an important project, but it is a project that others are better positioned to advance. My approach, therefore, is to articulate an argument that seeks to expand—or perhaps rupture—important aspects of the Western tradition largely on its own terms. In this sense, it constitutes an argument from within, rather than from without. Nonetheless, my argument constitutes an invitation to those who are grounded in myriad non-Western or subaltern intellectual traditions to contribute toward this same end, through arguments from without—as so many have already done. With that invitation and acknowledgement, I return to the argument at hand.

PHYSICALISM

In popular usage, *materialism* often signifies attachment to material things, preoccupation with the material world, or the elevation of material success as an ultimate value. But in Western philosophy, *materialism* is the ontological view that reality is nothing more than a material phenomenon.[144] According to this view, all biological, psychological, and social dimensions of reality derive, in their entirety, from underlying physical conditions and causes. Human consciousness and subjectivity are thus viewed as nothing more than epiphenomena or emergent properties of material systems.

Some philosophers consider the term *physicalism* to be a more nuanced and sophisticated term than *materialism*.[145] *Physicalism* signifies a recognition that the physical universe is characterized by more than matter. The physical universe also includes a range of forces, such as gravity, electromagnetism, strong and weak nuclear forces, that operate on matter; it exists in a space-time continuum; and so on, as the science of physics has demonstrated. *Physicalism* thus denotes all the foundational features of reality that are encompassed by the study of physics, along with the chemical, biological, neurological, and social phenomena that emerge through the causal interplay of those foundational features of physical reality. Nonetheless, many philosophers use the concepts *materialism* and *physicalism* interchangeably, as I will also do at times.

The earliest records of materialist or physicalist philosophies trace back to ancient Greece (e.g., Thales, Anaxagoras, Epicurus, Democritus), India (e.g., Ajita Kesakambali, Payasi, Kanada), and China (e.g., Xunzi, Yang Xiong, Wang Chong). But the modern ascendancy of such philosophies began in the context of religious attacks on early enlightenment science, along with devastating religious wars following the Reformation. Against this background of anti-scientific religious orthodoxies and violent religious conflicts, materialist philosophies (espoused by thinkers such as Pierre Gassendi, Jean Meslier, Julien Offray de La Mettrie, Baron d'Holbach, Denis Diderot, John Stewart, Ludwig Feuerbach, and Karl Marx) were undoubtedly very appealing. If modernizing societies could not advance while in the grips of religious orthodoxy and conflict, new systems of thought were clearly needed. Materialism emerged as an attractive, rational, and compelling alternative.

Materialist philosophy was closely associated with secularism, or the commitment to reason as one of the highest governing principles of the enlightenment. As a political philosophy, secularism sought to separate governance from the direct influence or control of any given religious institution, community, or belief system. One of its primary aims was to ensure that all citizens were free from religious rule or the coercive imposition of religious laws. One of its secondary aims was to end religious conflicts over control of state institutions. As processes of secularization advanced, along with the spread of materialist worldviews, many modern thinkers naturally began to assume religion had become entirely anachronistic. According to this *secularization thesis*, religious modes of thought and practice were predicted to decline steadily through the rise of more sophisticated and purely scientific forms of rationality—a process that was to liberate humanity from the ignorance and oppression of religious orthodoxies.[146]

The experience of two devastating world wars, the eugenics movement and the Holocaust, the invention of weapons of mass destruction and instruments of mass manipulation, and other disturbing developments of the twentieth century began to cast doubt on the view that a purely scientific rationality had the potential to solve humanity's problems or the potential to create a more peaceful and just world. After all, the leading protagonists of these horrific developments were generally at the vanguard of scientific rationality. In addition, the tenacity of religious thought and the contribution of religious communities to many progressive social movements in the twentieth century, along with the resurgence of religious fanaticism in the twenty-first century, cast doubt on the secularization thesis, even among influential secular thinkers.[147] As a result, a normative discourse on the role of religion in the modern public sphere, alluded to in previous chapters, is now emerging.[148]

The purpose of this brief historical sketch is to illustrate that modern materialist philosophies emerged in a specific historical context, within which they appeared rational and compelling to many people. But the limits of purely materialist philosophies are becoming apparent. Such philosophies are incapable of yielding a normative framework even for the application of the physical sciences, let alone for the many other normative questions facing humanity today. Physicalism may be appropriate for the internal work of the physical sciences. But it is too limited to explore, explain, predict, or guide every aspect of human reality, including collective expressions of human agency. We need a wider framework.

To consider what it means to adopt a wider frame of reference in efforts to understand reality, we can draw an analogy from physics. Classical Newtonian mechanics has proven to be remarkably useful for exploring, explaining, and predicting the movements and inter-actions of macroscopic objects that are neither extremely massive nor travelling near the speed of light. But studying aspects of phys-ical reality outside those parameters requires other theoretical lenses that become imaginable only within a wider frame of reference. For instance, the study of subatomic phenomena requires the theory of quantum mechanics, the study of phenomena travelling near the speed of light requires the theory of special relativity, and the study of extremely massive objects requires the theory of general relativ-ity—and all these theories require a frame of reference that is more expansive than the classical Newtonian frame.

Similarly, in an overarching way, physicalism serves as a useful lens for inquiry into all purely physical dimensions of reality. But this frame of reference does not encompass all of reality. Two ob-vious dimensions of reality, subjectivity and normativity, cannot be encompassed by physicalism.

This point is made in a compelling manner by Thomas Nagel in *The View from Nowhere*.[149] Nagel accepts the basic ontological prem-ise on which the physical sciences rest: that reality is governed by an underlying order that is independent of the degree to which subjec-tive human minds understand it. He also accepts the basic episte-mological premise on which the physical sciences rest: that, by using appropriate methods, human minds can explore and explain aspects of this underlying order in a relatively objective manner. In relation to these premises, Nagel suggests that the physical sciences require us to strive for *objectivity*, which he conceptualizes as an approach to understanding.

Through this approach, the empirical observations we make through our physical senses regarding the appearances of reality that we encounter become the means of exploring deeper, hid-den, structural properties of reality. Our efforts to explore these foundational properties of reality constitute an attempt to develop a more objective understanding. That understanding is never complete or infallible because human comprehension will always be incomplete and fragmented. But through an objective approach, aspects of reality can become objects of ongoing systematic inquiry. Nagel refers to this approach as *objective inquiry*.

Elaborating on this approach, Nagel contrasts an objective standpoint with a subjective standpoint. A subjective standpoint arises from an individual's unique psychological makeup, social position, life experience, and so forth. It is, in this sense, a highly particular "view from somewhere."[150] An objective standpoint, on the other hand, arises from shared forms of understanding that are accessible to a wide range of reasoning subjects. Thus, this becomes, in this sense, a "view from nowhere."[151] But the distinction between subjectivity and objectivity is a matter of degree. In this sense, the move from subjectivity to objectivity can be understood as "a set of concentric spheres, progressively revealed as we detach gradually from the contingencies of the self."[152] Or stated another way, "what really happens in the pursuit of objectivity is that a certain element of oneself, the impersonal or objective self, which can escape from the specific contingencies of one's creaturely point of view, is allowed to predominate."[153] In the physical sciences, the move from subjectivity to objectivity follows this path:

> The development goes in stages, each of which gives a more objective picture than the one before. The first step is to see that our perceptions are caused by the action of things on us, through their effects on our bodies, which are themselves parts of the physical world. The next step is to realize that since the same physical properties that cause perceptions in us through our bodies also produce different effects on other physical things and can exist without causing any perception at all, their true nature must be detachable from their perceptual appearance and need not resemble it. The third step is to try to form a conception of that true nature independent of its appearance either to us or to other types of perceivers. This means not only not thinking of the physical world from our own particular point of view, but not thinking of it from a more general human perceptual point of view either:

not thinking of how it looks, feels, smells, tastes, or sounds. These secondary qualities then drop out of our picture of the external world, and the underlying primary qualities such as shape, size, weight, and motion are thought of structurally.[154]

This move toward objectivity, as an approach to inquiry, has proven incredibly fruitful in the physical sciences. It has yielded a steadily growing body of knowledge that has transformed our relationship with the material world. Nagel points out, however, that the purely physical conception of objectivity on which the natural sciences operate constrains objective inquiry into other aspects of reality. The most obvious of these is inquiry into human subjectivity itself. Yet human subjectivity is clearly part of reality. Indeed, the entire process described above would not be possible without the existence of human subjectivity, because subjectivity is the starting point of objective inquiry.

A purely physical conception of objectivity has been unable to conceptualize or explain subjectivity—the conscious thought and perception of individuals—in any meaningful way. As Nagel points out, physicalism assumes that subjectivity is a mere epiphenomenon of biochemical processes in the brain. But physicalism offers no evidence to support this assumption, and it offers no causal explanation regarding how consciousness, or subjectivity, can arise from the interaction of purely physical elements.

Nagel argues that to explore the nature of human consciousness, we will need to move beyond the physical reductionism alluded to above by adopting an expanded conception of objectivity. In this regard, he suggests that "the subjectivity of consciousness is an irreducible feature of reality—without which we couldn't do physics or anything else—and it must occupy as fundamental a place in any credible world view as matter, energy, space, time, and numbers."[155] As he goes on to explain, "Even though the manifestations of mind evident to us are local—they depend on our brains and similar organic structures—the general basis of this aspect of reality is not local, but must be presumed to inhere in the general constituents of the universe and the laws that govern them."[156]

Recognizing this requires an expanded conception of objective reality—or an expanded conception of reality that can still be approached through objective methods of inquiry. The methods of inquiry appropriate for this expanded conception, Nagel admits, have not yet been developed because the dominance of a purely physical conception of objectivity precludes their development. Nagel's argument thus constitutes an appeal for intellectual humility. His purpose is not to invalidate physicalism but to expand on it, in the same way that Einstein's theory of relativity did not invalidate Newtonian mechanics but expanded on it. Nagel thus asks us to recognize that inherited conceptions of objectivity are unnecessarily narrow and therefore the methods, concepts, and theories needed to investigate foundational aspects of reality such as human subjectivity may not yet exist. And he calls us to get on with this work.

It should be noted that Nagel makes this call from a secular standpoint. He is avowedly not religious. He simply recognizes that a purely physical conception of objectivity cannot explain certain foundational aspects of reality. In this regard, Nagel suggests that the expanded conception of objective reality needed to explore human consciousness will be comparable to the leap that was needed to move from Newtonian physics to James Clerk Maxwell's theory of electromagnetism. The latter required the articulation of entirely new types of concepts, like the concept of electromagnetic *fields*, which did not exist in classical mechanics. Similarly, Nagel argues:

> To insist on trying to explain the mind in terms of concepts and theories that have been devised exclusively to explain non-mental phenomena is, in view of the radically distinguishing characteristics of the mental, both intellectually backward and scientifically suicidal. The difference between mental and physical is far greater than the difference between electrical and mechanical. We need entirely new intellectual tools, and it is precisely by reflection on what appears impossible—like the generation of mind out of the recombination of matter—that we will be forced to create such tools.[157]

In his call for new intellectual tools to explore the phenomena of subjectivity, Nagel also suggests that we will need new tools for exploring the phenomena of normativity. As he explains:

> The problem of the place of value in the natural world includes but goes beyond the problems of the place of consciousness

and of cognition in general, because it has to do specifically with the practical domain—the control and assessment of conduct. It is clear that the existence of value and our response to it depend on consciousness and cognition, since so much of what is valuable consists in or involves conscious experience, and the appropriate responses to what is good and bad, right and wrong, depend on the cognitive recognition of the things that give us reasons for and against. Practical reasoning is a cognitive, largely conscious process. I have argued so far that the reality of consciousness and cognition cannot be plausibly reconciled with traditional scientific naturalism, either constitutively or historically. I believe that value presents a further problem for scientific naturalism. Even against the background of a world view in which consciousness and cognition are somehow given a place in the natural order, value is something in addition, and it has consequences that are comparably pervasive.[158]

Elaborating on this theme, Nagel states that "an adequate conception of the cosmos must contain the resources to account for how it could have given rise to beings capable of thinking successfully about what is good and bad, right and wrong, and discovering moral and evaluative truths that do not depend on their own beliefs."[159] He again suggests this is possible only within an expanded conception of objectivity, through which inquiry can move from subjective appearances of normativity toward objective understandings of normativity.

If we understand our prereflective impressions of value—instinctive attractions and aversions, inclinations and inhibitions—as appearances of real value, then the cognitive process of discovering a systematic and consistent structure of general reasons and practical and moral principles can be thought of as a way of moving from appearances to reality in the normative domain.[160]

With this argument, Nagel is adopting a position of *value realism*—or *normative realism*—which is the assumption that normative truths have an existence that is independent of the purely subjective desires of individuals. In other words, he argues for a conception of universal normative truths that can be discerned through detached forms of ethical reasoning that transcend subjective desires, interests, and motivations.[161] Nagel thus believes it should be possible to adopt an objective approach to inquiry that leads to the articulation of normative truths that increasingly reflect "the view from nowhere." He illustrates this by considering the move from subjectivity to objectivity in a case where an agent has the potential to harm a victim. The key, Nagel explains, is "the distinction between the internal viewpoint of the agent or victim and an external, objective viewpoint which both agent and victim can also adopt. Reasons for action look different from the first two points of view than from the third."[162]

Nagel admits that value realism is not a position that can be proven at this time. But the same is true of the opposite position that values have no real existence. Furthermore, Nagel argues that "the burden of proof has often been misplaced in this debate," and "a defeasible presumption that values need not be illusory is entirely reasonable until it is shown not to be."[163] On this note, Nagel demonstrates that no logically coherent or empirically verifiable proofs have been marshalled against value realism, and he thus returns to his call for intellectual humility.[164] Value realism, as well as the denial of value realism—or anti-realism—remain equivalent premises at this stage in our understanding of normativity. The ultimate test of each will be their relative fruitfulness in producing results that improve the human condition. Indeed, this is the same test by which the basic ontological and epistemological premises underlying the entire enterprise of the physical sciences, alluded to above, have historically been assessed.

Nagel thus offers an alternative to *moral anti-realism*, which rejects the possibility that values, or normative truths, have an objective existence of any kind. Moral anti-realism became popularized in part through the rise of *positivism* in the philosophy of science. Positivism, as discussed earlier in this chapter, asserts a strong dichotomy between facts and values—or between empirical truths and normative beliefs. According to this view, facts are associated with objective phenomena, but values are purely subjective expressions or social constructs.[165]

This dichotomous conception of facts and values leads toward moral anti-realism. One of the most influential versions of this is *error theory*.[166] Error theory presumes that reality has no normative properties or features. According to this logic, there can be no normative truths, and there can be no valid normative truth claims; the fact that normative language often takes the form of truth claims merely reflects a cognitive error in our understanding of reality. In other words, error theory states that all normative truth claims are based on the erroneous presupposition that normative facts exist.

There are other variations on the theme of moral anti-realism, but they all share the assumption that normative truths do not exist. One premise that underlies such theories is that we should always assume the non-existence of something unless and until its existence can be empirically or scientifically proven. But there are many problems with this argument. One problem is that it privileges the assumption of non-existence over existence in a manner that would have precluded many great scientific discoveries. If scientists simply assumed the non-existence of everything that was not yet empirically proven, science would never have advanced because there would have been no motivation to discover yet unknown or unproven features of reality. The true scientist adopts a posture of humility and curiosity in the face of the unknown.

Another problem with the presumption of non-existence is that it rests on a naïve conception of what it means for something to be "proven." Strictly speaking, science is not in the business of "proving" things. Science is in the business of helping us assess the degree of confidence specific truth claims warrant. Confidence is a relative and highly complex condition. It derives not only from our observations of reality, but also from how we interpret those observations. Which interpretations we have confidence in can derive, in part, from an intuitive sense of how elegant, compelling, and attractive different interpretive theories are. Of course, such theories also need to explain observations in effective ways. But if competing theories appear to explain the same observations in equally effective ways, scientists tend to prefer the more parsimonious and elegant theory.

Moreover, many theories emerge long before it is possible to engage in observations by which they can be tested. Indeed, some theories raise entirely new possibilities about what might be observed. Many of Einstein's ideas—from the prediction that light could bend to the prediction that gravitational waves exist—were of this sort. Newtonian physics did not suggest these possibilities, and there was not yet any observational basis for them when Einstein formulated them. The ideas, in themselves, prompted the subsequent search for ways these phenomena might be observed. In both the examples alluded to above, those observations were eventually made. In the case of gravitational waves, it took one hundred years to create the technology that could even make such an observation possible.

Yet another problem with the presumption of non-existence is that it tends to assume every aspect of reality is susceptible to the investigations of the empirical sciences within a physicalist conception of objectivity. But this is another questionable assumption. For instance, we know that time is an aspect of reality, and we know that the future is an aspect of time, but the future is not readily susceptible to investigation by the empirical sciences. Likewise, as the previous discussion of Nagel demonstrates, we know that human subjectivity is an aspect of reality, but the empirical sciences have never been able to penetrate deeply into this feature of reality. Why should it not be the case that the empirical sciences, within a physicalist conception of objectivity, are ill-suited to investigate other features of reality, such as normativity?

Finally, it is important to note that science often tells us very little about the essence of things. Rather, science tells us about their effects. Gravity is a good example. Science tells us very little about the essence of "what gravity is." Rather, science tells us about the effects of gravity, and how to predict those effects, and how to harness those effects, and what the consequences will be if we ignore them. Why should we not understand normative truths—such as justice—in the same way? We do not need to answer the question "What is the essence of justice?" to observe the effects when we apply, or violate, the principle of justice as we construct social phenomena. When altruistic people strive to apply the principle of justice in their social endeavors, does this not lead, quite predictably, to the intersubjective experience of well-being and empowerment by those who are impacted by those endeavors? When egoistic people ignore the principle of justice in their social endeavors, does this not lead, quite predictably, to the intersubjective experience of suffering and oppression by those who are impacted by those endeavors? Can we not make corresponding predictions about other normative principles, such as truthfulness, and how their application or violation not only affects the health of basic social relationships, but also advances or retards the attainment of economic prosperity?

If we know things by their effects and by our ability to predict those effects, then there seems to be considerable evidence supporting the existence of normative truths. But to grasp this, we need to move beyond naïve conceptions of science, knowledge, and empirical proof. In so doing, we can dispense with the bias that we should simply assume the non-existence of something unless and until its existence can be empirically proven. The process of investigating reality is too nuanced and complicated for such simplistic assertions.

At best, *normative foundationalism* (or normative realism) and *normative anti-foundationalism* (or normative anti-realism) are equivalent and equally plausible premises at this time, neither of which yet warrants an extremely high degree of confidence. But when we consider how predictable the effects of applying or violating various normative principles are, it seems reasonable to conclude that the weight of initial evidence tilts in favor of normative foundationalism. Moreover, it seems equally reasonable that we should search for increasingly systematic and purposeful ways to test this premise further.

Additionally, if we reject this provisional evidence due to a narrowly materialist bias, then we foreclose the possibility of finding a route out of the grave normative impasse alluded to at the outset of this book—the inability to agree on how to live together successfully in an increasingly interdependent world. This impasse now represents an existential threat. If for no other reason, then, it appears pragmatic to operate on the assumption that foundational normative truths exist. Ironically, pragmatism, as a philosophical tradition, has rejected the possibility of foundational normative truths. It is therefore toward the tradition of pragmatism that we now turn our attention.

PRAGMATISM

In popular usage, *pragmatism* signifies everyday practicality or the ability to get things done within the constraints imposed by life. In philosophy, *pragmatism* is a broad tradition of thought that generally abandons the search for foundational normative truths as a basis for social progress, based on the premise that even if such truths exist, there is no way to prove them or agree on them. Although there are different currents of thought within pragmatism, most tend to focus on the discovery of practical measures on which people can try to agree in efforts to improve the human condition. Accordingly, human thought tends to be viewed as an instrument for guiding action toward what works, or how to best cope with contingent phenomena, rather than for discovering, representing, or knowing foundational aspects of reality. The successful solution of problems is thus seen as the measure of progress. But this is progress toward efficacy, not progress toward truth.

In this sense, all pragmatists need not be materialist. But pragmatism tends toward a materialist frame of reference as a lowest common denominator within pluralistic secular societies. Reality may have dimensions that transcend the material, as some people clearly believe, but these are seen by most pragmatists as articles of faith that must be bracketed off for the purposes of rational inquiry and decision-making in pluralistic societies.

The emergence of modern pragmatism as a philosophical position is generally traced to the work of Charles Sanders Peirce, William James, and John Dewey—American philosophers whose pragmatic ideas became influential in the last quarter of the nineteenth century. The explicit influence of pragmatist philosophy waned in the mid-twentieth century but then re-emerged in a broader form through the work of Rorty, Putnam, Robert Brandom, Richard Bernstein, and others. Moreover, as Bernstein demonstrates, many of the central themes of pragmatism have exerted an implicit influence on the entire field of philosophy for the past 150 years. Hence, "today, the vigorous creative discussion of pragmatic themes by thinkers all over the world is more widespread than it has ever been in the past."[167]

In a historical context, pragmatism, as a broad tradition of thought, is a laudable effort to overcome several problematic tendencies of Western philosophical thought. Those tendencies include naïve conceptions regarding the relationship between human knowledge and reality, the divorce of philosophical inquiry from practical concerns, and the construction of unproductive dualisms or false dichotomies. Pragmatist responses to each of these tendencies will be examined briefly below.

The first of these, tendencies toward naïve conceptions of the relationship between human knowledge and reality, have both rationalist and empiricist versions. On the one hand, naïve rationalists have assumed that essential truths about reality can be directly explored, discovered, and represented through pure reason. In response, pragmatists have pointed out that the human mind is too limited to represent, or mirror, infinitely complex or inaccessible aspects of reality in their essence. On the other hand, naïve empiricists have assumed that human observations are unmediated forms of sensory data that serve as reliable foundations for theory development. In response, pragmatists have pointed out that all observations are theory laden. In other words, what we notice and how we interpret it is enabled and constrained by the theories we bring to our observations. Since theories are fallible, observations cannot serve as infallible foundations for human knowledge.

In both these ways, pragmatists tend to reject the view that reliable bodies of knowledge can, through the correct rational and/or empirical methods, be confidently constructed on infallible foundations. At the same time, many pragmatists are agnostic regarding the possibility that foundational truths about reality exist independent of human knowledge. In other words, pragmatists tend to reject *epistemological foundationalism* while remaining agnostic regarding *ontological foundationalism*. Or to use the language employed in the first chapter of this book, pragmatists tend to be skeptical about ontological *truth claims* while remaining ambivalent about the existence of ontological *truths*.

In this regard, pragmatists tend to adopt a posture of epistemological humility. Even if ontological truths exist, pragmatists assume it is not possible to agree on them because there is no infallible method for discovering or proving them. Better to focus, instead, on what seems "to work," rather than what seems "to be true." And "what works" is conceptualized in a foundationless manner. An oft-cited expression of this is Otto Neurath's conception of the ship of human knowledge. According to Neurath, a body of knowledge is like a ship at sea that does not rest on any foundations. Thus:

We are like sailors who must rebuild their ship on the open sea, never able to dismantle it in dry-dock and to reconstruct it there out of the best materials. Where a beam is taken away a new one must at once be put there, and for this the rest of the ship is used as support. In this way, by using the old beams and driftwood the ship can be shaped entirely anew, but only by gradual reconstruction.[168]

Neurath thus saw systems of human knowledge as free-floating aggregate structures. The theories, concepts, and assumptions comprising them can never be built up with perfect confidence on solid foundations. Rather, elements of the system can be fashioned and refashioned only in relation to the aggregate logic of the system itself. According to this view, bodies of knowledge can be internally coherent, but they cannot be infallibly constructed from the ground up on foundational truths.

Neurath's conception of knowledge is a laudable attempt to push back against arguments that were being advanced by his contemporaries, such as Rudolf Carnap, who were seeking infallible methods by which human knowledge could be built up from secure foundations. Neurath was arguing against such foundationalist epistemologies. René Descartes penned the most well-known early modern version of a foundationalist epistemology. He argued that reliable bodies of knowledge could be built up systematically from foundational forms of *a priori* knowledge, or self-evident truths. In contrast to Descartes' rationalism, Carnap argued for a foundational epistemology based on logical empiricism, in which reliable bodies of knowledge could be built up systematically through a set of logical rules on the foundation of elementary experiential statements. But Carnap's aim, like Descartes', was to clarify a method by which to construct infallible systems of knowledge.

The analysis laid out in the first chapter of this book shares Neurath's general view—and the view generally held by pragmatists—that all epistemological truth claims, theories, or bodies of knowledge must ultimately be considered fallible. At the same time, this book posits the existence of ontological truths, and it offers the concept of *relative attunement* as a more nuanced alternative to Neurath's free-floating ship of knowledge. This book thus suggests a way to reconcile a non-foundational epistemology with a foundational ontology.

The second philosophical tendency pragmatists reject, closely related to their rejection of foundationalist epistemologies, is the divorce of philosophical inquiry from the practical concerns of citizens and the applied project of improving the human condition. Rather than concern themselves with the pursuit of ahistorical and universal truths, the role of the pragmatist philosopher is to inquire into the practical consequences of ideas. According to this logic, theories and models can never correspond with, or mirror, reality in its essence. They are merely instruments for solving problems, achieving goals, and coping with reality. As such, they should be judged by their relative fruitfulness. If one theory works better than another by solving a problem more effectively, it should be accepted—unless or until a more fruitful theory is constructed. The quest for truth and certainty is thus abandoned in favor of the quest for utility, empirical adequacy, and practical agreement.

Moreover, pragmatists assert that the fruitfulness of a theory cannot be assessed through abstract proofs and logical deductions. It should be assessed primarily through its application. Pragmatism is thus committed to learning in action. It focuses on testing ideas through experience in specific socio-historical contexts. It aims to generate insights by pressing on reality to see what happens. To do this, knowers must be agents of change engaged in reflective forms of action. The role of the philosopher, in this regard, is not to legislate eternal truths from on high, but to explore and make explicit the reasoning behind best practices. This requires more than a passive intellectualism because it is not possible to observe unless one acts.

Furthermore, pragmatists often assume there is a communal nature to such inquiry. As Dewey emphasized, learning through action requires collective action. Learning is both a participatory and experiential enterprise. This is the basis for the generation of knowledge in democratic societies. It is the means by which citizens can evaluate, criticize, and reform social norms, institutions, and practices.[169]

In all these ways, pragmatism is a philosophy of *praxis*—or a philosophy premised on the complete interdependence of theory and practice. For pragmatists, if a theory has no practical consequences, it has no real meaning.

The argument laid out in this book agrees with many of these ideas, including the need to test theories based on their fruitfulness, and the importance, in this regard, of reflective forms of collective action. But this book suggests there are methods by which these methods and commitments can be applied toward increasing the embodiment of foundational normative truths in social constructs.

The third broad philosophical tendency pragmatists reject is the tendency toward unproductive dualisms or false dichotomies. These include dichotomous conceptions of theory versus practice, mind versus body, appearance versus reality, thought versus experience, subject versus object, knowledge versus action, ends versus means, and facts versus values—all of which were central concerns of Dewey.[170] Dewey did not deny the general usefulness of conceptual distinctions. What concerned him was the tendency to move from fluid and contextualized distinctions to rigid and reified dualisms that provoke fruitless and irresolvable metaphysical debates.

Of most direct relevance to the discussion at hand is the fact/value dualism. Putnam traces the modern development of this false dichotomy through several stages.[171] His narrative begins with David Hume's doctrine that one cannot infer an "ought" from an "is" because the latter involves "matters of fact," but the former does not. Hume's distinction foreshadowed the rise of logical positivism, alluded to above. Logical positivism attempted to classify all truth claims as analytic, synthetic, or meaningless. Analytic statements were those that could be judged true or false based on logical rules and axioms (such as mathematical proofs). Synthetic statements were those that could be judged true or false based on empirical assessments (such as physics experiments). All other truth claims—including normative, aesthetic, and metaphysical claims—were considered cognitively meaningless and hence unworthy of philosophical or scientific inquiry.

Ironically, this distinction drawn by logical positivism is, itself, a metaphysical truth claim derived from a reductive form of physicalism. It is a claim about what is real and what can be known through objective forms of inquiry. Hence the logical positivist distinction that rejects metaphysical claims as meaningless is based on a metaphysical claim. Despite the self-contradictory nature of this distinction, logical positivism exerted a powerful influence on scientific and social scientific thought through a substantial part of the twentieth century, from which it also entered popular consciousness through the widely but uncritically accepted fact/value dichotomy, which views facts as truths and values as foundationless subjective preferences or emotional expressions.

Putnam demonstrates the untenable nature of this dichotomy by exploring the deeply entangled nature of facts and values. He begins by showing how the concept of a "fact" is, itself, a concept that is impossible to demarcate with precision. For instance, whether one calls a mathematical proof a "fact" or merely a logical "convention" is, itself, determined by intersubjective linguistic conventions on which different schools of thought do not agree. Putnam also shows how values and judgments permeate all human experience, including the practice of science itself. Values such as intellectual honesty are fundamental to the integrity of the scientific enterprise. In addition to ethical values such as honesty on which the practice of science rests, science also rests on epistemic values about how scientists "ought" to reason. These include the value placed on coherence, plausibility, reasonableness, simplicity, and even the aesthetic beauty of theories—all of which are widely accepted criteria for assessing the relative merits of scientific truth claims. But these normative commitments are not substantiated by empirical facts beyond the general "fruitfulness" of such commitments, which is precisely the point of the pragmatist argument against logical positivism.

Furthermore, facts and values are also entangled by the lines of inquiry that different scientists pursue, which yield scientific facts. Those lines of inquiry are shaped by the personal values held by scientists regarding what is important to research and by the values of those funding their research. So, in this sense, values make possible the discovery of facts. Putnam marshals additional arguments to demonstrate the thorough entanglement of facts and values, but the forms of entanglement discussed in this paragraph and the preceding one are sufficient for the discussion at hand.

After deconstructing fact/value dualism in these ways, Putnam discusses the normative relativism to which this false dichotomy gives rise. If, in contrast to facts, all values are meaningless subjective or emotional expressions, then there is little basis for constructing a more just social order. This problem can be transcended only by adopting an objective approach to at least some kinds of values and, like Nagel, Putnam argues that this requires an expanded conception of objectivity. To formulate this expanded conception, Putnam suggests we need to move beyond the physicalist "supposition that 'objectivity' means *correspondence to objects*."[172] He illustrates this by showing that mathematical and logical truths, or principles, are examples of "objectivity without objects."[173] He thus argues:

> it is time we stopped equating *objectivity* with *description*. There are many sorts of statements—bona fide statements, ones amenable to such terms as "correct," "incorrect," "true," "false,"

"warranted," and "unwarranted"—that are not descriptions, but that are under rational control, governed by standards appropriate to their particular functions and contexts. Enabling us to describe the world is one extremely important function of language; it is not the only function, nor is it the only function to which questions such as, "Is this way of achieving this function reasonable or unreasonable? Rational or irrational? Warranted or unwarranted?" apply.[174]

To further grasp Putnam's point, consider a normative statement such as "Honesty and trustworthiness are moral duties." This statement is not an empirical "description" of any "objects." Yet its honesty and trustworthiness are fundamental to human prosperity and, as such, the preceding statement can be considered an objective statement. Moreover, the entire enterprise of science would be impossible if scientists did not accept the validity of the preceding statement. How, then, can an epistemological system that aims for objective inquiry into myriad aspects of reality depend on a premise that has no objective reality? When this premise is violated, as it sometimes is by unscrupulous individuals pretending to practice science, scientific inquiry becomes compromised and meaningless. Therefore, the advancement of science is impossible without honest and trustworthy scientists. In this sense, the statement "honesty and trustworthiness are moral duties" is not merely a subjective opinion. Nor is it merely an intersubjective agreement. It is an objective statement describing a fundamental requisite of the entire scientific enterprise—and of any other human endeavor leading to collective advancement and shared prosperity.

Moving beyond the fact/value dichotomy and adopting the expanded conception of objectivity thus enables us to recognize, as Putnam explains, that "evaluation and description are interwoven and interdependent" aspects of human rationality.[175] In other words, values and facts are deeply entangled.

In arguing for an expanded conception of objectivity that encompasses normativity in this way, Putnam does not adopt the Platonic view that normativity has ontological foundations that are independent of human thought. On the contrary, in *Ethics without Ontology*, Putnam attempts to write an obituary for all ontological thought, arguing instead for a purely pragmatic approach to normativity.[176]

Pure pragmatism of this kind, however, runs into its own prob-lems. On the one hand, the value pragmatists place on the fruit-fulness of a premise or theory is laudable. As discussed in chapter 1, the entire enterprise of science rests on the twin premises that reality is governed by a hidden order and that the human mind can, with the proper methods, gain at least some partial insights into this order. Yet to this day, the only "proof" of these premises is their fruitfulness, as demonstrated by the astonishing power of the applied sciences to transform humanity's material conditions.

Such fruitfulness seems to be an excellent standard by which to assess such premises. By this same standard, what if premises re-garding the existence of foundational normative truths also prove to be fruitful? Pragmatists such as Putnam try to foreclose this pos-sibility by constructing logical arguments that preclude it. In doing so, ironically, Putnam contradicts his own pragmatic framework by invoking the kinds of timeless, abstract, universalizing arguments that pure pragmatists reject in favor of seeing "what works." What if the premise that foundational normative truths exists ends up being "what works"?

The limits of pure pragmatism can be further understood when one recognizes that to answer the question of "what works" one has to clarify the normative standards by which one evaluates "what works." Therefore, the question of "what works" can only be answered within an antecedent normative frame. For instance, within the normative frame of those who enslaved others, slavery "worked" quite well. Within the normative frame of colonists, the subjugation of non-European nations "worked" quite well. Within the normative frame of patriarchal males, the subjection of women "works" quite well. Within the normative frame of capitalists, the extraction of surplus value from working people "works" quite well.

It is thus impossible to arrive at conclusions about "what works" through purely pragmatic processes that do not begin with norma-tive presuppositions. Pure pragmatism can never escape this circular trap to arrive at unprejudiced conclusions about the relative fruit-fulness of different normative logics. Some pragmatists try to avoid this trap by adopting a strictly utilitarian framework in which the al-legedly objective measure of maximizing human pleasure and mini-mizing human pain becomes the only guiding standard. But from a purely pragmatic perspective, who is to say that the maximization of human pleasure and the minimization of human pain is an objective standard? This is clearly not the standard that slaveholders, colonists, capitalists, and other social Darwinists would invoke. And why should a purely pragmatic argument place a higher value on maximizing *human* pleasure and minimizing human pain, as opposed to *non-human* pleasures and pains? Critics of such an anthropocentric worldview have argued that humanity itself is the primary source of pain on a planet that would be better off without us.

The point is that extreme forms of pragmatism—such as the position Putnam adopts in his obituary for ontology—become incoherent. There is no coherent way to argue that contingent normative truths should derive from "what works" in the absence of foundational or antecedent normative principles that frame our assessment of what works. Of course, not all pragmatists adopt Putnam's position, and pragmatism has much to commend it. The fruitfulness of a premise or theory is one very good standard for assessing it. Likewise, there is a need to transcend false dichotomies, including the fact/value dichotomy. But these basic pragmatic commitments can be coupled with the premise that foundational normative truths exist, that we can become progressively attuned to them over time, and that we can construct a social reality that embodies such truths to increasing degrees.

PROCEDURALISM

In an effort to solve the problem just identified (that all assessments of "what works" ultimately rest on antecedent normative commitments), some pragmatists adopt a position known as *proceduralism.* Proceduralism is an approach to inquiry and decision-making that assumes the best we can do in pluralistic societies, in the absence of shared, foundational, or transcendent values, is agree on procedures that will presumably lead to the best outcomes. Proceduralism is commonly, but not exclusively, associated with theories of deliberative democracy. Within this tradition of thought, Habermas is among the most nuanced and influential thinkers of the last half century.

Since the 1960s, Habermas has been one of the leading voices in the tradition of critical theory that emerged from the Frankfurt

School in Germany. Critical theory is premised on the critique of oppressive features of the existing social order coupled with a commitment to emancipatory social change. Like many critical theorists, and most pragmatists, Habermas rejects normative realism—or the existence of foundational normative truths that are external to human subjectivity, social discourse, and processes of practical reasoning. At the same time, Habermas recognizes the need for some kind of normative principles that transcend the values governing specific cultural and historical contexts. Without such context-transcending principles, the entire project of critical theory has no solid footing because it lacks any real basis for social criticism, reform, and progress. Habermas has thus spent much of his career trying to construct a normative basis for the project of critical theory. Yet his materialist framework prompts him to do this in a "postmetaphysical" manner.[177]

Habermas attempts this through an approach he calls *epistemic proceduralism*, which rests on the view that social progress can be achieved through rational processes of collective social learning.[178] Although such processes are neither linear nor inevitable, Habermas asserts that they can advance as societies develop more mature forms of public reasoning. He views this in a manner that is roughly analogous to the psychological maturation of an individual. Like individual reasoning and learning processes, collective reasoning and learning always remain fallible, but progress toward a more just and mature social order is possible.

Within this broad framework, Habermas has attempted to articulate the ideal conditions and procedures through which deliberative processes in pluralistic societies can foster collective learning that leads to increasingly just outcomes. To do this, he conceptualizes speech as a form of action and then distinguishes between "strategic action" and "communicative action."[179] Strategic action is intended to influence others according to the actor's own interests and goals or the interests and goals of one's group. Communicative action is intended to foster shared understanding through rational and cooperative processes leading toward consensus regarding shared goals.

The rationality associated with communicative action entails the articulation of claims supported by reasons that are open to processes of criticism and justification in a reflective mode of discourse. Such claims include empirical ones and normative ones, among others. Empirical claims can refer to material or social aspects of reality that are independent of, or external to, the human mind. Normative claims, according to Habermas, do not refer to independent or external phenomena. But they still can be the objects of reasoning, criticism, and justification leading to normative consensus—or intersubjective validity—under the right conditions.

For Habermas, such conditions include the following: All relevant voices must be included and must have an equal voice. All participants must be free to initiate discussion, share their views, and question others in honest and open ways. And all participants must be free from coercion when they speak. Under such conditions, Habermas asserts that it is possible to arrive at some context-transcending normative principles. Such principles do not exist outside of human reasoning and discourse. Rather, the linguistic structure of human reasoning and discourse can, under the right conditions, yield them. In this sense, context-transcending normative truths are not ontologically foundational. They are derivative. Yet Habermas submits that they can be universal because the underlying structure of human language and reasoning is a universal species characteristic. Thus, when language and reason are collectively exercised through the right deliberative procedures under the right deliberative conditions, the process can allegedly yield context-transcending normative truths.

Other influential theorists of deliberative democracy, such as Seyla Benhabib, share these general views.[180] Proceduralists such as Habermas and Benhabib recognize that these ideal conditions are rarely met in practice and can never be guaranteed. But such conditions provide standards by which deliberative discourse can itself be critiqued and assessed within learning processes that, much like science, can be self-correcting over time.

Habermas is not naïve about the political and economic systems that distort deliberation in the modern public sphere. Indeed, much of his work has focused on a critique of these systems, such as systems of commercial mass media.[181] Nonetheless, he has been criticized for presenting an idealistic view of the world that overstates the potential for human rationality while failing to adequately account for power dynamics as well as irreconcilably conflicting identities and interests.[182] Such criticisms generally lead toward more adversarial—or *agonistic*—forms of social theory and practice. The insights, and limitations, of *agonism* as a tradition of thought will be explored in the next section of this chapter.

In the meantime, the analysis laid out in previous chapters of this book suggests that Habermas offers valuable insights into humanity's potential for more mature and constructive modes of public deliberation—even if much of that potential is yet unrealized and the path toward its realization will be long and difficult. In short, Habermas makes a compelling argument that more reflective and deliberative modes of collective learning are needed to address the exigencies of the age; he explores some of the conditions needed to support those learning processes; he does this in a way that acknowledges the ultimate fallibility of human knowledge while retaining the possibility of progress toward a more just social order; and, with appropriate humility, he has fostered a searching global conversation about if, or how, we might advance on this developmental path. Given the social and ecological stakes that are now at play on this planet, it would be irresponsible to dismiss the significance of this conversation or his contributions to it.

At the same time, it is important to examine critically the underlying assumptions about normativity that led Habermas—along with many other materialist thinkers—toward purely pragmatic procedural arguments. This brings us back to one of the fundamental problems inherent in pure pragmatism: the question of "What works?" presumes the existence of antecedent normative standards for assessing "what works." This problem is also inherent in the question of "What procedures work?"

Broadly speaking, antecedent normative standards can come from one of two sources. They can come from the internal normative logic of the culturally and historically specific social formations within which people are asking "What works?" Or they can come from some source that transcends all culturally and historically specific social formations. Philosophers refer to this as a distinction between immanent critique and transcendent critique.

The problem with immanent critique is that normative standards internal to a given social formation offer no ultimate basis for challenging social norms within that social formation. For instance, Nazism had an internal normative logic. That logic offered standards for assessing "what worked" within the Third Reich. If a critic could appeal only to this internal logic, there would be no ultimate basis for critiquing Nazism. The same is true of every social formation. To critique a given social formation one must be able to appeal to some transcendent normative standards.

Habermas, having grown up in post-war Germany, understands this problem. Yet like many modern thinkers, he rejects a metaphysical basis for transcendent normative truths. This is why he has tried so valiantly to come up with an argument for context-transcending normative truths that derive purely from the linguistic structure of communicative rationality and reasoned public discourse. He has thus tried to argue that context-transcending normative truths can, under the right conditions, be socially constructed. These include, ironically, the socially constructed normative truths that determine what those "right conditions" are for constructing normative truths.

It is not difficult to see the circularity of this argument—or to recognize the leap of logic it takes to conclude that the universal structure of human language and reasoning, exercised within an immanent frame, can yield context-transcending normative truths. Few have examined these problems more thoughtfully than Maeve Cooke. In an article titled "Argumentation and Transformation," Cooke lauds Habermas's deliberative procedures even as she unpacks the problematic ontology on which Habermas has tried to set them.[183]

Cooke agrees with Habermas that critical social theory is a socially transformative project that requires context-transcending normative truths. She also shares Habermas's epistemic view of this project as one of collective learning. She refers to this as *socio-cultural learning*, which she distinguishes from personal learning (and technical learning). Cooke sees personal learning and socio-cultural learning as mutually connected forms of cognitive transformation. Personal learning entails individual cognitive transformation. But socio-cultural learning entails transformation at the level of a shared episteme—or a shared system of knowledge and meaning—along with the linguistic resources with which the episteme is constructed. Socio-cultural learning thus includes, among other things, progressive transformation at the level of shared normative standards by which personal learning, and all other normative practices, are understood and assessed. Also, due to the intimate connection between thought and language, socio-cultural learning includes progressive transformation at the level of the language, or vocabulary, needed to understand, communicate, justify, and apply progressively transformed normative standards.

Cooke accepts Habermas's conditions and procedures for communicative rationality as a requisite of socio-cultural learning. But she asserts that "an adequate account of socio-cultural learning requires more than this. Habermas's account is deficient insofar as he neglects the question of the *sources* of such learning."[184] By sources, Cooke is referring to the question of *what* we are learning about when our normative standards are transformed and *where* the language comes from that enables this learning.

To elaborate this point, she compares sources of empirical learning with sources of moral learning. Empirical learning, as Habermas acknowledges, occurs through our interactions with an external, recalcitrant, material reality against which we can test our perceptions, interpretations, and vocabularies over time. According to Habermas, however, our moral learning can advance, not through testing against reality, but only through deliberation with other socially constituted beings. By this logic, "It is not the resistance of an independent world that necessitates revision of our moral vocabulary . . . . The protests that call upon us to change our moral norms and principles come from within a *linguistically constructed* social world and are assessed according to standards of validity that are *socially constructed* in processes of argumentation."[185]

Given Habermas's assertion that context-transcending normative truths can be formulated discursively in support of social transformation, Cooke concludes that his insistence that these truths lack any relation to a world independent of our linguistic practices is problematic. In short, Habermas's "denial of the existence of non-linguistic sources of moral validity makes it hard to see how context-transcending moral learning is even conceivable."[186] The reason for this is that Habermas cannot explain the source of radically new forms of normative reasoning or the linguistic resources that make such reasoning possible. In other words, if normative truths derive from cognitive-linguistic structures, yet cognitive-linguistic structures are immanent to a given socio-cultural formation, how do transformative cognitive-linguistic structures emerge? Logically speaking, there must be some external source.

Given this problem, Cooke suggests that we turn to Taylor's conception of moral sources, which have some independence from the immanent cognitive-linguistic structures of specific social formations.

> For Taylor, moral sources have a constitutive and enabling power that is to some degree independent of our abilities to articulate it; to this extent he appears to affirm a metaphysically based moral realism. One advantage of this kind of realist approach is that it makes it easier to answer the question of the sources of the new semantic contents that result in an enriched or renewed socio-cultural moral vocabulary. For, by postulating sources of moral meaning that have some independence of human interpretations, Taylor avoids the problem of how interpretive practices can produce new interpretations that call their own defining features into question. In addition, his postulate of non-linguistic sources of moral learning enables us to account for the sense that moral truth has an *irruptive* power, the perception that moral truth can burst into our lives and explode existing contexts of thought and action—a perception that is inexplicable on Habermas's account. It also helps to make sense of the idea of unconditionality traditionally attached to the idea of moral truth—an idea that Habermas clearly wants to retain but is unable to adequately account for.[187]

Cooke is careful to point out, however, that a realist conception of moral truths does not mean that the human mind can have infallible knowledge of such truths. Hence the perpetual need for individual and collective humility within interconnected processes of personal and socio-cultural learning. Toward this end, Cooke calls us to couple a realist account of normative sources with a deliberative approach to normative learning and social change. "At the very least," she argues, there is a "need for renewed debate on the status of transcendental arguments and, more generally, of the role of metaphysics in critical social theory."[188]

In contrast to Cooke, many skeptics reject the possibility of context-transcending normative principles altogether—whether they are understood in a realist or a language-derivative manner. This would also entail rejecting any universal commitments to rational and cooperative procedures for public deliberation, since rationality and cooperation are normative principles that would have no context-transcendent basis. By extension, this view entails rejecting the idea of socio-cultural learning, since the rejection of normative truths precludes the possibility that we can learn about their application to the betterment of society in a progressive manner. Not surprisingly, these views are associated with the belief that human interests and identities will inevitably conflict and that public deliberation will therefore always be characterized by self-interested and competitive expressions of power—which leads toward a very different form of pragmatic proceduralism known as *agonism*.

AGONISM

Agonism is a proceduralist tradition of thought that views conflict as an inescapable and desirable feature of social reality. This tradition rejects Habermas's epistemic proceduralism and other approaches to social change premised on collective learning as naïve. What is called for, instead, are perpetual struggles for power. In this context, normative forms of knowledge are viewed merely as functions of hegemonic power relations.

As with most traditions of thought, there are variations on this underlying theme.[189] The discussion that follows will focus primarily on the theory of agonism advanced by Chantal Mouffe, due to its relatively wide influence. Mouffe's thinking also represents a middle ground between minimalist and maximalist theories of agonism. Minimalist theories have been articulated by figures such as Hannah Arendt, who asserts that conflict plays an essential and productive role in liberal democracies even though it is sometimes possible to achieve normative consensus.[190] Maximalist theories have been articulated by figures such as Carl Schmitt, who asserts the inevitability of violent antagonisms between friends and enemies seeking to destroy one another.[191] Mouffe rejects the minimalist belief that normative consensus is possible. She agrees with the maximalists that violent conflict is part of the human condition, but she argues that violent conflict can be sublimated by a system of radical democracy that institutionalizes domesticated forms of perpetual conflict.

Mouffe began to develop her theory of agonism with Ernesto Laclau as a new socialist theory that expands the Marxist focus on class conflict by fully integrating identity politics.[192] Their theory rests on the ontological premise that conflict is a foundational property of human existence that cannot be transcended. Based on this premise, they abandon the Marxist view that social conflict will eventually be resolved through a historical dialectic that concludes with a stable, cooperative, communist order that transcends all historical divisions. Mouffe and Laclau argue that social arrangements can never be anything more than contingent expressions of oppressive power relations. All social relations are part of a never-ending succession of temporary hegemonic orders and counter-hegemonic struggles between oppositionally formed identity groups. According to this logic, every social order is an articulation of dominant identities and interests that excludes the identities and interests of marginalized social groups. Every social order thus represents only a temporary stabilization of conflictual power relations. Such power relations can be re-articulated in different ways over time but can never be rationally or cooperatively resolved.

Mouffe elaborates the relationship between these political processes and processes of identity formation.[193] All social identities, she argues, are formed oppositionally. According to this logic, there can be no "us" unless there is a "them" because all identities are mutually constituted through difference. Therefore, humanity "cannot be envisaged as 'one' . . . . It is only when division and antagonism are recognized as being ineradicable that it is possible to think in a properly political way."[194] In addition, Mouffe argues that there are no universal objective values or foundational normative truths that diverse identity groups can discover or rationally agree on. For both the preceding reasons, Mouffe assumes that a shared human identity and shared human interests are ontologically impossible, as is a fully inclusive or harmonious social order based on a rational, universal, normative consensus.[195] What is possible, Mouffe argues, is a form of democracy she calls "agonistic pluralism."[196]

The model of agonistic pluralism rests on a distinction between *antagonism* and *agonism*. Mouffe defines *antagonism* as a relationship between enemies that represent existential threats to one another—as in the maximalist views of Schmitt alluded to above.[197] Mouffe defines *agonism* as a relationship between adversaries who have fundamental disagreements but respect one another's right to exist and to compete within democratic processes. Agonism becomes possible when diverse identity groups agree on, and adhere to, the political principles of liberty and equality along with the institutional arrangements needed to preserve them by regulating conflict within stable boundaries. But this social contract still entails conflict over how to interpret and apply those principles in ongoing struggles to construct and reconstruct the social order. Agonistic pluralism thus requires that competing identity/interest groups "are not seen as enemies to be destroyed, but as adversaries whose ideas must be fought, even fiercely, but whose right to defend those ideas is not to be questioned."[198]

According to this logic, conflict is not only inevitable, it is desirable. Mouffe believes that the absence of conflict could only reflect the permanent exclusion of some social groups through failed democratic processes within a hegemonic social order without viable challengers. The absence of conflict thus entails a condition of political apathy—the loss of a sense of agency and the failure to identify with democratic processes—among those who are excluded or oppressed. Over time, however, this condition will unleash pent-up antagonisms in destructive ways. As Mouffe explains:

> When the agonistic dynamics of pluralism are hindered because of a lack of democratic forms of identification, then passions cannot be given a democratic outlet. The ground is therefore laid for various forms of politics articulated around essentialist identities of a nationalist, religious or ethnic type, and for the multiplication of confrontations over non-negotiable moral values, with all the manifestations of violence that such confrontations entail.[199]

Therefore, domesticated forms of non-violent political contestation are required to ensure the conditions for ongoing counter hegemonic struggles. These conditions keep alive the ever-present possibility of constructing a new social order by articulating new hegemonic relations. This possibility and the means to act on it allegedly sublimate dangerous antagonisms into more productive forms of conflict. But the goal of these productive forms of conflict can never be to arrive at a rational normative consensus that ends conflict, because such a consensus will always be illusory and will merely suppress dissent, which would eventually cause deeper antagonisms to erupt in destructive ways.

In short, agonistic pluralism calls on diverse social groups to enter into a social contract that entails perpetual but contained forms of political contestation to avoid a Hobbesian war of all against all. "The central question for democratic politics," Mouffe thus argues,

> is not how to negotiate a compromise among competing interests, nor is it how to reach a "rational", i.e., fully inclusive, consensus without any exclusion. Despite what many liberals want to believe, the specificity of democratic politics is not the overcoming of the we/they opposition, but the different way in which it is established. The prime task of democratic politics is not to eliminate passions or to relegate them to the private sphere in order to establish a rational consensus in the public sphere. Rather, it is to "sublimate" those passions by mobilizing them towards democratic designs, by creating collective forms of identification around democratic objectives.[200]

This requires forms of identity characterized by a posture of "agonistic respect" toward the other—a concept Mouffe borrows from William Connolly—in which political adversaries are granted the right to pursue conflicting political interests.[201] But such respect, Mouffe argues, extends only to those who accept the social contract of agonistic pluralism.[202] If "the other" adopts of a posture of existential antagonism, they should be met with existential antagonism. Agonistic pluralism thus has boundaries, which must be policed. Outside of those boundaries, Schmitt's rules of existential conflict apply. The challenge, according to this logic, is how best to establish and regulate the boundaries between agonistic pluralism and destructive antagonism and how to foster processes of identity formation that draw most, if not all, social groups into the contract of agonistic pluralism.

Mouffe's theory offers important insights into the prevailing culture of contest, and it raises important questions about how to contain the culture of contest within non-violent boundaries. But her assertion that the culture of contest is an inescapable feature of human existence is a questionable premise, if not a self-fulfilling prophecy. There is no doubt that we live in an era when many, if not most, social institutions have been organized according to the logic of conflict and competition.[203] Inter-group and intra-group conflict and competition have also played a significant role in past eras. Within this frame of reference, Mouffe's theory of agonism offers useful explanatory insights and, perhaps, some useful prescriptions. But this frame of reference does not encompass all human experience, past and present, and there is no reason to assume it must encompass all future experience. It is equally plausible to assume that humanity is capable of social progress, or spiritual maturation, in ways that might enable us to transcend, to a significant degree, the culture of contest. This is not to suggest that social progress is easy or linear or without substantial periodic setbacks. Nor does this imply that such progress is synonymous with the Western liberal project of modernity, which has clearly revealed its inability to construct a just and inclusive social order.

Furthermore, the existence or non-existence of social conflict need not be understood in a binary manner. It can be understood in a relative manner. To say that every trace of conflict or tension can one day be eliminated from our social existence, in an absolute binary sense, would undoubtedly be a naïve assertion. But Mouffe goes well beyond this assertion. She argues that domesticated forms of conflict should always remain the defining feature of social existence—at least in the sphere of governance.

In contrast, this book argues that the exigencies of the age require us to develop new patterns of social life on a planet with over seven billion people wielding technologies that multiply our social and ecological interdependence and impact a thousandfold. Historically speaking, this changes everything. These unprecedented conditions require unprecedented forms of social adaptation. To construct a more adaptive social reality, we must learn our way forward. Failure to adapt in these ways now carries existential risks not merely for some social groups, but for all of humanity. Furthermore, intellectual humility requires us to recognize that Mouffe's premise about the desirability of a culture of conflict, and the alternative premise that we need to transcend the culture of conflict, are equally plausible premises that need to be tested against reality.

It is also important to examine other secondary premises underlying Mouffe's theory of agonism. One of these is that all collective identities form oppositionally, a premise that is widely held today across the social sciences and in much popular culture. But, as Arash Abizadeh points out, there is no logical or empirical basis for this premise.[204] Abizadeh demonstrates that even if one assumes that on a psychological level, all individual identities arise through distinction with individual others, there is no empirical evidence and no defensible logical argument that can support the claim that all collective identities arise through distinction with collective others. Furthermore, even if one grants, for the sake of argument, that collective identities arise only through distinctions, it is still plausible that a shared human identity—a cosmopolitan identity—can arise in contrast to imagined or historical identities. As Abizadeh explains:

> To be sure, a collective identity might be formed in contrast to, or even in combat with, an actually existing external other excluded from its membership. But it might also be constructed on the basis of difference from hypothetical values and the imagined collective identities centered on them, or on the basis of difference from the values of a past historical identity from which one wishes to mark one's distance . . . humanity's own past provides a rich and terrifying repository in contrast to which cosmopolitan identity could constitute its "difference."[205]

Elaborating on this point, Abizadeh states:

> None of this is to deny the empirical fact of actual exclusion, antagonism, and conflict in our world. It is, indeed, an empirically observable phenomenon that collective identities often *do* constitute themselves via the exclusion of external others from membership. Perhaps there are even empirical (psychological, sociological, economic, and political) reasons why collective identities, particularly political collective identities, are most easily formed in this way—at least in the world as we know it. . . . But one must be careful not to redescribe the empirical phenomena in terms of conceptual or metaphysical necessity. . . . While a merely empirical observation that collective identities have usually been formed contrastively would certainly raise difficulties for cosmopolitanism, those difficulties might turn out to be dependent on contingent (say, structural) features of the current sociopolitical order—and hence in principle surmountable.[206]

The presumption that all identities are oppositional also becomes problematic when one considers empirical evidence to the contrary. Some of the most striking evidence in this regard has emerged through research into the empirical basis of altruism. Within the culture of contest, and its underlying assumption that human nature is fundamentally self-interested, altruism is an anomaly that the self-interest paradigm has never been able to adequately explain. Many attempts have been made to explain away altruism as self-interest in disguise. But a political psychologist named Kristen Monroe decided to take a fresh look at altruism.[207] Monroe defined *altruism* as "behavior intended to benefit another, even when this risks possible sacrifice to the welfare of the actor."[208] She initially examined the cases of twenty-five altruists, ranging from philanthropists who had given away much of their wealth, to heroes who had risked their own lives to save the lives of strangers in emergencies, to Germans who had sheltered Jews in Nazi Germany at the risk of death to their own families, even though some of those Jews were strangers. Monroe conducted extensive interviews with all twenty-five individuals, supplemented by written responses from each. When analyzing her data, she found that prevailing explanations of altruism from the fields of psychology, economics, and evolutionary biology that were rooted in the self-interest paradigm were completely inadequate to explain these cases. Rather, she discovered that every one of these cases had only one common denominator. "World views," she writes,

> constitute extremely powerful influences on altruism, with the critical factor being the altruist's perception of self in relation to others. But . . . this perception is not framed in terms of group ties. . . . Rather, it is a reflection of the perceived relationship between the altruist and all other human beings. . . . This view appears to bond them to all humanity in an affective manner that encourages altruistic treatment.[209]

"Altruists," she continues, "have a particular perspective in which all mankind is connected through a common humanity, in which each individual is linked to all others."[210] She concludes that "[a]ltruists share a view of the world in which all people are one."[211] In other words, altruistic individuals are inspired by a consciousness of the

oneness of humanity, to which they subordinate all secondary identities and interests. And these findings were confirmed and elaborated by Monroe in two major follow-up studies.[212]

Ultimately, every individual holds multiple, overlapping, non-ex-
clusive identities derived from their social circumstances, talents,
education, and experiences. There is no reason to assume, however, that a global "we" cannot accommodate countless secondary
identities. The latter need not be formed or enacted in a conflictual
manner.

The experience of the Bahá'í community, discussed in chapter 4,
illustrates this point. It is a steadily growing global community of
people drawn from every cultural, racial, economic, national, and
religious background on earth who have voluntarily adopted a set
of universally held spiritual beliefs that enable them to value the infinite diversity that characterizes the secondary aspects of their lives.
Within this framework of unity in diversity, Bahá'ís are, in turn, engaging ever-widening circles of friends, neighbors, and co-workers
on every continent in an expanding range of activities intended to
uplift, in an unprejudiced manner, the spiritual and material conditions of humanity as a whole. Although it may be premature to draw
definitive conclusions from the Bahá'í experience, that experience
certainly suggests the need to remain open about the possibility that
identities need not be oppositional. Alternative hypotheses, already
supported by provisional evidence, must be tested in an unprejudiced manner.

Another premise on which Mouffe's theory rests is the premise
that power invariably operates in adversarial and oppressive ways.
This narrow conception of power was examined, contextualized,
and expanded in chapter 2 of this book. There is no need to repeat
that discussion here. Suffice it to say that humanity is clearly able
to draw on more mutualistic and ennobling expressions of power.
The question, of course, is whether a new social order can be constructed in ways that more fully embody and foster these ennobling
expressions of power. Again, this is a hypothesis that needs to be
tested against reality.

Yet another premise on which Mouffe's theory rests is that no
objective values or foundational normative truths exist. As the discussion of Nagel's work earlier in this chapter demonstrates, equally
plausible alternatives exist. This is a theme on which the next chapter

will further elaborate. In the meantime, suffice it to say that once again, intellectual humility requires us to recognize that divergent hypotheses regarding the existence or non-existence of normative truths need to be tested against reality.

To Mouffe's credit, if one is committed to the principles of liberty and equality, agonistic pluralism is arguably more desirable than imposed or coerced forms of pseudo-harmony that are oppressive, stifle dissent, and give rise to political apathy among marginalized and exploited populations. But the choice between unchallenged hegemonic oppression and perpetual social conflict may be a false choice. Moreover, in a world of perpetual social conflict, Mouffe offers no reliable way to prevent the slide from agonistic pluralism into violent antagonisms. Therefore, framing humanity's future as a choice between unchallenged oppression and perpetual conflict carries profound risks. In an age where ever-more-powerful weapons of mass annihilation can easily be wed to ever-more-powerful means of mass manipulation, this agonistic frame puts the future of our entire species at risk. Therefore, it seems worthwhile to explore and test an alternative set of premises about social reality to find out if there is a more viable way forward.

Chapter 6

Looking Forward

Each of the traditions of thought discussed in the previous chapter offers, within its respective frame of reference, valid insights regarding existing social formations that we have inherited from the past. But the imperatives of social existence now require us to explore a more expansive frame of reference through which we can begin to construct more adaptive social forms. Toward this end, the discussion that follows offers additional thoughts, beyond those sketched earlier in this book. These thoughts are organized as follows: first, I discuss some further ontological implications; second, I discuss some further epistemological implications; and third, I discuss some implications for our theory and practice of social change.

Some Ontological Implications

In *Ethics without Ontology*, Putnam wrote an obituary for ontology. But rumors of its death seem to be greatly exaggerated. Ontology has been a topic of interest for millennia, and there is no indication this interest is waning. Every religion embodies a system of ontological thought and traditions of ontological inquiry. Philosophers have been similarly concerned with ontology for as long as we have written records, and this interest continues. In addition, many social scientists today recognize the relevance of ontological assumptions to projects of social inquiry and social change. Indeed, a growing number of social scientists and philosophers have recently begun to organize conferences and journals around the concept of *social ontology*.[213]

Social ontology, broadly speaking, is concerned with the foundational nature and properties of the social world, including the fundamental constituents of social phenomena. Within this broad field of inquiry, *critical realism* has emerged as a metatheory, or a set of philosophical positions, of direct relevance to the discussion at hand. Critical realism received its initial impetus in part from the work of Roy Bhaskar.[214] Bhaskar's thinking combined ontological realism (including normative realism) with epistemological relativism—akin to the line of reasoning presented in the first chapter of this book.[215] Since Bhaskar's initial work, many critical realists have been systematically exploring ways to move beyond the fact/value dichotomy that is a legacy of positivism, as alluded to in chapter 5. In this regard, they are exploring an ontology of values and developing theories and methods for their empirical investigation, but this work is in an early stage of development.[216]

Comprehensive overviews of social ontology in general, and critical realism in particular, are beyond the scope of this book. The purpose of alluding to them here is merely to demonstrate that ontology is far from dead, that social ontology is a growing field of interest, that critical realism provides a social ontology framework that is coherent with some of the central premises of this book, and that, within that framework, thoughtful people are beginning to articulate modern versions of normative realism.

In philosophy, normative realism is often traced back to Plato. Plato posited the ontological existence of normative truths through his conception of *Eidos* or *Morphē*—*Ideas* or *Forms*—which he viewed as abstract, timeless, universal essences that find imperfect but substantive expression in our material and social worlds.[217] These include the Form of *The Good* and the Form of *Justice*, which were both considered by Plato to be foundational phenomena. Aristotle rejected Plato's ontological view of normative truths, as do many contemporary philosophers. Even Nagel, whose defense of normative truths was discussed in the last chapter, rejects Plato's version of normative realism. Nonetheless, the debate over Platonic realism offers an insightful entry point to the exploration of normative truths.

Few contemporary scholars have examined Platonic realism or the concept of Platonic Forms more closely or thoughtfully than Thomas Seung. In *Intuition and Construction: The Foundation of*

Normative Theory, Seung argues that the modern world is in a state of crisis due to the widespread rejection of any ontological or transcendent basis for normative agreement, along with the consequent adoption of purely relativistic theories of social constructivism.[218] He argues that this crisis will be overcome only when we recognize that rational processes of social construction inevitably depend on the exercise of intuition regarding foundational normative truths. The most relevant points of his argument are as follows.

Seung begins by defining *constructivism* as the view that all normative propositions and standards are created by humans and lack ontological foundations. When confronted with the problems of normative anarchy or oppression, constructivists turn to proceduralist solutions, as discussed in chapter 5. They ask: What is the most just way to construct social norms, policies, and laws without appealing to foundational normative truths?

Before examining various proceduralist attempts to answer that question, Seung draws a contrast between *proceduralism* and *intuitionism*. He defines *intuitionism* as the view that normative truths exist and can be discovered by rational intuition. The constructivist rejection of normative truths also constitutes a rejection of normative intuition. According to this view, normative statements are merely subjective or emotive expressions that have no relation to any objective reality. Procedural approaches to constructing a more just society thus tend to focus on either the deliberative exercise of reason or the agonistic struggle for power.

As Seung demonstrates, however, *every* procedure for constructing a more just society rests on intuitive assertions of normative truths—whether explicit or implicit. One example Seung examines in depth to illustrate this point is Rawls's influential theory of justice. As a constructivist, Rawls developed his procedural theory as an attempt to minimize, if not eliminate, reliance on normative intuition. Rawls's procedure requires rational deliberation from behind a veil of ignorance that prevents all those who are deliberating from knowing what their position in society is or will be (e.g., their gender, race, economic status). Rational individuals deliberating together from behind such a veil will allegedly come up with the most just possible rules for governing a society because they will want to maximize their well-being, regardless of whatever their social position turns out to be. Toward this end, Rawls suggests that justice should be understood in terms of two constituent principles, liberty and equality, which all rational agents will support and apply in their deliberations. No matter how hard Rawls tries, however, his procedural formulation still relies on antecedent normative intuitions about justice, liberty, equality, and even rationality.

Seung identifies similar problems with the prescriptions of other proceduralists, such as Habermas. Proceduralists and, more broadly, constructivists ultimately cannot escape a dependence on normative intuition if they aspire toward a more *just* society. All such approaches rely on an intuitive recourse to some foundational principle of justice, or to constituent normative principles from which a conception of justice derives, or to normative principles associated either with the proper exercise of human rationality or the proper way to organize contests of power. Ontologically, any critically informed project of social construction (i.e., any project that is concerned with justice) depends on normative intuition. "One way or another," Seung explains, "we have to rely on our normative intuition in any constructivist project, though our reliance may be covert."[219]

Seung also demonstrates that the exercise of normative intuition in efforts to create a more just society always depends on the reciprocal processes of social construction. This is because at best, normative intuitions reflect compelling yet indeterminate truths that must be translated into social reality in particular socio-historical contexts. In other words, if normative truths exist, people must still figure out how best to apply them in different contexts. Seung's central thesis is, therefore, that normative intuition and social construction are mutually necessary and mutually dependent.[220] Both are inescapable features of social existence, and neither is possible without the other.

To help the reader grasp this mutually dependent relationship, Seung revisits the concept of Platonic Forms. In his careful reading of Plato, Seung demonstrates that the Platonic realism many people reject today is a naïve conception of normative truths that even Plato came to reject as his thinking matured. In brief, there is an immature and a mature version of Platonic Forms, which reflect the evolution of Plato's thought over the course of his life. Seung refers to the immature version as the "skyscraper" version and the mature version as the "bedrock" version of Forms.[221] According to the skyscraper version, normative truths constitute a complete, determinate, concrete system of normative rules and standards for all conditions and all time. They are, in this sense, superstructural. According to the bedrock version, however, normative truths are general, indeterminate, abstract ideals that must be applied in context-dependent ways. They are, in this sense, substructural. Seung demonstrates that the only sensible way to understand normative truths is the bedrock version, as the mature Plato also came to understand. He then demonstrates why "constructivism is essential for completing the bedrock version of Platonism."[222]

To illustrate this point, Seung compares a Platonic view of normative truths with a Platonic view of mathematical truths. According to the skyscraper version, the realm of Platonic Forms would contain the complete superstructure of all mathematics, from arithmetic and geometry to calculus and topology, prior to and independent of human thought. According to the bedrock version, however, the realm of Platonic Forms need contain only essential underlying truths about reality from which mathematical systems can be constructed through human thought. As Seung demonstrates, mathematics (and elementary logic itself) are impossible without the latter version of Platonism.[223]

Similarly, the construction of a more just society is also impossible without a bedrock version of normative truths. By definition, constructing a more *just* society requires some intuitive sense of *justice*. Yet any sense of justice must derive from one of two sources: transcendent normative truths or inherited cultural norms. If the latter is the only basis for normative intuition, then we become prisoners of inherited norms that are often unjust and oppressive. Only if we can intuit transcendent normative truths can we hope to transcend oppressive cultural norms and construct a more just society. As Seung explains:

> By the power of Platonic Forms, we can take a critical stance toward prevailing norms. By virtue of their transcendent standards, we can feel even the injustice inflicted on strangers on the other side of the globe. By virtue of those standards, we can feel indignation at the oppression of the weak, not only in our age but even in antiquity. Platonic Forms enable us to have a sense of justice that cuts across national boundaries and cultural barriers. They give us a transcendental intersubjectivity

of values that is neither propped up by our voluntary mutual assurance nor imposed on us by external coercion. There is no way of accounting for this dimension of our intersubjective experience without accepting Platonic Forms.[224]

In other words, without a bedrock version of foundational normative truths, we become denizens of the Platonic Cave, confusing the shadows of our own cultural forms for normative truths.[225] Moreover,

[t]he syndrome of the Platonic Cave need not be limited to the tribal consciousness of a primitive society; it is equally present in the positivistic consciousness of our scientific world. For the positivistic consciousness is governed as much as the tribal consciousness by its own provincial norms and standards. Positivism has its own cave, the cave of an exclusively materialistic universe, and this cave is so deep and dark that it allows no view of any other dimension of reality.[226]

Elaborating on this theme, Seung explains that

from Socrates, Plato learned that the life of reason can be understood in two contexts, materialism and spiritualism. If materialism is true, human reason is only an appendage to the physical world and can never have norms and standards other than those produced by the workings of the physical universe. Materialism dictates the life of reason in accordance with positive norms, which emerge as products of nature. But Plato believed that materialism is proven false by our capacity for critical reflection, which attests to our power of transcendence. Such power of transcendence is the foundation of the open society. Yet the open society leads only to normative anarchy, and the transcendence of reason, unless guided by the light of transcendent Forms, is but an uncharted flight into the darkness of nihilism. This is the essence of Plato's teaching, and it is his everlasting legacy to the life of reason.[227]

Of course, Plato is only one of many people to argue for the existence of foundational normative truths. His conception of Forms is, at best, only one source of limited insight. We also need to look to other sources of insight and other language for exploring the basis of normativity. For instance, beyond the language of Forms, it is possible to understand normative truths as abstruse *forces* or even *laws* that act on human subjectivity and social relationships and that can be harnessed for social progress in a manner that is analogous to the ways gravity and electromagnetism, along with the strong and weak nuclear forces, act on matter and can be harnessed for the betterment of humanity. When violated, such forces or laws have socially destructive and oppressive consequences. We can thus know them, in part, by learning how to discern their effects. But this is not a simple thing. It has taken humanity tens of thousands of years to understand, let alone harness, basic electromagnetic forces. Only a few centuries ago we were unable to conceptualize, explain, or channel these forces in any meaningful way. But thanks to science, no one doubts that they exist today. Our systems of communication, transportation, and power transmission, along with most other modern technologies, were made possible only by the application of laws derived from systematic study of what are now relatively well-understood forces. It is not irrational to assume that there are other forces acting on us that are less well understood.

It is also possible to understand normative truths as abstruse *properties* of social norms and structures that can be intuited, to some degree, through the development of one's powers of normative discernment. The language of virtues reflects this conception of normative truths. And it is possible to apply the language of normative properties, or virtues, not only to individual character but to the character of entire social systems. One can thus conceptualize a virtuous social order as one that promotes human nobility, peace, justice, and shared prosperity. Virtue, in this sense, is a relative property of social constructs or social systems that can be discerned in an intersubjective but rational manner to the degree that we cultivate the capacity for normative discernment within ourselves.

Furthermore, it is also possible to understand normative truths as spiritual *principles* that we can learn how to apply to improve the human condition—principles that derive from and reflect something about the fabric of reality. The language of spiritual principles links ontological truths with practical actions.[228] Spiritual principles allude to relatively inscrutable aspects of reality that humans are nonetheless capable of intuitively recognizing and responding to. Recognition of such principles stirs the human spirit to find ways to apply them in individual and collective actions for the progressive reconstruction of social reality.

The terms *forces*, *laws*, *properties*, and *principles* all provide potentially useful language for exploring the same underlying phenomena—as might the more archaic language of Platonic Forms. The precise nature or essence of foundational normative truths will undoubtedly continue to defy human comprehension or easy description. But the premise that such truths exist—independent of the degree to which we understand them—may be essential to social progress. In other words, if normative truths exist, then we must take their enabling and constraining properties seriously. Seung's argument invites us to explore this possibility. Nagel's expanded conception of objectivity discussed in the last chapter draws us further into this exploration. And the concept of *relative embodiment* introduced earlier in this book provides one way (not the only way) we can begin to conceptualize the work of constructing a new social reality that embodies normative truths to greater degrees.

The concept of relative embodiment also suggests the need to reconcile processes of social construction with the concept of *teleology*. Teleology, broadly speaking, refers to efforts to understand or explain phenomena in terms of some intrinsic *end* or *purpose*. Such thinking is often traced back to Aristotle.[229] Aristotle argued that all living things have a natural telos and the fulfillment of that telos constitutes the ultimate good of a thing. For instance, an acorn's telos is to become an oak tree. According to Aristotle, the telos of a human being is, among other things, the exercise of practical reason in pursuit of a virtuous social order. Aristotelian virtues are thus conceptualized in terms of striving for excellence in self-realization or self-fulfillment.[230] At an ontological level, this Aristotelian view assumes an underlying unity of physical properties and normative values. For instance, if one could know the essence of a dog, one could know something about what a good or bad dog is or what the purpose of a dog is. The descriptive and normative dimensions are inseparable.

Teleological thinking fell into disfavor with the rise of materialism in modern science and philosophy as mechanistic models of the universe were adopted alongside the fact/value dichotomy of positivism. But it is not only the telos of individual species (e.g., the purpose of canine existence or human existence) that has been widely rejected in the modern world. Teleological conceptions of biological evolution as a whole have also been rejected. Within a materialist frame of reference, all evolutionary processes are assumed to be purely accidental—without any direction, end, or purpose. Likewise, within a materialist frame of reference, teleological conceptions of history or social evolution or grand narratives have also been widely rejected. All of this has, in turn, tended to reinforce a nihilistic conception of human existence.

Against this backdrop, Nagel makes a compelling argument for remaining open to certain teleological explanations. His thinking once again warrants consideration. For reasons discussed in the previous chapter, Nagel believes that purely physical conceptions of objectivity are inadequate to explain the nature and rise of human consciousness. Nagel's critique extends, in this regard, to purely physical conceptions of the evolution of life. Nagel accepts the basic mechanics of Darwinian natural selection, but he suggests the need to expand the framework within which we understand how those mechanisms operate. As he explains:

> Consciousness presents a problem for evolutionary reductionism because of its irreducibly subjective character. This is true even of the most primitive forms of sensory consciousness, such as those presumably found in all animals. The problem . . . concerns mental functions such as thought, reasoning, and evaluation that are limited to humans, though their beginnings may be found in a few other species. These are the functions that have enabled us to transcend the perspective of the immediate life-world given to us by our senses and instincts, and to explore the larger objective reality of nature and value.[231]

In this context, Nagel asks, "Is it credible that selection for fitness in the prehistoric past should have fixed capacities that are effective for theoretical pursuits that were unimaginable at the time?"[232] He then points out that

> if we hope to include the human mind in the natural order, we have to explain not only consciousness as it enters into

perception, emotion, desire, and aversion but also the conscious control of belief and conduct in response to the awareness of reasons—the avoidance of inconsistency, the subsumption of particular cases under general principles, the confirmation or disconfirmation of general principles by particular observations, and so forth. This is what it is to allow oneself to be guided by the objective truth, rather than just by one's impressions. It is a kind of freedom—the freedom that reflective consciousness gives us from the rule of innate perceptual and motivational dispositions together with conditioning.[233]

In other words, an adequate theory of evolution needs to explain not only the initial emergence of life, and then the emergence of consciousness, but also "the development of consciousness into an instrument of transcendence that can grasp objective reality and objective value."[234] Yet the materialist conception of evolution has been unable to explain any of these three singularly important developments—even the initial emergence of biological life itself. Clearly, we should remain open to the possibility that such developments might only be explained within a wider, but still rational, frame of reference.

Toward this end, Nagel suggests that the world must have properties that make the appearance of life, then simple consciousness, and then transcendent consciousness, not a complete accident. Rather, "in some way the likelihood must have been latent in the nature of things."[235] Nagel is thus suggesting that evolutionary processes must have some minimal teleological properties. In this regard, Nagel is drawn toward "natural teleology, or teleological bias, as an account of the existence of the biological possibilities on which natural selection can operate."[236] And he suggests that "this would probably have to involve some conception of an increase in value through the expanded possibilities provided by the higher forms of organization toward which nature tends" and "that would make value an explanatory end."[237]

Elaborating on this theme, Nagel asserts that "an adequate conception of the cosmos must contain resources to account for how it could have given rise to beings capable of thinking successfully about what is good and bad, right and wrong, and discovering moral and evaluative truths that do not depend on their own beliefs."[238] In this regard, Nagel points out that the history of value in the world . . . seems to coincide with the history of life. First, with the appearance of life even in its earliest forms, there come into existence entities that *have* a good, and for which things can go well or badly. Even a bacterium has a good in this sense, in virtue of its proper functioning, whereas a rock does not. Eventually in the course of evolutionary history there appear conscious beings, whose experiential lives can go well or badly in ways that are familiar to us. Later some descendants of those beings, capable of reflection and self-consciousness, come to recognize what happens to them as good or bad, and to recognize reasons for pursuing or avoiding those things. They learn to think about how these reasons combine to determine what they should do. And finally they develop the collective capacity to think about reasons they may have that do not depend only on what is good or bad for themselves.[239]

"[O]nce we recognize that an explanation of the appearance and development of life must at the same time be an explanation of the appearance and development of value," Nagel concludes, "a teleological explanation comes to seem more eligible. This would mean that what explains the appearance of life is in part the fact that life is a necessary condition of the instantiation of value, and ultimately of its recognition."[240] In the social domain, Nagel suggests that this process can advance, in turn, because humans are able not only to detect value but to be motivated by it and to engage in conscious efforts to increase it through the exercise of free will.[241] In other words, Nagel invites us to consider that there may well be normative dimensions to the broad arc of both biological and social evolution, and if so, that arc begins with latent potentialities that are gradually realized through developmental processes—the latter stages of which can advance only through the conscious exercise of human agency.

With appropriate humility, Nagel does not assert that he has proven this argument. His claim is more modest. In the face of reductionist modes of scientific materialism, he has thought it necessary to explore possible alternatives and to extend the boundaries of what is thinkable, "in light of how little we really understand about the world."[242] In making his argument, Nagel declares his atheist standpoint along with his rejection of the crude religious arguments that often arise in fundamentalist attacks on the theory of evolution.

Nagel accepts the basic mechanisms in Darwin's theory of evolution and tries to contextualize that theory in an expanded frame of reference. He points out, for example, that the rejection of value realism and teleology by materialists derives from anti-realism and anti-teleological premises that are unsupported by any empirical evidence. Nagel then invites us to explore the theoretical possibilities that emerge if we start from other, equally plausible, premises. In this regard, Nagel also admits that certain religiously inspired premises, if consistent with established science, cannot be ruled out based on the empirical data. This includes, most notably, the possibility of Divine intention behind an evolutionary telos that bends toward increasing value and onward toward the recognition and enactment of value by conscious subjects.

If we regard religion as an evolving system of knowledge and practice, as suggested in chapter 3 and illustrated in chapter 4, it is not difficult to reconcile religious thought with established science and with the teleological conception of evolution that Nagel sketches. It is worth exploring this theme briefly, given its implications for social ontology.

To reconcile religious thought with a scientific and teleological theory of evolution, one clearly needs to move beyond literal interpretations of the figurative language found in ancient religious texts addressed to pre-scientific populations. Fortunately, most serious students and scholars of religion in the modern world understand the role of hermeneutics—or textual interpretation—in efforts to advance religious insight and understanding. In this regard, many thoughtful believers today have moved beyond literal interpretations of figurative language in ancient texts.

With this hermeneutic principle in mind, we can understand that most religious texts use figurative language to indicate, in ways that would have been culturally and historically sensible to the populations to which they were addressed, that humanity has a unique essence or *spirit* that distinguishes us in some ways from other animals. In many traditions, this unique nature is understood in terms of a *soul* that transcends our material existence, that is capable of moral reasoning, and that must be developed through the thoughtful exercise of free will in ways that require spiritual discipline, self-restraint, the acquisition of latent virtues, and so forth.

Although Nagel does not share this belief in the existence of a transcendent soul, he acknowledges that faith in the existence of a soul is no more or less rational than faith in its non-existence and that the empirical evidence does not yet tilt in favor of either. In other words, belief in the existence or non-existence of the soul are equally rational premises. To work out the basic implications of the first premise—the existence of the soul—for a teleological theory of evolution, we can consider some of the relevant Bahá'í teachings on this theme. As a religion that emerged in the modern era, that recognizes the validity of all major religious texts (while noting the figurative dimension of those texts), and that is committed to the harmony of science and religion, the Bahá'í teachings offer a fresh perspective on evolution and the existence of the soul. Moreover, this perspective helps illustrate how an expanded ontological frame of reference can remain coherent with reason, empirical evidence, and science.

The concept of *evolution* permeates Bahá'í ontology. In 'Abdu'l-Bahá's writings and publicly recorded talks, we find numerous references to "the evolution of existence,"[243] "evolution in the world of matter,"[244] "anatomical evolution,"[245] "human evolution,"[246] "the evolution or progress of the spirit,"[247] and "evolution in civilization."[248]

Likewise, the teleological concept of *latency* is also central to Bahá'í ontology, and it is a key to reconciling belief in a transcendent soul with the theory of evolution. The concept of latency is often conveyed in the Bahá'í writings through organic metaphors. For instance, Bahá'u'lláh writes:

Consider . . . how the fruit, ere it is formed, lieth potentially within the tree. Were the tree to be cut into pieces, no sign nor any part of this fruit, however small, could be detected. When it appeareth, however, it manifesteth itself, as thou hast observed, in its wondrous beauty and glorious perfection.[249]

Similarly, 'Abdu'l-Bahá writes that "the whole of the great tree is potentially latent and hidden in the little seed. When this seed is planted and cultivated, the tree is revealed."[250] Building on such analogies, 'Abdu'l-Bahá explains that humans are "the fruit of the tree of creation."[251] As he states elsewhere, "If man did not exist in this world, it would have been like a tree without fruit."[252] "This world is," therefore, "even as a tree and man as the fruit."[253] The relationship between the seed, the tree, and the fruit also enables us to recognize how things can have qualitatively distinct natures even though they come from the same origin. We understand that the fruit is qualitatively different from any other part of the tree, though it grows from the same seed. In the same sense, 'Abdu'l-Bahá acknowledges that biologically speaking, the human form emerged from the same evolutionary tree as all other life forms. As he explains, "the origin of all material life is one."[254] Elaborating on this theme, he states:

> There is no doubt that initially there was a single origin: There cannot have been two origins. For the origin of all numbers is one and not two; the number two is itself in need of an origin. It is therefore evident that originally matter was one, and that one matter appeared in a different form in each element. Thus various forms appeared, and as they appeared, they each assumed an independent form and became a specific element. But this distinction attained its full completion and realization only after a very long time. Then these elements were composed, arranged, and combined in infinite forms; in other words, from the composition and combination of these elements countless beings appeared.[255]

At the same time, he emphasizes that humanity is distinct from all other life forms due to the existence of the human soul, which, as the previously quoted passages indicate, is associated with the fruit of the tree of evolution. For instance, in response to questions on this topic by early Western believers, 'Abdu'l-Bahá states that "the form, appearance, and organs of man have evolved over time. But man has always been a distinct species; he has been man, not an animal."[256] This reference appears to refer to the spiritual reality of the human being—the reality of the soul—rather than our animal form, because, in many other contexts, 'Abdu'l-Bahá clearly acknowledges "the animal nature of man"[257] and the fact that all life evolved from the same origin, as cited above. But "the reality of man," he reminds us, is "the human spirit."[258] And this inner reality, he explains, "is clad in the outer garment of the animal."[259]

Therefore, when 'Abdu'l-Bahá states that "man has always been a distinct species," he appears to be using the concept of *species* to signify our intrinsic spiritual nature rather than our biological form. In this regard, he states elsewhere that "in man there are two natures; his spiritual or higher nature and his material or lower nature."[260] It is because of our spiritual nature that "the world of humanity is distinct from the animal kingdom."[261]

One can thus accept the scientific theory of biological evolution, including the mechanisms of natural selection that it identifies, while also recognizing a qualitative difference between the human species and other species. By analogy, humans can be understood as the fruit of the tree of evolution because we are characterized by a transcendent soul that makes us qualitatively distinct from the rest of the tree. At the same time, we can understand that the entire tree, including the fruit, comes from the same seed, or origin. We can understand how the fruit was only a latent reality for much of the life of the tree. And we can understand how the latent presence of the fruit in the seed constitutes the intrinsic purpose, or telos, of the seed. None of this contradicts the prevailing theory of biological evolution and its mechanisms of natural selection—if that theory is understood within the expanded frame of reference that Nagel invites us to explore, with its normative and teleological dimensions.

Moreover, if any doubt were to remain among Bahá'ís about how to interpret relevant statements from the primary Bahá'í writings regarding evolution, they would need only call to mind the fundamental Bahá'í teaching that "religion must stand the analysis of reason. It must agree with scientific fact and proof."[262] "Religion and science," 'Abdu'l-Bahá emphatically states, must "walk hand in hand, and any religion contrary to science is not the truth."[263] And again: "Weigh carefully in the balance of reason and science everything that is presented to you as religion. If it passes this test, then accept it, for it is truth! If, however, it does not so conform, then reject it, for it is ignorance!"[264] And yet again: "Put all your beliefs into harmony with science; there can be no opposition, for truth is one."[265]

Given that science has furnished overwhelming evidence in support of evolution by natural selection, Bahá'ís have no reason to object to the prevailing scientific consensus regarding the basic mechanisms of evolution. Of course, the science of evolution continues to advance, and secondary aspects of the theory of evolution continue to be modified. For instance, recent insights into the important role epigenetics play in how the expression of genes can be

affected within the life cycle of individuals, and how those epigene-
tic expressions can be inherited by offspring, is causing evolutionary
scientists to revisit some previously rejected notions. Other aspects
of evolutionary science will undoubtedly continue to advance, or
be revisited, in similar ways. But many of the basic mechanisms of
biological evolution appear to be well understood, and there is no
reason for Bahá'ís to doubt them.

Like Nagel, however, Bahá'ís question the materialist frame of
reference within which the mechanisms of evolution are widely in-
terpreted today. That materialist framework not only obscures, as
Nagel argues, the possibility of subtle teleological processes at play
in biological evolution; it also obscures a potentially significant distinction between humans and other species: the existence of a soul
that transcends our biological form. Both of these interpretations
are neither supported nor refuted by the empirical evidence.

In addition to obscuring this possible qualitative distinction between humans and all other species, the materialist frame of reference also leads many evolutionary biologists to reject the view
that evolution moves in a directional or teleological manner. For
instance, materialists tend to reject the notion that evolution always
moves from simple to more complex life forms. And indeed, there
are examples of natural selection operating in ways that reduce the
complexity of life forms over time in some environments. Evolutionary theories thus tend to conceptualize evolution as a process
that moves in all possible directions (rather than in one direction)
as it responds to the myriad selective pressures at play in diverse,
ever-changing environments.

It should be noted, however, that this omnidirectional feature of
evolution is not incompatible with the idea that human consciousness was a latent evolutionary reality. Nor is it incompatible with the
idea that human consciousness is qualitatively distinct from all other
evolutionary outcomes. Nor has any empirical evidence ruled out
the possibility that biological evolution has an intrinsic telos leading
toward the emergence of this distinct reality—even if the mecha-
nism by which that telos unfolds is through movement in all possible directions. Nagel offers a compelling argument for why these
possibilities should all be taken seriously. Bahá'ís concur.

Building on this premise, the Bahá'í writings also suggest a rational way to understand the appearance of the human spirit in the

material world when the tree of biological evolution reached its fruition. They suggest that once the biological human form evolved, it enabled the transcendent human spirit to become manifest in the contingent world in a manner that is analogous to the property of magnetism becoming manifest when iron atoms are organized in the appropriate way, or analogous to the light of the sun becoming manifest in a mirror once the mirror has been created. As 'Abdu'l-Bahá explains:

> The members, constituent parts, and composition that are found within man attract and act as a magnet for the spirit: The spirit is bound to appear in it. Thus, when a mirror is polished, it is bound to attract the rays of the sun, to be illumined, and to reflect splendid images. That is, when these physical elements are gathered and combined together, according to the natural order and with the utmost perfection, they become a magnet for the spirit, and the spirit will manifest itself therein with all its perfections.
>
> From this perspective one does not ask, "Why is it necessary for the rays of the sun to fall upon the mirror?"; for the relationships that bind together the realities of all things, whether spiritual or material, require that when the mirror is polished and turned towards the sun it should manifest the rays thereof. In like manner, when the elements are composed and combined according to the noblest order, arrangement, and manner, the human spirit will appear and manifest itself therein.[266]

The latent reality of the human spirit can thus be understood as a transcendent reality that became manifest in the material world only when the tree of biological evolution reached its fruition and produced the human form, thus laying the basis for higher-order evolutionary processes with moral and social dimensions. This understanding is an article of faith—or an ontological premise. It has not been empirically proven. But it is a rational premise that is just as plausible as the contrasting premise that human subjectivity or consciousness can be explained in a materially reductionist manner as a mere biochemical epiphenomenon that emerged through pure chance, that might not have emerged at all, and that has no purpose or meaning.

Consider, in this regard, the current state of neuroscience. Human brain imaging studies, using technology such as functional magnetic resonance imaging (fMRI) or electroencephalograms (EEG), yield correlational rather than causal results. Based on such studies, we can conclude there is a correlation between the specific pattern of activity in brain region X and the specific thought or behavior Y. But we cannot determine whether X causes Y, or whether Y causes X, or whether X and Y co-emerge through a causal dialectic, or whether X and Y are both caused by a third variable Z. Nor can we explain how a correlation between X and Y is associated with the subjective experience of consciousness. All we can say is that the X brain region is active in a specific way when a person is thinking or doing Y.

For instance, if brain region X becomes active in some way when certain people meditate on altruistic thought Y (or engage in altruistic behavior Y), it could be that people with a genetic predisposition toward certain patterns of activity in brain region X are naturally predisposed toward Y. Or it could also be that people who are raised to engage in Y develop specific patterns of activity in brain region X. Or it could be that both X and Y co-emerge through a complex dialectical interaction between nature and nurture. Or it could be that the relation between X and Y is, in part, the result of a third variable, including a variable we don't yet recognize or understand. Moreover, none of these explanatory models might prove capable of explaining the subjective experience of consciousness. Therefore, the humble—and truly scientific—approach would be to acknowledge that if subjective mental states are linearly correlated with biochemical brain states, then we should be open to models that examine causality in either direction or that consider even more complex forms of causality.

Granted, some techniques, such as transcranial magnetic stimulation (TMS) and deep brain stimulation (DBS), can probe simple kinds of causality in which altering a human brain state changes a mental or behavioral state. Likewise, more invasive techniques such as optogenetics, which makes neurons light-sensitive through genetic manipulation, are being widely used with lab animals such as rodents. These latter techniques offer more powerful ways to probe the same kinds of causality that flow from brain state manipulations to mental or behavioral changes. And these causal relationships are likely to have been passed on to humans through evolutionary mechanisms.

But reverse forms of causality—including the extent to which *conscious* and *intentional* changes in mental or behavioral states can cause changes in brain states—remain an open question. Research on brain plasticity suggests that some forms of causality clearly run in this direction.[267] But to what extent can such change be attributed to consciousness and intentionality, as distinct from environmental forces that shape mental and behavioral states? Furthermore, what are *consciousness* and *intentionality*? And how do they arise, or where do they come from? And how can we explain the *subjective experience* of consciousness? Is it merely an illusion created from a complex set of biochemical interactions in the brain, shaped by the brain's interactions with its material environment? Or is it something more ontologically fundamental? Likewise, how can we explain the role that *meaning* and *purpose* play in human consciousness, and how they arise, and why they can play such powerful motivating forces in human lives?

We should be cautious before assuming any models conceived within a purely materialist framework will ever be able to adequately answer such questions. If we adopt a corresponding posture of humility, it opens new avenues of inquiry, of the kind Nagel invites, regarding the systematic exploration of human nature and consciousness.

For instance, the analogy of the mirror and the light alluded to above suggests a complex relationship between body and spirit, the interaction of which gives rise to a human soul. In this context, Bahá'ís believe that "the mind forms a link between the soul and the body, and the two interact on each other."[268] Thus, the soul might inspire the exercise of free will in intentional ways that can affect the operation of the mind and that, over time, might mold the plasticity of the brain. Such forms of intentionality might include spiritual disciplines such as prayer, meditation, and fasting, along with altruistic acts, sacrificial service to a higher cause, and the development of other life habits that cannot be easily explained as mere epiphenomena of biochemical processes.

There is, of course, much work to be done to explore a potentially complex relationship of the kind alluded to above and to clarify whether such an exploration might offer new insight and understanding. But such work becomes possible only if we are willing to entertain the underlying premises discussed above and explore their implications, which requires the expanded conception of objectivity for which Nagel makes a case. Thoughtful and fair-minded scientists, characterized by a humble posture of learning and free from dogmatic biases, should welcome this avenue of inquiry.

The expanded conception of objectivity and the teleological conception of evolution Nagel invites us to explore also have implications for how we understand humanity's collective social evolution. In this regard, it is possible to recognize that consciousness has a collective expression. No mind can develop its latent potentialities independent of other minds. Individual minds grow and mature within wider fields of consciousness that are constituted, at least in part, through complex behavioral interactions, diverse modes of communication, evolving bodies of knowledge, and rich systems of meaning.

In this sense, while individuality is clearly a characteristic of human consciousness, individual minds are also like nodes in larger networks of collective consciousness. Based on this insight, we can recognize that the seeds of existence appear to have contained within them another latent reality, or telos, related to collective consciousness. This is the latent reality of a peaceful, just, and mutually prosperous global civilization—or what Bahá'ís often refer to as divine civilization—which embodies the principle of the oneness of humanity in a mature form. Bringing this latent reality into existence will require the conscious exercise of agency. It needs to be constructed.

The Bahá'í writings suggest that this divine civilization, like the human soul, is one of the intrinsic purposes of the universe that was latent in the seeds of existence. In this regard, Bahá'u'lláh writes that God "cherisheth in His heart the desire of beholding the entire human race as one soul and one body."[269] Elaborating on this theme, a document commissioned by the Universal House of Justice explains:

In a letter addressed to Queen Victoria over a century ago, and employing an analogy that points to the one model holding convincing promise for the organization of a planetary society, Bahá'u'lláh compared the world to the human body. There is, indeed, no other model in phenomenal existence to which we can reasonably look. Human society is composed not of a mass of merely differentiated cells but of associations of individuals, each one of whom is endowed with intelligence and will; nevertheless, the modes of operation that characterize man's biological nature illustrate fundamental principles of existence. Chief among these is that of unity in diversity. Paradoxically, it is precisely the wholeness and complexity of the order constituting the human body—and the perfect integration into it of the body's cells—that permit the full realization of the distinctive capacities inherent in each of these component elements. No cell lives apart from the body, whether in contributing to its functioning or in deriving its share from the well-being of the whole. The physical well-being thus achieved finds its purpose in making possible the expression of human consciousness; that is to say, the purpose of biological development transcends the mere existence of the body and its parts.

What is true of the life of the individual has its parallels in human society. The human species is an organic whole, the leading edge of the evolutionary process. That human consciousness necessarily operates through an infinite diversity of individual minds and motivations detracts in no way from its essential unity. Indeed, it is precisely an inhering diversity that distinguishes unity from homogeneity or uniformity. What the peoples of the world are today experiencing, Bahá'u'lláh said, is their collective coming-of-age, and it is through this emerging maturity of the race that the principle of unity in diversity will find full expression. From its earliest beginnings in the consolidation of family life, the process of social organization has successively moved from the simple structures of clan and tribe, through multitudinous forms of urban society, to the eventual emergence of the nation-state, each stage opening up a wealth of new opportunities for the exercise of human capacity.

Clearly, the advancement of the race has not occurred at the expense of human individuality. As social organization has increased, the scope for the expression of the capacities latent in each human being has correspondingly expanded. Because the relationship between the individual and society is a reciprocal one, the transformation now required must occur simultaneously within human consciousness and the structure of social institutions. It is in the opportunities afforded by this twofold process of change that a strategy of global development will find its purpose. At this crucial stage of history, that purpose must be to establish enduring foundations on which planetary civilization can gradually take shape.[270]

These premises have profound implications for our efforts to articulate a new social ontology. Although some of the points above go beyond Nagel's initial argument, they are compatible with his expanded conception of objectivity, his conception of consciousness as a fundamental property of existence, his realist conception of value, and his teleological conception of evolutionary processes that bend toward increasing instantiations of value. These premises also have profound implications for efforts to articulate a new social epistemology.

SOME EPISTEMOLOGICAL IMPLICATIONS

The first chapter of this book points out that the generation of knowledge about social reality cannot be separated from the construction of social reality. Both processes advance in simultaneous and codependent ways. But they need not be understood in entirely relativistic ways. The concepts of relative attunement and relative embodiment enable us to understand how these processes can advance in relation to foundational normative truths and their enabling and constraining properties. Chapter 2 then elaborates some of the conditions needed for this. Chapter 3 explores how these insights enable us to conceptualize science and religion as complementary systems of knowledge and practice that partially overlap. The natural sciences are focused, at least in part, on increasing our understanding of truths about the physical universe and learning how to apply those insights to the betterment of humanity. Religion is focused, at least in part, on increasing our understanding of normative truths and learning how to apply those. But how might the social sciences fit into this picture?

The social sciences, as we know them today, emerged against the backdrop of rapidly advancing natural sciences that were making transformative contributions to the material life of humanity. Not surprisingly, many early social scientists attempted to apply philosophical and methodological principles underlying the natural sciences to the study of social reality. Positivism, as a philosophy of science, was embraced by many social scientists, along with its fact/value dichotomy. This led to an emphasis on allegedly value-neutral modes of descriptive and explanatory research regarding social phenomena. The clearest example of this emphasis can be seen in mainstream economics, which has attempted to model itself largely after physics, with a focus on elegant mathematical models and a pretense to value-neutrality that obscures its normative underpinnings. Similar aspirations have also influenced sociology, political science, and other fields in varying degrees. Such approaches are still common today, although they are increasingly contested by critical theorists from various disciplinary traditions.

The most influential and direct challenge to positivism in the social sciences traces back to the Frankfurt School of critical theory, which arose in the 1930s, drawing heavily upon the work of Marx and, to some degree, Sigmund Freud. At that time, confidence in the entire enlightenment project was eroding as the most advanced scientific societies in the world began using insights from the natural and social sciences to develop and employ weapons of mass destruction and techniques of mass manipulation. Against the backdrop of rising fascism in Germany and its deployment of such means, Frankfurt scholars such as Max Horkheimer and Theodor Adorno began to articulate strong critiques of positivism and other Enlightenment ideals in an effort to align the social sciences with projects of human emancipation.[271] These critiques contributed in part to the rise of a broader tradition of critical social theory that now spans the social sciences and humanities and continues to expand in influence. Although this broad intellectual movement has been characterized by a great diversity of theories and methods, it tends to rest on central commitments that include a rejection of positivism and its fact/value dichotomy, a commitment to justice as an organizing principle of social theory and research, and a corresponding critique of oppressive power relations in whatever sphere of social reality is under interrogation.

Critical social theory, understood in this broad sense, has been an important corrective to positivism, and it has yielded important insights into the countless ways self-interested expressions of power have shaped, and continue to shape, social reality. However, the critical theory project has generally adopted a narrow conception of power, discussed in chapter 2, that has limited it in various ways. Most notably, the project tends to foster deep skepticism regarding the human potential to transcend oppressive relations of power. In addition, because of its own materialist underpinnings, which results in a rejection of moral realism, the project of critical theory tends to lead once again to extreme normative relativism. Ironically, this ends up undermining the entire project of critical theory, because the pursuit of justice has no real basis without commitment to a transcendent principle of justice. Indeed, it is partly due to this normative incoherence that many social scientists continue to adopt positivist approaches. If there are no transcendent normative truths, positivism can appear as the only rational approach to the generation of knowledge about social reality.

In fairness, some prominent critical theorists, such as Habermas, have tried valiantly to find a path out of the cul-de-sac of normative relativism, as discussed in the previous chapter. Habermas does this by arguing that context-transcending normative truths can be socially constructed purely on the foundation of human language and reasoning. But as Cooke has illustrated, Habermas's denial of non-linguistic sources of normative truth makes it impossible to explain the source of transformations in normative reasoning or the linguistic resources that make such transformations possible. This is because if normative truths derive only from cognitive-linguistic structures, yet cognitive-linguistic structures are always products of a given socio-cultural formation, then transforming cognitive-linguistic structures requires some external, recalcitrant, irruptive source that is independent of the socio-cultural formation.[272]

How, then, can the social sciences advance beyond the limitations of positivism and critical theory? What might more mature social sciences look like? The answer to this question will undoubtedly take generations to clarify, and dogmatic pronouncements about the future of the social sciences should be viewed with skepticism. Nonetheless, it is important to begin exploring this question now, with an appropriate posture of humility.

Toward this end, it seems reasonable to assume that many of the descriptive and explanatory methodologies that initially arose within a positivist framework will continue to have some merit in the social sciences. These methodologies yield valuable insights into many of the social forces that have shaped past and present social formations. But on their own, such methodologies can tell us little about latent social possibilities or about how to increase the embodiment of normative truths in the construction of a new social reality.

Likewise, it seems reasonable to assume that many of the insights offered by critical methodologies will also continue to have merit in the social sciences. These methodologies yield valuable insights into how forces of oppression, especially self-interested expressions of power, have shaped past and present social formation. But again, such methodologies tell us little about latent social possibilities or about how to increase the embodiment of normative truths in the construction of a new social reality.

Mature social sciences, it seems, will need to develop and include methodologies for normative inquiry into unfolding processes of social construction. In other words, if the analysis in this book is correct, social scientists should be able to contribute to the systematic generation of knowledge about the conscious application of normative principles to the construction of a new social reality. This would entail the ability to assess emergent social phenomena, or unfolding social patterns, as they are being brought into existence through collective agency. This would require the ability to draw on evolving intersubjective assessments regarding the application of normative principles. And when principles such as justice are involved, these intersubjective assessments will need to be informed by marginalized segments of society who are most familiar with the experience of injustice.

Such methodologies are well beyond most of what occurs in the social sciences today. However, emerging approaches to community-based participatory action research offer glimpses into what some of these methodologies might look like. The term *participatory action research*, as it is used here, encompasses a range of methodologies that began to emerge in the latter decades of the twentieth century. Even though these methods remain on the margins of mainstream social sciences, they are gaining credibility and popularity. At their core tend to be the following commitments: the generation of knowledge in the context of lived communities outside the academy; a focus on the betterment of the community; a recognition of the wealth of knowledge and capacity that resides in the community; participatory approaches that entail collaboration and parity between social scientists and other community members in the formulation and investigation of research questions that arise from community needs; as well as sound, coherent, and reflective processes of learning through action.[273]

One of the great strengths of participatory action research, when it is done well, is its ability to raise the capacity of a community to become protagonists in the systematic generation of knowledge. Another strength is its ability to generate locally contextualized knowledge in ways that are relevant to the needs and conditions of particular communities. However, it is not yet clear how universal patterns can be systematically distilled from the locally contextualized knowledge generated through participatory action research. Some efforts toward this end have occurred within international development organizations such as the United Nations Educational, Scientific and Cultural Organization (UNESCO) or the United Nations Development Programme (UNDP). Their move toward "participatory development" models in the late 1980s was informed in part by a recognition that locally generated knowledge was more relevant to development processes than ideas generated by experts who were far removed from the communities and processes they were theorizing. These UN agencies therefore worked to share locally generated knowledge and practices across nation states in the service of development.

Similarly, the concept of micro-credit for community empowerment came out of an action research project called "Grameen Bank" by Muhammad Yunus in Bangladesh. In the 1990s, Grameen Bank went from being a local action research project to a national institution that challenged conventional banking wisdom. The insights gained from that experience led to a global emergence of micro-credit programs and learning processes, along with a rich body of associated knowledge.

A maturing social science, it seems, will need to build on this kind of experience. It will need to further systematize methods for identifying and disseminating universally applicable insights that emerge from participatory action research carried out in diverse local contexts, along with corresponding forms of theory development that scale globally, while continuing to recognize the intrinsic value of locally contextual knowledge. In the absence of better understood and more widely employed methods that can move from the particular to the universal and back, it is not clear whether the sum of participatory action research efforts in most fields amounts, yet, to a social *science*—despite the obvious value of such methods for the betterment of local communities.

In addition, although participatory action research has an obvious normative dimension, it does not yet rest on a coherent normative ontology. Learning how to address a specific social need through participatory action is not necessarily the same as consciously learning how to apply foundational normative principles to the construction of a new social reality that embodies those principles to increasing degrees. The latter requires an evolving conceptual framework capable of generating insights into the nature of a highly complex undertaking with local and global dimensions.

This is not to suggest that participatory action research should become the only approach to the generation of knowledge within the social sciences. Conventional methodologies, as they are applied outside a participatory action framework, have merit for examining many aspects of past or present social formations. But social scientists arguably need to expand and refine their methodological palette if the social sciences are to mature in the manner implied by the line of reasoning outlined in this book.

Furthermore, if the argument laid out in this book is sound, social scientists will need to arrive at a new relationship with maturing forms of religion. Religious communities, at their best, are active protagonists in the generation of knowledge about the application of normative principles in the construction of a new social reality. It follows that the maturing practice of religion and the maturing practice of social sciences can also be understood in terms of a complementary relationship. The precise nature of this relationship is impossible to discern when religious practices and social scientific practices are still in relatively immature stages of development. But a much deeper complementary can be imagined.

Toward this end, it may also be helpful to step back from the conception of science (including the social sciences) and religion as systems of knowledge and practice, to consider them from a wider perspective. The previous section of this chapter, along with the previous chapter, suggests that human consciousness might be understood as a latent potentiality inherent in the fabric of reality which became manifest through a process of biological evolution characterized by teleological properties. Once manifest, human consciousness has been developing in myriad ways on both individual and collective levels. This has been an exceedingly complex, non-linear process. In the aggregate, however, it is difficult to deny that human consciousness has expanded, advanced, or matured in at least some ways over time—the most obvious being advancements in our understanding of the many physical and biological forces operating in the material universe.

In this sense, science and religion can be viewed, at their best, as principle forces impelling the ongoing development of human consciousness itself. Science is contributing to our ever-deepening awareness and understanding of material reality—the substrate of our existence. Religion is contributing to our ever-deepening awareness and understanding of spiritual reality, a reality that transcends us and beckons us toward latent potentialities that are yet unrealized. On an individual level, those latent potentialities can be understood, at least in part, as the development of the soul through the acquisition of moral or spiritual virtues, the experience of Divine love and grace, salvation or spiritual enlightenment, and communion with the Source of our existence. On a collective level, those latent potentialities can be understood, at least in part, as the eventual emergence of a global civilization that fully and organically embodies the principle of the oneness of humanity, which will be possible only through the conscious application of a range of spiritual principles, or normative truths, to the construction of a new social reality. The most significant of these, perhaps, are the reciprocal principles of unity and justice.

Toward a Radical Constructive Program

Although the discussion in this book has been highly abstract at times, its ultimate purpose is very practical. Humanity cannot continue its present course much longer. Increasingly acute social and ecological crises, unfolding on a global scale, are awakening us to the need for radical change. But some of the ways we pursue social change continue to be informed by the same assumptions about social reality that have precipitated these crises. For many people, these include nihilistic assumptions about truth and relativity, cynical assumptions about the relationship between knowledge and power, and conflictual assumptions about the relationship between science and religion. These assumptions offer no route out of the crises we are facing.

The line of reasoning laid out in this book, and the premises on which it rests, offer a path out. In this regard, they have significant implications for how we pursue processes of radical or transformative social change in the face of injustice and oppression. In other words, how we understand the relationship between truth and relativity, knowledge and power, and science and religion has implications for how we approach social activism—or how we approach the reconstruction of social reality.

To explore these implications, let's begin by considering the thought and practice of Mohandas Gandhi, since his non-violent philosophy of social change has arguably exerted more influence on the practice of activism than any figure of the last century. Gandhi's thinking about social activism was inspired in part by observations of passive resistance movements playing out in other parts of the world when he was a young man. Gandhi also drew on his study of the Bhagavad Gita and other Hindu texts, his familiarity with the teachings of Jainism and Buddhism, and his subsequent study of the Christian Gospels as he formulated and refined his non-violent strategies of social change.[274]

Gandhi's deep spiritual commitments, combined with his observations of contemporary social movements, led him to the conclusion that passive resistance to injustice was not enough. The struggle for justice, Gandhi believed, entailed the proactive application of spiritual truths in struggles for transformative change. In Sanskrit, the word *satya* means "truth" and the word *agraha* means "holding firmly to." Gandhi thus coined the term *satyagraha* to denote the strategy of holding firmly to the truth in the face of oppression.[275] He later referred to satyagraha as "the Force which is born of Truth"[276] or the application of "Truth-Force."[277]

As Gandhi's language indicates, he held a realist conception of normative truths. He understood them in an ontologically foundational way. As he expresses it, "The world rests upon the bedrock of satya or truth. Asatya, meaning untruth, also means nonexistent, and satya or truth also means that which is. If untruth does not so much as exist, its victory is out of the question. And truth being that which is, can never be destroyed. This is the doctrine of satyagraha in a nutshell."[278] In this context, Gandhi conceptualized normative truths as ontological laws or forces. He writes, for instance:

The law of love will work, just as the law of gravitation will work, whether we accept it or not. Just as a scientist will work wonders out of various applications of the laws of nature, even so a man who applies the law of love with scientific precision can work greater wonders. For the force of nonviolence is infinitely more wonderful and subtle than the material forces of nature, like, for instance, electricity.[279]

Gandhi's view that satyagraha must be non-violent derived from his recognition that one cannot separate the *means* from the *ends* in any struggle for social change. As he states:

They say "means are after all means." I would say "means are after all everything." As the means so the end. There is no wall of separation between means and end. . . . Realization of the goal is in exact proportion to that of the means.[280]

Based on this premise, Gandhi understood that if we seek to construct a peaceful and just society, we must employ peaceful and just means. Since violence is a means of oppression, violent means can only beget further cycles of violence and oppression. Non-violence is thus the only rational way forward. In this regard, Gandhi envisioned an emerging science of non-violence, he understood himself and his compatriots as humble students of non-violence, and he saw the satyagraha campaigns he led as early experiments generating initial insights within this new science.[281]

In the struggle to free India from the oppressive yoke of the British Empire, one of the most well-known applications of satyagraha was the Dandi Satyagraha—or the Salt March—of 1930. This peaceful campaign consisted of a 240-mile march to the sea, where Gandhi and the ranks of those who joined him along the course of his march made salt in defiance of an unjust colonial law that prohibited independent Indian salt making to force dependence on the British salt monopoly. This campaign, which the British Raj first ignored as inconsequential and then attempted to suppress through incarceration and violence, attracted global media coverage and became one of a series of key moments in the struggle for independence because it exposed the manifestly unjust nature of British colonial rule to the entire world.

The Dandi Satyagraha was successful, at least in part, because it stirred the moral sentiments of populations at home and abroad. The campaign quickly attracted mass popular support among Indians, began to transform popular attitudes in Britain against its own colonial rule abroad, softened the hearts of some within the British Raj, and captured the imagination and the sympathy of observers around the world, including leaders of the American civil rights movement who would later adapt similar strategies in the struggle for racial justice in the United States.

The accumulated evidence from similar Gandhi-inspired approaches throughout the world, over the decades since his initial campaigns, points to the relative efficacy of Gandhian strategies.[282] To put it simply, collective actions that derive from Gandhi's premises have proven fruitful. Those premises include the assumption that normative truths have a foundational existence, that thoughtful people everywhere are capable of intuitively recognizing and responding to such truths, and that non-violent activism can increase the embodiment of such truths in social reality.

Of course, Gandhi's strategies are not only about stirring the moral sentiments of populations at home and abroad. The associated processes of mass mobilization on the home front, along with pressure from abroad, ultimately disrupt the power dynamics needed to govern through oppression. In short, satyagraha increases the costs of oppression while undermining the coercive powers of the oppressors. In the process, when non-violent strategies are successful, even members of oppressive classes whose hearts are not won over ultimately recognize that the status quo cannot be sustained.

Gene Sharp, one of the most influential scholars of non-violence in recent decades, focuses on this destabilizing power dynamic as the key to non-violent social change. In the process, he moves away from Gandhi's principled and religiously inspired approach to non-violence and articulates a purely pragmatic, secular, tactical approach to non-violence.[283] Even this purely pragmatic approach has proven relatively successful at achieving short-term political gains. For instance, it has been employed effectively to destabilize many oppressive regimes and force political change, including movements toward liberal democratic elections in parts of the former Soviet Union, the Arab world, and many other regions.[284] But liberal democracies are easily recaptured by powerful social classes or authoritarian elites—as experience has demonstrated in many of these same countries as well as in more established democracies.

For this reason and others, Gandhi rejected Western liberalism as the goal of satyagraha. He understood that liberal democracies merely reproduce the competitive power dynamics he wanted to transcend and, as a result, liberal democracies inevitably devolve toward oppressive social relations.[285] With this concern about competitive power dynamics in mind, Gandhi even acknowledged the limits of civil disobedience and other confrontational expressions of satyagraha that embodied a contest of power, albeit a non-violent one. In this regard, he viewed all oppositional tactics as a last resort necessitated only by the failure of an oppressed population to fully commit, in a unified manner, to a transformative *constructive program*.[286]

For Gandhi, the primary form of satyagraha was a radical constructive program through which populations struggle to actively build the more just society they aspire toward, even as they are living within the shell of an oppressive social order. As he explains, a population must actively "build up the structure of Swaraj [self-governance] from its very foundation."[287] Furthermore, he asserts, "Those who think that the major reforms will come after the advent of Swaraj are deceiving themselves. It will not drop from heaven one fine morning. But it has to be built up brick by brick by corporate self-effort."[288] Elaborating on this theme, Gandhi explains that "outward agitation cannot be given the first place. It is of subsidiary importance and it depends for its success entirely on the success of that which is internal, viz. constructive work."[289] Indeed, Gandhi asserts that civil disobedience would not even be necessary "if the cooperation of the whole nation is secured in the constructive programme."[290] He also warns that civil disobedience "without the co-operation of the millions by way of constructive effort is mere bravado and worse than useless."[291]

In this regard, Gandhi viewed non-violent confrontation as the negative side of satyagraha and the constructive program as its positive side. At best, non-violent confrontation could throw off the

yoke of oppression, but a robust constructive program was needed, in advance, to fill the eventual vacuum with new social norms,
relationships, practices, and institutions. Otherwise, new forms of
oppression would quickly reappear. Gandhi also viewed the constructive program as a vehicle by which an oppressed population
could educate itself and cure its own social ills in the process of
building its capacity for self-governance. This entailed the development of courage, moral discipline, self-reliance, and unity alongside
the construction of new institutional forms.

In sum, Gandhi understood the constructive program as the core
of the emerging science of non-violence. Regrettably, Gandhi's
constructive program was downplayed by many of his contemporaries in favor of non-violent confrontation. Likewise, many social
movements subsequently inspired by Gandhian non-violence also
downplayed this aspect of his thought and practice. Accordingly,
radical constructive programs have received relatively little attention among scholars of non-violence. But that is starting to change.
Karuna Mantena, Stellan Vinthagen, Sean Chabot, Kurt Schock,
Majken Jul Sørensen, Mark Mattaini, and others have begun to focus renewed attention on the Gandhian concept of constructive
programs.[292]

The closely related concept of *prefigurative politics* or *prefiguration*—
initially coined by Carl Boggs—helps us further understand the
nature of transformative constructive programs.[293] This concept
arose in the 1970s to explain the ways that some New Left, feminist, and anarchist movements sought to embody the relationships
they aspired toward within their modes of political organizing.[294]
Such movements recognized, in varying degrees, that the means of
a struggle should *prefigure* the ends the struggle sought. Otherwise,
even if a movement succeeded in throwing off some system of
oppression, its adherents would not have developed the capacities
to create the more just social order toward which they aspired. For
example, if people aspired to live in a society that did not mar-
ginalize or oppress any social groups, they should work for change
in ways that were mutually empowering for all groups. The means
would thereby prefigure the ends. Similarly, if people aspired to live
in a society that was not characterized by oppressive hierarchies,
they should organize their movement in ways that did not reproduce
oppressive hierarchies. The means would thereby prefigure the ends.

As Sean Chabot and Stellan Vinthagen illustrate, constructive programs that employ prefigurative means are often combined with contentious means in the same movements.[295] Gandhi himself did this, reluctantly. But as Majken Jul Sørensen points out, constructive means of social change can also be pursued independently of contentious means.[296]

With the concept of prefiguration in mind, we can appreciate why a radical constructive program might intentionally avoid contentious politics. Western civilization has constructed a culture of conflict and competition in which most social institutions and many social practices are characterized by contests of power. Contests of power inherently privilege self-interested actors who enter such contests with the most power. The prevailing culture of contest therefore inherently tends toward oppressive power relations. It should not be surprising, then, that some people reject the prevailing culture of contest as an unjust model of social organization.[297] If moving beyond the culture of contest is the *end* sought, then it makes sense to pursue it through *means* that prefigure that end.[298]

Or stated another way, if we expand our analysis of power in the manner alluded to in chapter 2, we can recognize the value of pursuing transformative social change through approaches that fall entirely on the right side of figure 8 from that chapter—the domain of mutualistic power relations. After all, if we aspire to a world that is characterized by such relations, we should pursue that aspiration through means that prefigure it. This expanded conception of power thus enables us to imagine and explore radically non-adversarial—or radically constructive—approaches to overcoming oppression.

Even though some constructive programs eschew confrontational strategies, this does not imply passivity in the face of injustice. Gandhi conceptualized constructive programs as active and urgent responses to oppression. They require collective agency, struggle, and sacrifice. They must attract and mobilize growing numbers of protagonists. They entail training, discipline, focus, and the generation of knowledge. And they require participants to question deeply held assumptions about social reality, to root out prejudices, to rethink inherited social norms, to develop new social practices, and to build entirely new social structures. These are not passive responses to injustice.

Moreover, commitment to a purely non-adversarial constructive program need not imply judgment or criticism of those who work for justice through more contentious means. Purely constructive programs can co-exist with contentious strategies of non-violence within a broader ecology of movements characterized by diverse forms of mobilization. Such movements would be generating different forms of knowledge and experience. They would, in a sense, be like different research programs testing slightly different premises within the wider science of non-violence. And their relative fruitfulness, as well as their potential complementarities, can be assessed only over time.

The Bahá'í approach to social change—including the Bahá'í response to oppression—is informed by much of the preceding logic. It is an active, rather than passive, response to injustice. It recognizes the importance of coherence between ends and means. And while it derives from a principled commitment to purely peaceful and constructive means, it need not entail criticism of more confrontational strategies of non-violent social change.

Bahá'ís have been learning how to translate principled commitments into action for many generations now. One insight that can be drawn from the experience of the Bahá'í community is that constructive programs aimed at deep social transformation, even when pursued through purely peaceful means, often encounter hostile responses from privileged or elite segments of society.[299] This is because radical constructive programs implicitly problematize, or denaturalize, aspects of the prevailing social order that benefit some segments of society. Thoughtful members of privileged segments of society will support a constructive program as they come to understand its moral necessity. But others will respond with hostility and even violence in efforts to preserve their narrowly conceived interests. Such hostility and violence creates a visible public contrast between the constructive program and the repressive program. This contrast can, in turn, become a source of attraction to thoughtful people from all walks of life who are moved to join or publicly defend the constructive program, as the experience of the Bahá'ís in Iran has demonstrated.[300]

This dynamic of repression and attraction is the same dynamic that many campaigns of civil disobedience actively seek to create. Since the time of Gandhi, such campaigns have been staged to set up precisely these dynamics. Gandhi understood this. Martin Luther King understood this. Sharp wrote extensively about this.

However, unlike campaigns of civil disobedience, Bahá'ís do not seek to actively provoke repression. Rather, Bahá'ís are exhorted to direct all their time and energy toward constructing a new social order through unifying means, independent of how they are perceived by vested interests. And when Bahá'ís encounter repression, they are exhorted to adopt a posture of resilience, confident that such repression cannot ultimately stop their constructive program.[301] Of course, some Bahá'ís have suffered trauma in this process, and that trauma should not be understated. But the Bahá'í teachings emphasize that social transformation is impossible without sacrifice, and Bahá'ís are thus able to find meaning in this suffering, which has fortified their "constructive resilience."[302]

Not surprisingly, the necessity for resilience is often recognized in discourses on social change. As Schock explains, *resilience*, in this context, refers to the ability of a movement to withstand and recover from acute repression or to sustain a campaign despite the actions of others who try to destroy, constrain, or inhibit the movement.[303] The Indian independence movement and the US civil rights movements are excellent examples of such resilience in the face of acute repression.

It is worth noting, however, that resilience can also be understood in relation to more generalized, less acute forms of oppression. For instance, the materialism that is aggressively propagated in capitalist societies today can be understood as a pervasive form of oppression that undermines the psychological and spiritual well-being of all people, fosters cynicism and lethargy, alienates people from their true nature and one another, and retards social progress.[304] Under conditions of generalized oppression such as this, every effort to labor for the betterment of humanity and contribute to the advancement of civilization requires some form of resilience. Resilience can therefore be understood as an essential feature of all struggles for social change, whether those struggles are pursued in the context of acute or generalized forms of oppression. Efforts to reconstruct social reality require it.

Conclusion

This book began by pointing out that the global challenges facing humanity today are without precedent and constitute existential threats. Our technological and reproductive success as a species has transformed the conditions of our own existence. But we have not yet adapted to these new conditions. We have not yet learned how to live together as a single global community. We now, urgently, need to do this.

Although there are many practical obstacles that will need to be overcome on this path of learning, some of the most significant obstacles are products of Western thought itself that have, to varying degrees, been exported around the world by centuries of Western hegemony. These include dichotomous views regarding truth and relativity, cynical views regarding knowledge and power, and conflictual views regarding science and religion. Based on these deeply ingrained and at times unconscious habits of thought, many people today have all but given up hope that we can learn how to live together on this planet.

Against this backdrop, I have argued that normative truths exist; that human knowledge can, to some degree, become attuned to such truths; that under the right conditions, the generation of such knowledge need not be corrupted by power and privilege; and that it is possible to learn our way toward a new social order that embodies normative truths such as peace, justice, and the inherent worth of every soul, to increasing degrees. To do these things, however, we need a conceptual framework that reconciles truth and relativity, knowledge and power, and science and religion in rational and constructive ways. I suggested a way to do this—namely, by reconciling ontological foundationalism and epistemological relativism within a moderate social constructionist framework. I then examined the experience of the Bahá'í community to illustrate these possibilities.

The line of reasoning laid out in this book rests on premises that have been made explicit along the way. These premises are not universally accepted—especially within Western intellectual traditions. Many influential Western thinkers, some of whom have been cited in this book, have argued from opposite premises.

Ultimately, all premises must be assessed by their fruitfulness as we test them against reality. The premises examined in this book cannot be tested until sufficient numbers of people translate them into social practices on a large enough scale that their fruitfulness can be assessed. In this context, we would do well to ask ourselves: Do the premises laid out in this book warrant testing? Conversely, in the face of mounting existential crises precipitated in part by hegemonic Western premises, what might be the consequence of not testing the alternative premises brought into focus by this book?

To test the premises laid out in this book, we need to take seriously a program of radical constructive activism. This is among the most important practical implications of the argument developed in the preceding chapters. Within the shell of an oppressive social order, efforts to construct a new social reality that embodies normative truths to increasing degrees constitute radical social activism.

Radical forms of constructive activism are not new, yet they rarely make it into history books, scholarly journals, or the news, because they do not embody the conflictual dynamics on which conventional storytellers typically focus. Therefore, if we are to advance a constructive program of activism in conscious and intentional ways, we will need to begin to learn more systematically from past and present experiences that are often overlooked. We will also need to generate new experiences from which we can draw new insights.

Within the culture of cynicism and nihilism that has become widespread in the West, some people believe such talk is naïve. In my experience, however, many people—especially young people—yearn for a more peaceful and just world, want to believe it is possible, and are willing to work for it if they are presented with a meaningful and coherent framework that offers practical opportunities to do so.

The human spirit longs for meaning, purpose, hope, and constructive agency. Cynicism and nihilism are cultivated forms of oppression that perpetuate the status quo by forestalling the exercise of socially transformative agency. Empowering a population to move beyond cynicism and nihilism is, itself, a significant form of activism. It is an important dimension of a radical program to construct a more peaceful, just, and mutually prosperous social reality. My hope is that the line of reasoning laid out in this book contributes, in some small measure, to this end.

Acknowledgements

I am grateful to numerous people who contributed to this project in different ways. First and foremost, many of the central ideas contained in this book evolved through ongoing conversations and collaborations with Todd Smith. Todd also provided detailed and invaluable feedback on the manuscript, as well as ongoing encouragement throughout the process. My mother, Kathy Roesch, who is an excellent editor, read the first complete draft of the manuscript and provided valuable suggestions to make the structure of my argument and the language I employ as accessible as possible. Paul Lample, despite his heavy responsibilities, offered to read the manuscript, provided very helpful feedback on it, and expressed encouragement that was much appreciated. Likewise, Selvi Adaikkalam Zabihi, Michael Welton, David Palmer, Mark Gilman, Tara Raam, Steven Phelps, Shabnam Koirala, and Matt Weinberg all read the manuscript and provided encouragement, along with insightful feedback that enriched, and added nuance to, the line of reasoning laid out in the book. I am also grateful to John Hatcher, publications editor for the Association for Bahá'í Studies, for seeing value in my work and stewarding it through the peer review and editing process. I am similarly indebted to Nilufar Gordon, who stewarded the logistical aspects of the publication process on behalf of the Association, and to Jennifer Janechek, whose copyediting was meticulous and thoughtful. I am thankful to my wife, Anne Marie Karlberg, for her ongoing encouragement and support through the long process that led to the publication of this book. Finally, I am grateful to Bahá'ís around the world who have been generating an ever-expanding body of practical insight and experience at the frontiers of knowledge, from which I have learned so much and without which this book would have been impossible to write. Among other things, the Bahá'í community has shown me what humanity is capable of and given me confidence that we can eventually learn how to live together on this planet in peace, justice, and shared prosperity.

Notes

1. Bahá'u'lláh, *Tablets of Bahá'u'lláh* (Haifa, Israel: Bahá'í World Center, 1982), 171.
2. Farzam Arbab, "The Intellectual Life of the Bahá'í Community," *Journal of Bahá'í Studies* 26, no. 4 (2016): 14.
3. Refer, for example, to Farzam Arbab, "An Inquiry into the Harmony of Science and Religion," in *Religion and Public Discourse in an Age of Transition: Reflections on Bahá'í Thought and Practice*, ed. Geoffrey Cameron and Benjamin Schewel (Waterloo, ON: Wilfrid Laurier University Press, 2018); Farzam Arbab, "Promoting a Discourse on Science, Religion, and Development," in *The Lab, the Temple, and the Market: Reflections at the Intersection of Science, Religion, and Development*, ed. Sharon M. P. Harper (Ottawa: International Development Research Center and Kumarian Press, 2000); Farzam Arbab, "Knowledge and Civilization: Implications for the Community and the Individual," in *The Bahá'í World 1997–1998* (Haifa, Israel: Bahá'í World Center, 1998); Paul Lample, *Revelation and Social Reality: Learning to Translate What Is Written into Reality* (West Palm Beach, FL: Palabra Publications, 2009); Paul Lample, "In Pursuit of Harmony between Science and Religion," *Journal of Bahá'í Studies* 26, no. 4 (2016).
4. Todd Smith, "The Relativity of Social Construction: Towards a Consultative Approach to Understanding Health, Illness and Disease" (PhD diss., University of Toronto, 1997).
5. If we accept religious identification as an indicator of belief in normative or spiritual truths, then more than 80 percent of the world's current population appears to hold such beliefs, according to the Pew Forum on Religion & Public Life. See "The Global Religious Landscape: A Report on the Size and Distribution of the World's Major Religious Groups as of 2010" (Washington, DC: Pew Research Center, 2012), 9.
6. For a sobering and thoroughly documented examination of this need, refer to Paul Hanley, *Eleven* (Victoria, BC, Canada: FriesenPress, 2014).
7. The most influential exponent of this view is arguably Michel

Foucault, whose thinking has impacted virtually every field across the social sciences and humanities in recent decades. Refer, for instance, to *Power/Knowledge* (Brighton, UK: Harvester, 1980) and *The Archaeology of Knowledge* (London: Tavistock, 1972).

8. Refer to discussions of this theme in Thomas Kuhn, *The Structure of Scientific Revolutions* (Chicago: University of Chicago Press, 1970); Imre Lakatos, *The Methodology of Scientific Research Programmes* (Cambridge, UK: Cambridge University Press, 1978).

9. Henry Shue, *Climate Justice: Vulnerability and Protection* (Oxford, UK: Oxford University Press, 2014).

10. Richard Rorty, *Consequences of Pragmatism* (Minneapolis, MN: University of Minnesota Press, 1982), 92.

11. Ibid. Refer also to discussions in Richard Bernstein, *Beyond Objectivism and Relativism: Science, Hermeneutics, and Praxis* (Philadelphia, PA: University of Pennsylvania Press, 1983); Bryan Turner, *Regulating Bodies: Essays in Medical Sociology* (London: Routledge, 1992).

12. Todd Smith and Michael Karlberg, "Articulating a Consultative Epistemology: Toward a Reconciliation of Truth and Relativism," *Journal of Bahá'í Studies* 19, no. 1 (2009).

13. In our article, Smith and I express this as "the dynamic relationship between foundational reality and the social construction of truths" (e.g., p. 81). However, for reasons that will become apparent as the argument of this book unfolds, I now find it important to distinguish the concepts of truth, truth claims, and knowledge. Whereas Smith and I use those concepts in interchangeable ways, I will elaborate upon and employ distinctions between them.

14. Paul Feyerabend, *Against Method*, 3rd ed. (London: Verso, 1993), 269.

15. Helen Longino, *Science as Social Knowledge: Values and Objectivity in Scientific Inquiry* (Princeton, NJ: Princeton University Press, 1990), 222.

16. Specifically, we maintain that while any given paradigmatic lens has the potential to yield valid insights into a phenomenon, some may be more attuned to that phenomenon, or aspects of it, than others. Such paradigms have a greater degree of what we refer to as specified attunement with such aspects. (Specified

attunement is contrasted with three other types of attunement, namely general, anomalous, and fabricated attunement). However, it is not always clear when and to what degree any given paradigm (or perspective, for that matter) has attained specified attunement, which is one of the reasons for pursuing a consultative epistemology.

17. For an even deeper exploration of some of these themes, the reader may want to refer to Smith, "The Relativity of Social Construction."

18. There are, of course, other ways to conceptualize truth. For instance, as discussed in chapter 5, logical positivism attempts to draw a distinction between analytic and synthetic truths. Analytic statements are those that can allegedly be judged true or false based on logical rules and axioms (such as mathematical proofs). Synthetic statements are those that can allegedly be judged true or false based on empirical assessments (such as physics experiments). All other truth claims—including normative, aesthetic, and metaphysical claims—are considered cognitively meaningless by logical positivists and hence unworthy of philosophical or scientific inquiry. This distinction is problematic for reasons discussed in that chapter. For the purpose of the argument at hand, the diction between ontological and contingent truths is sufficient.

19. Smith and Karlberg, "Articulating a Consultative Epistemology."

20. Ibid.

21. Carsten Held, "The Meaning of Complementarity," *Studies in History and Philosophy of Science* 25, no. 6 (1994).

22. Sandra Harding, ed., *The Feminist Standpoint Theory Reader* (New York: Routledge, 2004); Patricia Hill-Collins and Sirma Bilge, *Intersectionality* (Cambridge, UK: Polity Press, 2016).

23. Smith and Karlberg, "Articulating a Consultative Epistemology."

24. Alan Chalmers, *What Is This Thing Called Science?* (New York: Open University Press, 2011); Peter Godfrey-Smith, *Theory and Reality: An Introduction to the Philosophy of Science* (Chicago: University of Chicago Press, 2003).

25. For an insightful discussion of intuition as a form of intellectual perception, see Elijah Chudnoff, *Intuition* (Oxford, UK: Oxford

University Press, 2013).

26. Refer to a discussion of this theme in Smith and Karlberg, "Articulating a Consultative Epistemology."

27. Lample, "In Pursuit of Harmony." For an elaboration of this example, including the science and data behind it, refer to Hanley, *Eleven.*

28. Refer, for example, to Michael Huemer, *Ethical Intuitionism* (New York: Palgrave, 2005); Robert Audi, *The Good in the Right: A Theory of Intuition and Intrinsic Value* (Princeton, NJ: Princeton University Press, 2004); Philip Stratton-Lake, ed., *Ethical Intuitionism: Re-Evaluations* (Oxford, UK: Oxford University Press, 2002); T. K. Seung, *Intuition and Construction: The Foundation of Normative Theory* (New Haven, CT: Yale University Press, 1993).

29. See Kristen Monroe, "Biology, Psychology, Ethics, and Politics: An Innate Moral Sense?," in *On Human Nature: Biology, Psychology, Ethics, Politics, and Religion*, ed. Michel Tibayrenc and Francisco J. Ayala (Cambridge, MA: Academic Press, 2017); Kristen Renwick Monroe, Adam Martin, and Priyanka Ghosh, "Politics and an Innate Moral Sense: Scientific Evidence for an Old Theory?," *Political Research Quarterly* 62, no. 3 (2009); Paul Bloom, *Just Babies: The Origins of Good and Evil* (New York: Broadway Books, 2014); James Wilson, *The Moral Sense* (New York: Free Press, 1993).

30. David E. Nye, *Technology Matters: Questions to Live With* (Cambridge, MA: MIT Press, 2006); Kristin Shrader-Frechette and Laura Westra, eds., *Technology and Values* (New York: Rowman & Littlefield, 1997); Dennis Goulet, *Uncertain Promise: Value Conflicts in Technology Transfer* (New York: Apex Press, 1989).

31. Pertti J. Pelto, *The Snowmobile Revolution: Technology and Social Change in the Arctic* (Long Grove, IL: Waveland Press, 1987). Another classic study of this kind is Lauriston Sharp, "Steel Axes for Stone-Age Australians," *Human Organization* 11, no. 2 (1952). For many other examples of unintended consequences refer to Edward Tenner, *Why Things Bite Back: Technology and the Revenge of Unintended Consequences* (New York: Vintage Books, 1996).

32. Vandana Shiva, *The Violence of the Green Revolution: Third World Agriculture, Ecology, and Politics* (New York: Zed Books, 2000); Vandana Shiva, *Staying Alive: Women, Ecology, and Development* (Berkeley, CA: North Atlantic Books, 2016).

33. See, for example, Jürgen Habermas, *The Structural Transformation*

of the Public Sphere, trans. Thomas Burger and Frederick Lawrence (Cambridge, MA: The MIT Press, 1991); Jürgen Habermas, *Theory of Communicative Action*, trans. Thomas McCarthy (Boston: Beacon Press, 1984); Jürgen Habermas, *Between Facts and Norms: Contributions to a Discourse Theory of Law and Democracy*, trans. William Rehg (Cambridge, MA: The MIT Press, 1996); Craig Calhoun, ed., *Habermas and the Public Sphere* (Cambridge, MA: The MIT Press, 1992); Craig Calhoun, Eduardo Mendieta, and Jonathan VanAntwerpen, eds., *Habermas and Religion* (Cambridge, UK: Polity Press, 2013).

34. John Rawls, *A Theory of Justice*, 2nd ed. (Cambridge, MA: Harvard University Press, 1999); Amartya Sen, *The Idea of Justice* (Cambridge, MA: Harvard University Press, 2009); Christine Korsgaard, *The Sources of Normativity* (Cambridge, MA: Harvard University Press, 1996); Hilary Putnam, *Ethics without Ontology* (Cambridge, MA: Harvard University Press, 2004); Charles Taylor, *A Secular Age* (Cambridge, MA: Harvard University Press, 2007); Kwame Anthony Appiah, *The Honor Code: How Moral Revolutions Happen* (New York: W. W. Norton & Company, 2010); Alasdair MacIntyre, *After Virtue: A Study in Moral Theory*, 3rd ed. (Notre Dame, IN: University of Notre Dame Press, 2007).

35. Foucault, *Power/Knowledge.*

36. Stephen A. Marglin, *The Dismal Science: How Thinking Like an Economist Undermines Community* (Cambridge, MA: Harvard University Press 2010); Karl Polanyi, *The Great Transformation: The Political and Economic Origins of Our Time*, 2nd ed. (Boston: Beacon Press, 2001); Thomas Piketty, *The Economics of Inequality* (Cambridge, MA: Harvard University Press, 2015); Joseph E. Stiglitz, *The Price of Inequality: How Today's Divided Society Endangers Our Future* (New York: W. W. Norton & Company, 2013); Frederic Lee, *A History of Heterodox Economics: Challenging the Mainstream in the Twentieth Century* (New York: Routledge, 2009); Herman E. Daly and Joshua Farley, *Ecological Economics*, 2nd ed. (Washington, DC: Island Press, 2011); Naomi Klein, *This Changes Everything: Capitalism vs. The Climate* (New York: Simon & Schuster, 2015).

37. Paula A. Johnson et al., "Sex-Specific Medical Research: Why Women's Health Can't Wait" (Boston: Brigham and Women's

Hospital, 2014); Alison M. Kim, Candace M. Tinge, and Teresa K. Woodruff, "Sex Bias in Trials and Treatment Must End," *Nature* 465, no. 7299 (2010); Irving Zucker and Annaliese K. Beery, "Males Still Dominate Animal Studies," *Nature* 465, no. 7299 (2010); Anita Holdcroft, "Gender Bias in Research: How Does It Affect Evidence Based Medicine?" *Journal of the Royal Society of Medicine* 100, no. 1 (2007); Kary L. Moss, ed., *Man-Made Medicine: Women's Health, Public Policy, and Reform* (Durham, NC: Duke University Press, 1996).

38. Richard Smith, *The Trouble with Medical Journals* (London: Royal Society of Medicine Press, 2006); Thomas E. Finucane and Chad E. Boult, "Association of Funding and Findings of Pharmaceutical Research at a Meeting of a Medical Professional Society," *The American Journal of Medicine* 117, no. 11 (2004); C. Seth Landefeld, "Commercial Support and Bias in Pharmaceutical Research," *The American Journal of Medicine* 117, no. 11 (2004); Joel Lexchin et al., "Pharmaceutical Industry Sponsorship and Research Outcome and Quality: Systematic Review," *British Medical Journal* 326, no. 7400 (2003); John Yaphea et al., "The Association between Funding by Commercial Interests and Study Outcome in Randomized Controlled Drug Trials," *Family Practice* 18, no. 6 (2001).

39. Stephen R. Gliessman and Eric W. Engles, *Agroecology: The Ecology of Sustainable Food Systems*, 3rd ed. (Boca Raton, FL: CRC Press/Taylor & Francis, 2015); Amy E. Guptill, Denise A. Copelton, and Betsy Lucal, *Food and Society: Principles and Paradoxes* (Cambridge, UK: Polity Press, 2013); Raj Patel, *Stuffed and Starved: The Hidden Battle for the World Food System* (New York: Melville House Publishing, 2012); Kevin Morgan and Jonathan Murdoch, "Organic vs. Conventional Agriculture: Knowledge, Power and Innovation in the Food Chain," *Geoforum* 31, no. 2 (2000); Shiva, *Violence*.

40. Naomi Oreskes and John Krige, eds., *Science and Technology in the Global Cold War* (Boston: The MIT Press, 2014); Michael E. O'Hanlon, *The Science of War* (Princeton, NJ: Princeton University Press, 2009); Stuart W. Leslie, *The Cold War and American Science: The Military-Industrial-Academic Complex at MIT and Stanford*, rev. ed. (New York: Columbia University Press, 1993).

41. Carol P. van Schaik, "Social Learning and Culture in Animals,"

in *Animal Behaviour: Evolution and Mechanisms*, ed. Peter Kappeler (Berlin: Springer, 2010).

42. Merritt Roe Smith and Leo Marx, eds., *Does Technology Drive History?: The Dilemma of Technological Determinism* (Boston: The MIT Press, 1994).

43. Aristotle, *The Nicomachean Ethics*, trans. David Ross (Oxford, UK: Oxford University Press, 1980).

44. Michael Karlberg, "The Power of Discourse and the Discourse of Power: Peace as Discourse Intervention," *International Journal of Peace Studies* 10, no. 1 (2005); Michael Karlberg, *Beyond the Culture of Contest: From Adversarialism to Mutualism in an Age of Interdependence*, George Ronald Bahá'í Studies Series (Oxford, UK: George Ronald, 2004).

45. Discussions of this distinction can be found in numerous sources, including Nancy Hartsock, "Political Change: Two Perspectives on Power," *Quest: A Feminist Quarterly* 1, no. 1 (1974); Lewis Coser, "The Notion of Power: Theoretical Developments," in *Sociological Theory: A Book of Readings*, ed. Lewis Coser and Bernard Rosenberg (New York: Macmillan, 1976); Steven Lukes, ed., *Power, Readings in Social & Political Theory* (New York: New York University Press, 1986); Keith Dowding, *Power* (Buckingham, UK: Open University Press, 1996).

46. Thomas E. Wartenberg, *The Forms of Power: From Domination to Transformation* (Philadelphia, PA: Temple University Press, 1990), 27.

47. Thomas Hobbes, *Leviathan* (Oxford, UK: Oxford University Press, 2012 [1651]); Karl Marx and Friedrich Engels, *The German Ideology*, ed. C. J. Arthur, trans. W. Lough, C. Dutt, and C. P. Magill (London: Lawrence & Wishart, 1967 [1846]); Max Weber, "Domination by Economic Power and by Authority," in *Power (Readings in Social & Political Theory)*, ed. Steven Lukes (New York: New York University Press, 1986).

48. Anthony Giddens, *The Constitution of Society: Outline of the Theory of Structuration* (Cambridge, UK: Polity Press, 2013 [1984]), 256–57.

49. Refer, for example, to Antonio Gramsci, *Selections from the Prison Notebooks of Antonio Gramsci*, ed. Quinton Hoare and Geoffrey N. Smith (New York: International Publishers, 1971); Steven Lukes, *Power: A Radical View*, 2nd ed. (London: Palgrave, 2005).

50. Wartenberg, *Forms of Power.*

51. Lukes, *Power: A Radical View*, 30–31.

52. Foucault, *Power/Knowledge*, 102.

53. Giddens, *The Constitution of Society*, 15, 257.

54. Robin Lakoff, *Language and Woman's Place* (New York: Harper & Row, 1975); Janice Moulton, "A Paradigm of Philosophy: The Adversary Method," in *Discovering Reality: Feminist Perspectives on Epistemology, Metaphysics, Methodology, and Philosophy of Science*, ed. Sandra Harding and Merrill Hintikka (Boston, MA: Kluwer, 1983).

55. Birgit Brock-Utne, *Feminist Perspectives on Peace and Peace Education* (New York: Pergamon Press, 1989); Betty Reardon, *Women and Peace: Feminist Visions of Global Security* (New York: State University of New York Press, 1993).

56. Jean Baker Miller, *Toward a New Psychology of Women*, 2nd ed. (Boston: Beacon Press, 1976); "Colloquium: Women and Power," Stone Center for Developmental Services and Studies Work in Progress, no. 882–01 (1982).

57. Nancy Hartsock, *Money, Sex, and Power: Toward a Feminist Historical Materialism* (New York: Longman, 1983), 253.

58. Kenneth E. Boulding, *Three Faces of Power* (London: SAGE, 1990).

59. For a discussion of "power with," refer to Mary Parker Follett, "Power," in *Dynamic Administration: The Collected Papers of Mary Parker Follett*, ed. Henry C. Metcalf and L. Urwick, *The Early Sociology of Management and Organizations* (New York: Harper, 1942), 72–95.

60. For a discussion of "power against," refer to Dennis H. Wrong, *Power: Its Forms, Bases, and Uses* (New Brunswick, NJ: Transaction Publishers, 1997).

61. For discussions of "balance of power," refer to Peter Blau, *Exchange and Power in Social Life* (New York: John Wiley and Sons, 1964); William A. Gamson, *Power and Discontent* (Homewood, IL: Dorsey Press, 1968).

62. Immanuel Kant, *Groundwork of the Metaphysic of Morals*, trans. Mary Gregor and Jens Timmermann (Cambridge, UK: Cambridge University Press, 2012 [1785]); Rawls, *Theory of Justice.*

63. David Palmer offers a useful way to conceptualize "spiritual principles" as expressions of foundational normative truths. As

Palmer explains, "The concept of 'spiritual principles' provides us with a useful lens through which to think about the contexts in which the spiritual yearning for solidarity can be properly developed and expressed. Bahá'í discourse often discusses the oneness of humankind, justice, the equality of men and women, and environmental stewardship, among others, as 'spiritual principles.' What makes these widely accepted principles specifically spiritual? The term 'spiritual principles' refers in this discourse to a certain set of normative concepts that are expressions of a deeper spiritual reality; as such, they link ontological foundations and practical action. The concept of spiritual principle ties motivation, goals, and action to an ontological foundation that is understood as spiritual. First, it describes an aspect of spiritual reality. Second, it refers to the consciousness of this reality within us, which causes a deep yearning of our soul. Third, it describes an outer social state in which this inner consciousness finds its expression; it thus refers to the motivation and imperative to translate consciousness into social reality. Fourthly, it guides our action in the realization of the inner yearning toward its outer expression." David Palmer, "Religion, Spiritual Principles, and Civil Society," in *Religion and Public Discourse in an Age of Transition: Reflections on Bahá'í Thought and Practice*, ed. Geoffrey Cameron and Benjamin Schewel (Waterloo, ON: Wilfrid Laurier University Press, 2018), 54.

64. Pew Forum on Religion & Public Life, "Global Religious Landscape."
65. Refer, for example, to Arbab, "Inquiry into the Harmony"; Arbab, "Promoting a Discourse"; Lample, *Revelation and Social Reality*.
66. Benjamin Schewel, *Seven Ways of Looking at Religion: The Major Narratives* (New Haven, CT: Yale University Press, 2017).
67. Arbab, "Promoting a Discourse."
68. Chalmers, *What Is This Thing*; Godfrey-Smith, *Theory and Reality*.
69. Karl Popper, *The Logic of Scientific Discovery* (London: Hutchinson, 1975).
70. Paul Weindling, *Victims and Survivors of Nazi Human Experiments: Science and Suffering in the Holocaust* (New York: Bloomsbury Academic, 2015); Susan M. Reverby, *Examining Tuskegee: The*

Infamous Syphilis Study and Its Legacy (Chapel Hill, NC: University of North Carolina Press, 2009).

71. Refer, for example, to Timothy Shah, Alfred Stepan, and Monica Duffy Toft, eds., *Rethinking Religion and World Affairs* (Oxford, UK: Oxford University Press, 2012); Eduardo Mendieta and Jonathan VanAntwerpen, eds., *The Power of Religion in the Public Sphere* (New York: Columbia University Press, 2011); Daniel Philpott, "Has the Study of Global Politics Found Religion?," *Annual Review of Political Science* 12, no. 1 (2009); José Casanova, "Public Religions Revisited," in *Religion: Beyond the Concept*, ed. Hent de Vries (New York: Fordham University Press, 2008); Armando Salvatore, *The Public Sphere: Liberal Modernism, Catholicism, Islam* (New York: Palgrave, 2007); José Casanova, *Public Religions in the Modern World* (Chicago: University of Chicago Press, 1994); Calhoun, Mendieta, and VanAntwerpen, *Habermas and Religion*.

72. See Brian Temple, *Philadelphia Quakers and the Antislavery Movement* (Jefferson, NC: McFarland, 2014); Joerg Rieger and Kwok Pui-lan, *Occupy Religion: Theology of the Multitude* (New York: Rowman & Littlefield, 2012); Susan Berrin, ed., *Sh'ma: A Journal of Jewish Responsibility* (Special Issue: Social Movements), 43 (2012); Fred Kniss and Gene Burns, "Religious Movements," in *The Blackwell Companion to Social Movements*, ed. David Snow, Sarah Soule, and Hanspeter Kriesi (Oxford, UK: Blackwell Publishing, 2011); Helene Slessarev-Jamir, *Prophetic Activism: Progressive Religious Justice Movements in Contemporary America* (New York: New York University Press, 2011); Melissa Snarr, *All You That Labor: Religion and Ethics in the Living Wage Movement* (New York: New York University Press, 2011); Daniel Philpott and Gerard Powers, eds., *Strategies of Peace: Transforming Conflict in a Violent World* (Oxford, UK: Oxford University Press, 2010); David Cortright, *Peace: A History of Movements and Ideas* (Cambridge, UK: Cambridge University Press, 2008); Charles Marsh, *The Beloved Community: How Faith Shapes Social Justice, from the Civil Rights Movement to Today* (New York: Basic Books, 2004); Christopher Queen, *Engaged Buddhism: Buddhist Liberation Movements in Asia* (Albany, NY: State University of New York Press, 1996); Christian Smith, *Disruptive Religion: The Force of Faith in Social Movement Activism* (New York: Routledge, 1996); *The Emergence of Liberation Theology: Radical Religion and Social Movement Theory* (Chicago: University of

Chicago Press, 1991).

73. Lucas Johnston, *Religion and Sustainability: Social Movements and the Politics of Environment* (New York: Routledge, 2014); Richard Bohannon, ed., *Religions and Environments: A Reader in Religion, Nature and Ecology* (Oxford, UK: Bloomsbury Academic, 2014); Clifford Chalmers Cain, ed., *Many Heavens, One Earth: Readings on Religion and the Environment* (Plymouth, UK: Lexington Books, 2013); Roger Gottlieb, ed., *This Sacred Earth: Religion, Nature, Environment*, 2nd ed. (New York: Routledge, 2004).

74. Robert Holmes and Barry Gan, *Nonviolence in Theory and Practice*, 2nd ed. (Long Grove, IL: Waveland Press, 2005); Mark Kurlansky, *Nonviolence: The History of a Dangerous Idea* (New York: Modern Library, 2008); Thomas Merton, *Gandhi on Non-Violence* (New York: New Directions, 1964); Ira Chernus, *American Nonviolence: The History of An Idea* (Maryknoll, NY: Orbis Books, 2004).

75. Refer, for example, to Manav Ratti, *The Postsecular Imagination: Postcolonialism, Religion, and Literature* (New York: Taylor & Francis, 2013); Jürgen Habermas, "Secularism's Crisis of Faith: Notes on Post-Secular Society," *New Perspectives Quarterly* 25 (2008); Taylor, *Secular Age*; Calhoun, Mendieta, and VanAntwerpen, *Habermas and Religion*.

76. Allan Brandt, "Racism and Research: The Case of the Tuskegee Syphilis Study," *The Hastings Center Report* 8, no. 6 (1978).

77. Brent Nongbri, *Before Religion: A History of a Modern Concept* (New Haven, CT: Yale University Press, 2012).

78. Steven M. Wasserstrom, "Islamicate History of Religions?" *History of Religions* 27, no. 4 (1988).

79. Schewel, *Seven Ways*, 112.

80. Ibid., 119.

81. Ibid., 120.

82. Ibid., 121.

83. The Bahá'í Faith is widely recognized as the second most geographically widespread religion after Christianity. See "Worldwide Adherents of All Religions by Six Continental Areas, Mid-2002," in *Encyclopædia Britannica* (2002); Denis MacEoin, "Baha'ism," in *The New Penguin Handbook of Living Religions*, 2nd ed., ed. John Hinnells (New York: Penguin, 2000).

84. Thomas Headland, Kenneth Pike, and Marvin Harris, eds.,

Emics and Etics: The Insider/Outsider Debate (Newbury Park, CA: SAGE, 1990).

85. Bahá'u'lláh, *Gleanings from the Writings of Bahá'u'lláh* (Wilmette, IL: Bahá'í Publishing Committee, 1939), 213.

86. 'Abdu'l-Bahá, *The Secret of Divine Civilization* (Wilmette, IL: US Bahá'í Publishing Trust, 1957), 38.

87. Shoghi Effendi, *The World Order of Bahá'u'lláh* (Wilmette, IL: US Bahá'í Publishing Trust, 1938), 42–43.

88. 'Abdu'l-Bahá, *'Abdu'l-Bahá in London* (London: Bahá'í Publishing Trust, 1982), 19.

89. 'Abdu'l-Bahá, *'Abdu'l-Bahá on Divine Philosophy* (Boston: The Tudor Press, 1918), 26.

90. 'Abdu'l-Bahá, *The Promulgation of Universal Peace* (Wilmette, IL: Bahá'í Publishing Trust, 1982), 126.

91. Ibid., 105–06.

92. Bahá'u'lláh, *The Proclamation of Bahá'u'lláh to the Kings and Leaders of the World* (Haifa, Israel: Bahá'í World Centre, 1978), 119.

93. Ibid., 114.

94. Bahá'u'lláh, *Gleanings*, 215.

95. Bahá'u'lláh, *Tablets of Bahá'u'lláh Revealed after the Kitáb-i-Aqdas* (Haifa, Israel: Bahá'í World Centre, 1982), 220.

96. Bahá'u'lláh, 95.

97. 'Abdu'l-Bahá, *'Abdu'l-Bahá in London*, 28.

98. 'Abdu'l-Bahá, *Promulgation*, 181.

99. Ibid., 124.

100. 'Abdu'l-Bahá, *Paris Talks*, 12th ed. (London: Bahá'í Publishing Trust, 1995), 141.

101. 'Abdu'l-Bahá, *Promulgation*, 103.

102. 'Abdu'l-Bahá, *Paris Talks*, 130–31.

103. Ibid., 147.

104. Shoghi Effendi, Statement to the Special United Nations Committee on Palestine, 1947.

105. The Universal House of Justice, Letter to the World's Religious Leaders, 2002.

106. Ibid., 2.

107. Ibid., 3.

108. Ibid., 3–4.

109. Ibid., 4–5.

110. Ibid., 5.

111. Ibid., 6.

112. Ibid.

113. Ibid.

114. Ibid., 7.

115. Ibid.

116. Lample, *Revelation.*

117. The Universal House of Justice, Letter to the Bahá'ís of the World, January 17, 2003.

118. The Ruhi Institute, *Learning About Growth* (Cali, Colombia: The Ruhi Institute, 1991).

119. The Universal House of Justice, Ridván Message to the Bahá'ís of the World, 1996.

120. Bahá'í World News Service, "Statistics," *Bahá'í World News Service*, Bahá'í International Community, 2018, http://news.bahai.org/media-information/statistics.

121. The Universal House of Justice, Letter to the Conference of the Continental Boards of Counsellors, December 27, 2005.

122. International Teaching Centre, *The Five Year Plan 2011–2016: Summary of Achievements and Learning* (Haifa, Israel: Bahá'í World Centre, May 2017); The International Teaching Centre, *Insights from the Frontiers of Learning* (Haifa, Israel: Bahá'í World Center, 2013).

123. The nature and functions of this institution were outlined by the Universal House of Justice in a document titled *The Institution of the Counsellors* (Haifa, Israel: Bahá'í World Centre, 2001).

124. The Universal House of Justice, Letter to the Bahá'ís of the World, November 9, 2018.

125. See, for example, Soli Shahvar, *The Forgotten Schools: The Bahá'ís and Modern Education in Iran, 1899–1934* (London: Tauris Academic Studies, 2009); Seena Fazel and Minou Foadi, "Bahá'í Health Initiatives in Iran: A Preliminary Survey," in *The Bahá'ís of Iran: Socio-Historical Studies*, ed. Dominic Parviz Brookshaw and Seena Fazel (New York: Routledge, 2008).

126. Bahá'í International Community, *For the Betterment of the World: The Worldwide Bahá'í Community's Approach to Social and Economic Development* (New York: Bahá'í International Community, 2018).

127. Pascal Molineaux, "Strengthening Local Economies and Community Identity: FUNDAEC's Experience," trans. Paul

Hanley, in *The Spirit of Agriculture*, ed. Paul Hanley (Oxford, UK: George Ronald, 2005); Michael Karlberg and Bita Correa, "Development at Systematic Learning and Capacity Building," in *Education, Learning and the Transformation of Development*, ed. Amy Skinner et al. (New York: Routledge, 2016).

128. Shahriar Razavi, "Bahá'í Participation in Public Discourse: Some Considerations Related to History, Concepts, and Approaches," in *Religion and Public Discourse in an Age of Transition: Reflections on Bahá'í Thought and Practice*, ed. Geoffrey Cameron and Benjamin Schewel (Waterloo, ON: Wilfrid Laurier University Press, 2018).

129. Shoghi Effendi, Statement to the Special United Nations Committee on Palestine.

130. The Universal House of Justice, Letter to the World's Religious Leaders, 2002.

131. 'Abdu'l-Bahá, *Promulgation*, 16, 69, 91; 'Abdu'l-Bahá, *Some Answered Questions* (Haifa, Israel: Bahá'í World Centre, 2014), 228–32.

132. 'Abdu'l-Bahá, *Some Answered Questions*, 324.

133. Bahá'u'lláh, *Gleanings*, 249.

134. The Universal House of Justice, Ridván Message to the Bahá'ís of the World, 2010.

135. The Universal House of Justice, Letter to the Bahá'ís of Iran, March 2, 2013.

136. Ibid.

137. The Universal House of Justice, Ridván Message to the Bahá'ís of the World, 2010.

138. Refer to examples discussed in International Teaching Centre, *Five Year Plan 2011–2016*.

139. Arjen Bolhuis, "Bahá'í World Statistics August 2001 CE," (Haifa, Israel: Department of Statistics, Bahá'í World Centre, 2001).

140. Bahá'u'lláh, *Gleanings*, 92.

141. Bahá'u'lláh, *Epistle to the Son of the Wolf* (Wilmette, IL: Bahá'í Publishing Trust, 1991), 122.

142. The Universal House of Justice, Ridván Message to the Bahá'ís of the World (2008).

143. Bahá'u'lláh, *Epistle*, 30.

144. Friedrich Lange, *The History of Materialism and a Critique of Its*

Current Significance, trans. Ernest Chester Thomas (New York: The Humanities Press, 1950 [1866]); Richard Vitzthum, *Materialism: An Affirmative History and Definition* (Amherst, NY: Prometheus Books, 1995); Paul Moser, ed. *Contemporary Materialism: A Reader* (New York: Routledge, 1995).

145. Jeffrey Poland, *Physicalism: The Philosophical Foundations* (Oxford, UK: Clarendon, 1994); Daniel Stoljar, *Physicalism* (New York: Routledge, 2010).

146. Peter Harrison, *Narratives of Secularization* (New York: Routledge, 2017); Owen Chadwick, *The Secularization of the European Mind in the Nineteenth Century* (Cambridge, UK: Cambridge University Press, 1975); Michael Warner, Jonathan VanAntwerpen, and Craig Calhoun, eds., *Varieties of Secularism in a Secular Age* (Cambridge, MA: Harvard University Press, 2010).

147. Rob Warner, *Secularization and Its Discontents* (London: Continuum Books); Habermas, "Secularism's Crisis of Faith."

148. Mendieta and VanAntwerpen, *Power of Religion*; Calhoun, Mendieta, and VanAntwerpen, *Habermas and Religion*; Shah, Stepan, and Toft, *Rethinking Religion*; Casanova, *Public Religions*; Salvatore, *Public Sphere*.

149. Thomas Nagel, *The View from Nowhere* (Oxford, UK: Oxford University Press, 1986).

150. Ibid.

151. Ibid.

152. Ibid., 5.

153. Ibid., 9.

154. Ibid., 14.

155. Ibid., 7–8.

156. Ibid., 8.

157. Ibid., 52.

158. Thomas Nagel, *Mind and Cosmos: Why the Materialist Neo-Darwinian Conception of Nature Is Almost Certainly False* (Oxford, UK: Oxford University Press, 2012), 97–98.

159. Ibid., 106.

160. Ibid., 108.

161. Nagel, *View from Nowhere*, 139.

162. Ibid., 185.

163. Ibid., 143.

164. Nagel, *Mind and Cosmos*. See discussion in chapter 5.

165. For a history and assessment of this fact/value dichotomy, refer to Hilary Putnam, *The Collapse of the Fact/Value Dichotomy* (Cambridge, MA: Harvard University Press, 2002).
166. The term "error theory" was coined by its most influential advocate, John Mackie. See John Mackie, *Ethics: Inventing Right and Wrong* (London: Penguin Books, 1977).
167. Richard Bernstein, *The Pragmatic Turn* (Cambridge, UK: Polity Press, 2010), xi.
168. Otto Neurath, translated and quoted in Nancy Cartright, *Otto Neurath: Philosophy between Science and Politics* (Cambridge, UK: Cambridge University Press, 2008), 191.
169. John Dewey, *Democracy and Education* (New York: The Free Press, 1966); John Dewey, *Liberalism and Social Action* (New York: Putnam, 1935).
170. See John Dewey, *Reconstruction in Philosophy* (London: University of London Press, 1921); John Dewey, *Experience and Nature* (Chicago: Open Court Pub. Co., 1925); John Dewey, *The Quest for Certainty: A Study of the Relation of Knowledge and Action: Gifford Lectures 1929* (New York: Putnam, 1960); John Dewey, *How We Think: A Restatement of the Relation of Reflective Thinking to the Educative Process* (Boston: Houghton Mifflin, 1998).
171. Putnam, *Collapse.*
172. Ibid., 33.
173. Ibid.
174. Ibid.
175. Ibid., 3.
176. Putnam, *Ethics without Ontology.*
177. Jürgen Habermas, *Postmetaphysical Thinking*, trans. W. M. Hohengarten (Cambridge, MA: The MIT Press, 1992).
178. Jürgen Habermas, *Communication and the Evolution of Society*, trans. Thomas McCarthy (Boston: Beacon Press, 1979).
179. Habermas, *Theory of Communicative Action*; Jürgen Habermas, "Some Further Clarifications of the Concept of Communicative Rationality," in *On the Pragmatics of Communication*, ed. Maeve Cooke (Cambridge, MA: The MIT Press, 1998).
180. Seyla Benhabib, "Toward a Deliberative Model of Democratic Legitimacy," in *Democracy and Difference: Contesting the Boundaries of the Political*, ed. Seyla Benhabib (Princeton, NJ: Princeton University Press, 1996); Seyla Benhabib, "Models of Public

Space: Hannah Arendt, the Liberal Tradition, and Jürgen Habermas," in *Habermas and the Public Sphere*, ed. Craig Calhoun (Cambridge, MA: The MIT Press, 1992).

181. For instance, his earliest and best-known work does precisely this. See Habermas, *Structural Transformation*.

182. Refer, for example, to the collection of essays in Calhoun, *Habermas and the Public Sphere*. See especially Nancy Fraser, "Rethinking the Public Sphere: A Contribution to the Critique of Actually Existing Democracy," in *Habermas and the Public Sphere*, ed. Craig Calhoun (Cambridge, MA: The MIT Press, 1992).

183. Maeve Cooke, "Argumentation and Transformation," Argumentation 16 (2002). Refer also to "Socio-Cultural Learning as a 'Transcendental Fact': Habermas's Postmetaphysical Perspective," *International Journal of Philosophal Studies* 9, no. 3 (2001).

184. Cooke, "Argumentation and Transformation," 90.

185. Ibid., 95.

186. Ibid.

187. Ibid., 96. Note: Cooke's in-text citations have been removed from this quote for clarity.

188. Ibid., 90.

189. Refer, for example, to Bonnie Honig, *Political Theory and the Displacement of Politics* (Ithaca, NY: Cornell University Press, 1993); William E. Connolly, *Pluralism* (Durham, NC: Duke University Press, 2005); John Gray, *Enlightenment's Wake: Politics and Culture at the Close of the Modern Age* (London: Routledge, 1996); Ewa Plonowska Ziarek, *An Ethic of Dissensus: Postmodernity, Feminism, and the Politics of Radical Democracy* (Stanford, CA: Stanford University Press, 2001).

190. Hannah Arendt, "Thoughts on Politics and Revolution," in *Crisis of the Republic* (New York: Harvest Books, 1969).

191. Carl Schmitt, *The Concept of the Political*, trans. George Schwab (Chicago: University of Chicago Press, 2007 [1932]).

192. Ernesto Laclau and Chantal Mouffe, *Hegemony and Socialist Strategy* (London: Verso, 1983).

193. Chantal Mouffe, *Agonistics: Thinking the World Politically* (London: Verso, 2013).

194. Ibid., 15.

195. Ibid.

196. Mouffe's theory of agonistic pluralism was initially developed and elaborated in *The Democratic Paradox* (New York: Verso, 2000); Chantal Mouffe, *The Return of the Political* (New York: Verso, 2005).

197. Mouffe, *Democratic Paradox*.

198. Mouffe, *Agonistics*, 7.

199. Ibid., 8.

200. Ibid., 9.

201. Connolly, *Pluralism*.

202. Mouffe, *Agonistics*.

203. Karlberg, *Beyond the Culture of Contest*.

204. Arash Abizadeh, "Does Collective Identity Presuppose an Other? On the Alleged Incoherence of Global Solidarity," *American Political Science Review* 99, no. 1 (2005).

205. Ibid., 58.

206. Ibid., 58–59.

207. Kristen Monroe, *The Heart of Altruism: Perceptions of a Common Humanity* (Princeton, NJ: Princeton University Press, 1998).

208. Ibid., 6.

209. Ibid., 198.

210. Ibid., 206.

211. Ibid., 198.

212. Kristen Monroe, *The Hand of Compassion: Portraits of Moral Choice During the Holocaust* (Princeton, NJ: Princeton University Press, 2004); Kristen Monroe, *Ethics in an Age of Terror and Genocide: Identity and Moral Choice* (Princeton, NJ: Princeton University Press, 2012).

213. Refer, for example, to the International Social Ontology Society, the European Network for the Philosophy of the Social Sciences, and the Philosophy of Social Science Roundtable, along with the Journal of Social Ontology and the Philosophy of the Social Sciences journal.

214. Roy Bhaskar, *A Realist Theory of Science* (Leeds, UK: Leeds Books, 1975); Roy Bhaskar, *The Possibility of Naturalism: A Philosophical Critique of the Contemporary Human Sciences* (Brighton, UK: Harvester, 1979).

215. Bhaskar, Realist Theory.

216. Margaret Archer, *The Relational Subject* (Cambridge, UK: Cambridge University Press, 2015); Philip Gorski, "Beyond

the Fact-Value Distinction: Ethical Naturalism and the Social Sciences," *Society* 50 (2013); Andrew Sayer, *Why Things Matter to People: Social Science, Values and Ethical Life* (Cambridge, UK: Cambridge University Press, 2011); Christian Smith, *What Is a Person?: Rethinking Humanity, Social Life, and the Moral Good from the Person Up* (Chicago: University of Chicago Press, 2010); Christian Smith, *To Flourish or Destruct: A Personalist Theory of Human Goods, Motivations, Failure, and Evil* (Chicago: University of Chicago Press, 2015).

217. Plato, *Republic*, trans. Robin Waterfield (Oxford, UK: Oxford University Press, 1993).

218. Seung, *Intuition.*

219. Ibid., xi.

220. Ibid., xiv.

221. Ibid., xii, 194–99.

222. Ibid., xiii.

223. Ibid., 69–70, 205.

224. Ibid., 209–10.

225. The Platonic Cave is an allegory employed in Plato's *Republic*. In the cave are inmates who have been chained their entire lives so they can see only shadows on the cave wall, created by objects passing in front of a fire behind them. They give names to these shadows, which they mistake for reality itself, and they don't desire to leave the cave because it is all they have every known.

226. Seung, *Intuition*, 210.

227. Ibid., 211.

228. See Palmer, "Religion."

229. Aristotle, *Metaphysics* (Indianapolis, IN: Hackett Publishing, 2016); Monte Johnson, *Aristotle on Teleology* (Oxford, UK: Oxford University Press, 2005); Mariska Leunissen, *Explanation and Teleology in Aristotle's Science of Nature* (Cambridge, UK: Cambridge University Press, 2010).

230. Aristotle, *Nicomachean Ethics.*

231. Nagel, *Mind and Cosmos*, 71.

232. Ibid., 74.

233. Ibid., 84.

234. Ibid., 85.

235. Ibid., 86.

236. Ibid., 91.

237. Ibid., 91–92.

238. Ibid., 106.

239. Ibid., 117–18.

240. Ibid., 121.

241. Ibid., 112–13.

242. Ibid., 127.

243. 'Abdu'l-Bahá, *Some Answered Questions*, 229.

244. 'Abdu'l-Bahá, *Paris Talks*, 71.

245. 'Abdu'l-Bahá, *Promulgation*, 359.

246. Ibid., 126.

247. 'Abdu'l-Bahá, *Paris Talks*, 88.

248. 'Abdu'l-Bahá, *Promulgation*, 39.

249. Bahá'u'lláh, *Gleanings*, 155.

250. 'Abdu'l-Bahá, *Promulgation*, 69.

251. 'Abdu'l-Bahá, *Divine Philosophy*, 123.

252. 'Abdu'l-Bahá, *Selections from the Writings of 'Abdu'l-Bahá* (Haifa, Israel: Bahá'í World Centre, 1978), 120.

253. 'Abdu'l-Bahá, *Some Answered Questions*, 232.

254. 'Abdu'l-Bahá, *Promulgation*, 349.

255. 'Abdu'l-Bahá, *Some Answered Questions*, 208.

256. Ibid., 212.

257. 'Abdu'l-Bahá, *Promulgation*, 41.

258. Ibid., 260.

259. Ibid., 465.

260. 'Abdu'l-Bahá, *Paris Talks*, 60.

261. 'Abdu'l-Bahá, *Promulgation*, 359.

262. Ibid., 175.

263. 'Abdu'l-Bahá, *Paris Talks*, 131.

264. Ibid., 144.

265. Ibid., 145.

266. 'Abdu'l-Bahá, *Some Answered Questions*, 232–33.

267. Refer, for example, to Norman Doidge, *The Brain That Changes Itself* (London: Penguin, 2007).

268. Shoghi Effendi, *Arohanui: Letters to New Zealand* (Fiji Islands: Bahá'í Publishing Trust of Suva, 1982 [1946]), 89.

269. Bahá'u'lláh, *Gleanings*, 213.

270. The Universal House of Justice, "The Prosperity of Humankind" (Haifa, Israel: Office of Public Information, 1995), Section I.

271. Refer, for instance, to Max Horkheimer, "The Latest Attack on Metaphysics," in *Critical Theory: Selected Essays* (New York: Continuum Publishing, 2002 [1937]); Theodor Adorno et al., *The Positivist Dispute in German Sociology* (London: Heinemann, 1976).

272. Cooke, "Argumentation and Transformation."

273. Sara Kindon, Rachel Pain, and Mike Kesby, eds., *Participatory Action Research Approaches and Methods: Connecting People, Participation and Place* (New York: Routledge, 2007); William Foote Whyte, ed., *Participatory Action Research* (London: SAGE, 1991).

274. For insightful discussions of Gandhi's deep religious beliefs and commitments, refer to Ira Chernus, "Mahatma Gandhi," in *American Nonviolence: The History of an Idea* (Marykoll, NY: Orbis Books, 2004); Cortright, *Peace*, 211–32.

275. Mohandas Gandhi, *Non-Violent Resistance* (Satyagraha) (Mineola, NY: Dover, 2001).

276. Mohandas Gandhi, *Satyagraha in South Africa*, trans. Valji Govindji Desai (Ahmedabad, India: Navajivan Publishing House, 1954), 109–10.

277. Mohandas Gandhi, *Non-Violent Resistance*, 3.

278. Quoted in E. Stanley Jones, *Gandhi: Portrayal of a Friend* (Nashville, TN: Abingdon Press, 1948), 82.

279. Mohandas Gandhi, "My Faith in Nonviolence," in *The Power of Nonviolence: Writings by Advocates of Peace* (Boston: Beacon Press, 2002 [1930]), 46.

280. Mohandas Gandhi, "An Appeal to the Nation (17-7-1924)," in *The Collected Works of Mahatma Gandhi* (New Delhi, India: GandhiServe Foundation, 1999), 28, 310.

281. Mohandas Gandhi, *The Story of My Experiments with Truth* (New York: Dover Publications, 1983 [1948]).

282. Erica Chenoweth and Maria Stephan, *Why Civil Resistance Works: The Strategic Logic of Nonviolent Conflict* (New York: Columbia University Press, 2011); Gene Sharp, *Waging Nonviolent Struggle: 20th Century Practice and 21st Century Potential* (Boston: Porter Sargent Publishers, 2005).

283. Sharp, *Waging Nonviolent Struggle*; Gene Sharp, *The Politics of Nonviolent Action* (Boston: Extending Horizons Books, 1973).

284. Chenoweth and Stephan, *Why Civil Resistance Works*.

285. Mohandas Gandhi, "Hind Swaraj," in *Gandhi: 'Hind Swaraj' and*

Other Writings, ed. Anthony Parel (Cambridge, UK: Cambridge University Press, 1997 [1909]); Anthony Parel, *Pax Gandhiana: The Political Philosophy of Mahatma Gandhi* (Oxford, UK: Oxford University Press, 2016).

286. Mohandas Gandhi, *Constructive Program: Its Meaning and Place* (Ahmedabad, India: Navajivan Publishing House, 1945).

287. Ibid., 14.

288. Ibid., 21.

289. Mohandas Gandhi, "My Notes (30-8-1925)," in *The Collected Works of Mahatma Gandhi*, vol. 32 (New Delhi, India: GandhiServe Foundation, 1999), 362–63.

290. Gandhi, *Constructive Program*, 27–28.

291. Ibid., 28–29.

292. Karuna Mantena, "Gandhi and the Means-Ends Question in Politics," *Occasional Papers of the School of Social Science*, Yale 46 (2012); Stellan Vinthagen, *A Theory of Nonviolent Action: How Civil Resistance Works* (London: Zed Books, 2015); Majken Jul Sørensen, "Constructive Resistance: Conceptualising and Mapping the Terrain," *Journal of Resistance Studies* 2, no. 1 (2016); Kurt Schock, *Civil Resistance Today* (Cambridge, UK: Polity Press, 2015); Sean Chabot and Stellan Vinthagen, "Decolonizing Civil Resistance," *Mobilization: An International Quarterly* 20, no. 4 (2015); Mark Mattaini, *Stategic Nonviolent Power: The Science of Satyagraha* (Edmonton, AB, Canada: Athabasca University Press, 2013).

293. Carl Boggs, "Revolutionary Process, Political Strategy, and the Dilemma of Power," *Theory & Society* 4, no. 3 (1977).

294. See also Sheila Rowbotham, "The Women's Movement and Organizing for Socialism," in *Beyond the Fragments: Feminism and the Making of Socialism*, ed. Sheila Rowbotham, Lynne Segal, and Hilary Wainwright (London: Merlin Press, 1979); Wini Breines, *Community Organization in the New Left: 1962–1968: The Great Refusal* (New Brunswick, NJ: Rutgers University Press, 1989).

295. Chabot and Vinthagen, "Decolonizing Civil Resistance."

296. Sørensen, "Constructive Resistance."

297. Karlberg, *Beyond the Culture of Contest*.

298. Michael Karlberg, "The Paradox of Protest in a Culture of Contest," *Peace and Change* 28, no. 3 (2003).

299. Michael Karlberg, "Constructive Resilience: The Bahá'í

Response to Oppression," *Peace & Change* 35, no. 2 (2010).

300. Ibid.

301. Ibid.

302. The phrase "constructive resilience" originates in letters from the Universal House of Justice. Refer, for example, to The Universal House of Justice, To the Bahá'í Students Deprived of Access to Higher Education in Iran, September 9, 2007; To the Believers in the Cradle of the Faith, March 21, 2011; Letter to an Individual Bahá'í in the United States, February 4, 2018.

303. Schock, "Practice and Study," 283.

304. Tim Kasser, *The High Price of Materialism* (Cambridge, MA: MIT Press, 2002); Abdu'l-Missagh Ghadirian, *Materialism: Moral and Social Consequences* (Oxford, UK: George Ronald, 2010).

Bibliography

'Abdu'l-Bahá. *'Abdu'l-Bahá in London*. London: Bahá'í Publishing Trust, 1982.

———. *'Abdu'l-Bahá on Divine Philosophy*. Boston: The Tudor Press, 1918.

———. *Paris Talks*. 12th ed. London: Bahá'í Publishing Trust, 1995.

———. *The Promulgation of Universal Peace*. Wilmette, IL: Bahá'í Publishing Trust, 1982.

———. *Secret of Divine Civilization*. Wilmette, IL: US Bahá'í Publishing Trust, 1957.

———. *Selections from the Writings of 'Abdu'l-Bahá*. Haifa, Israel: Bahá'í World Centre, 1978.

———. *Some Answered Questions*. Newly revised ed. Haifa, Israel: Bahá'í World Center, 2014.

Abizadeh, Arash. "Does Collective Identity Presuppose an Other? On the Alleged Incoherence of Global Solidarity." *American Political Science Review* 99, no. 1 (2005): 45–60.

Adorno, Theodor, Hans Albert, Ralf Dahrendorf, Jürgen Habermas, Harald Pilot, and Karl Popper. *The Positivist Dispute in German Sociology*. London: Heinemann, 1976.

Appiah, Kwame Anthony. *The Honor Code: How Moral Revolutions Happen*. New York: W. W. Norton & Company, 2010.

Arbab, Farzam. "An Inquiry into the Harmony of Science and Religion." In *Religion and Public Discourse in an Age of Transitoin: Reflections on Bahá'í Thought and Practice*, edited by Geoffrey Cameron and Benjamin Schewel, 131–62. Waterloo, ON: Wilfrid Laurier University Press, 2018.

———. "The Intellectual Life of the Bahá'í Community." *Journal of Bahá'í Studies* 26, no. 4 (2016): 9–21.

———. "Knowledge and Civilization: Implications for the Community and the Individual." In *The Bahá'í World 1997–1998*, 157–78. Haifa, Israel: Bahá'í World Center, 1998.

———. "Promoting a Discourse on Science, Religion, and Development." In *The Lab, the Temple, and the Market: Reflections at the Intersection of Science, Religion, and Development*, edited by Sharon M. P. Harper, 149–237. Ottawa, Canada: International Development Research Center and Kumarian Press, 2000.

Archer, Margaret. *The Relational Subject*. Cambridge, UK: Cambridge University Press, 2015.

Arendt, Hannah. "Thoughts on Politics and Revolution." In *Crisis of the Republic*, 199–234. New York: Harvest Books, 1969.

Aristotle. *Metaphysics*. Indianapolis, IN: Hackett Publishing, 2016.

———. *The Nicomachean Ethics*. Translated by David Ross. Oxford, UK: Oxford University Press, 1980.

Audi, Robert. *The Good in the Right: A Theory of Intuition and Intrinsic Value*. Princeton, NJ: Princeton University Press, 2004.

Bahá'í International Community. *For the Betterment of the World: The Worldwide Bahá'í Community's Approach to Social and Economic Development*. New York: Bahá'í International Community, 2018.

———. "The Prosperity of Humankind." Haifa, Israel: Office of Public Information, 1995.

Bahá'í World News Service. "Statistics." *Bahá'í World News Service*. Bahá'í International Community, 2018. http://news.bahai.org/media-information/statistics.

Bahá'u'lláh. *Epistle to the Son of the Wolf*. Wilmette, IL: Bahá'í Publishing Trust, 1991.

———. *Gleanings from the Writings of Bahá'u'lláh*. Wilmette, IL: Bahá'í Publishing Committee, 1939.

———. *The Proclamation of Bahá'u'lláh to the Kings and Leaders of the World*. 1967. Haifa, Israel: Bahá'í World Centre, 1978.

———. *Tablets of Bahá'u'lláh*. Haifa, Israel: Bahá'í World Center, 1982.

Benhabib, Seyla. "Models of Public Space: Hannah Arendt, the Liberal Tradition, and Jürgen Habermas." In *Habermas and the Public Sphere*, edited by Craig Calhoun, 73–98. Cambridge, MA: The MIT Press, 1992.

———. "Toward a Deliberative Model of Democratic Legitimacy." In *Democracy and Difference: Contesting the Boundaries of the Political*, edited by Seyla Benhabib, 67–94. Princeton, NJ: Princeton University Press, 1996.

Bernstein, Richard. *Beyond Objectivism and Relativism: Science, Hermeneutics, and Praxis*. Philadelphia, PA: University of

Pennsylvania Press, 1983.

———. *The Pragmatic Turn*. Cambridge, UK: Polity Press, 2010.

Berrin, Susan, ed. *Sh'ma: A Journal of Jewish Responsibility* (Special Issue: Social Movements), 43 (2012).

Bhaskar, Roy. *The Possibility of Naturalism: A Philosophical Critique of the Contemporary Human Sciences*. Brighton, UK: Harvester, 1979.

———. *A Realist Theory of Science*. Leeds, UK: Leeds Books, 1975.

Blau, Peter. *Exchange and Power in Social Life*. New York: John Wiley and Sons, 1964.

Bloom, Paul. *Just Babies: The Origins of Good and Evil*. New York: Broadway Books, 2014.

Boggs, Carl. "Revolutionary Process, Political Strategy, and the Dilemma of Power." *Theory & Society* 4, no. 3 (1977): 359–93.

Bohannon, Richard, ed. *Religions and Environments: A Reader in Religion, Nature and Ecology*. Oxford, UK: Bloomsbury Academic, 2014.

Bolhuis, Arjen. "Bahá'í World Statistics August 2001 CE." Haifa, Israel: Department of Statistics, Bahá'í World Centre, 2001.

Boulding, Kenneth E. *Three Faces of Power*. London: SAGE, 1990.

Brandt, Allan. "Racism and Research: The Case of the Tuskegee Syphilis Study." *The Hastings Center Report* 8, no. 6 (1978): 21–29.

Breines, Wini. *Community Organization in the New Left: 1962–1968: The Great Refusal*. New Brunswick, NJ: Rutgers University Press, 1989.

Brock-Utne, Birgit. *Feminist Perspectives on Peace and Peace Education*. New York: Pergamon Press, 1989.

Cain, Clifford Chalmers, ed. *Many Heavens, One Earth: Readings on Religion and the Environment*. Plymouth, UK: Lexington Books, 2013.

Calhoun, Craig, ed. *Habermas and the Public Sphere*. Cambridge, MA: The MIT Press, 1992.

Calhoun, Craig, Eduardo Mendieta, and Jonathan VanAntwerpen, eds. *Habermas and Religion*. Cambridge, UK: Polity Press, 2013.

Cartright, Nancy. *Otto Neurath: Philosophy between Science and Politics*. Cambridge, UK: Cambridge University Press, 2008.

Casanova, José. *Public Religions in the Modern World*. Chicago: University of Chicago Press, 1994.

———. "Public Religions Revisited." In *Religion: Beyond the Concept*, edited by Hent de Vries, 101–19. New York: Fordham University

Press, 2008.

Chabot, Sean, and Stellan Vinthagen. "Decolonizing Civil Resistance." *Mobilization: An International Quarterly* 20, no. 4 (2015): 517–32.

Chadwick, Owen. *The Secularization of the European Mind in the Nineteenth Century.* Cambridge, UK: Cambridge University Press, 1975.

Chalmers, Alan. *What Is This Thing Called Science?* New York: Open University Press, 2011.

Chenoweth, Erica, and Maria Stephan. *Why Civil Resistance Works: The Strategic Logic of Nonviolent Conflict.* New York: Columbia University Press, 2011.

Chernus, Ira. *American Nonviolence: The History of an Idea.* Marykoll, NY: Orbis Books, 2004.

Chudnoff, Elijah. *Intuition.* Oxford, UK: Oxford University Press, 2013.

Connolly, William E. *Pluralism.* Durham, NC: Duke University Press, 2005.

Cooke, Maeve. "Argumentation and Transformation." *Argumentation* 16 (2002): 79–108.

———. "Socio-Cultural Learning as a 'Transcendental Fact': Habermas's Postmetaphysical Perspective." *International Journal of Philosophal Studies* 9, no. 3 (2001): 63–83.

Cortright, David. *Peace: A History of Movements and Ideas.* Cambridge, UK: Cambridge University Press, 2008.

Coser, Lewis. "The Notion of Power: Theoretical Developments." In *Sociological Theory: A Book of Readings*, edited by Lewis Coser and Bernard Rosenberg, 150–61. New York: Macmillan, 1976.

Daly, Herman E., and Joshua Farley. *Ecological Economics.* 2nd ed. Washington, DC: Island Press, 2011.

Dewey, John. *Democracy and Education.* New York: The Free Press, 1966.

———. *Experience and Nature.* Chicago: Open Court Pub. Co., 1925.

———. *How We Think: A Restatement of the Relation of Reflective Thinking to the Educative Process.* Boston: Houghton Mifflin, 1998.

———. *Liberalism and Social Action.* New York: Putnam, 1935.

———. *The Quest for Certainty: A Study of the Relation of Knowledge and Action: Gifford Lectures 1929.* New York: Putnam, 1960.

———. *Reconstruction in Philosophy.* London: University of London

Press, 1921.

Doidge, Norman. *The Brain That Changes Itself.* London: Penguin, 2007.

Dowding, Keith. *Power.* Buckingham, UK: Open University Press, 1996.

Fazel, Seena, and Minou Foadi. "Bahá'í Health Initiatives in Iran: A Preliminary Survey." In *The Bahá'ís of Iran: Socio-Historical Studies*, edited by Dominic Parviz Brookshaw and Seena Fazel, 122–40. New York: Routledge, 2008.

Feyerabend, Paul. *Against Method.* 3rd ed. London: Verso, 1993.

Finucane, Thomas E., and Chad E. Boult. "Association of Funding and Findings of Pharmaceutical Research at a Meeting of a Medical Professional Society." *The American Journal of Medicine* 117, no. 11 (2004): 842–45.

Follett, Mary Parker. "Power." In *Dynamic Administration*, edited by Henry C. Metcalf and L. Urwick, 72–95. The Early Sociology of Management and Organizations. New York: Harper, 1942.

Foucault, Michel. *The Archaeology of Knowledge.* London: Tavistock, 1972.

———. *Power/Knowledge.* Brighton, UK: Harvester, 1980.

Fraser, Nancy. "Rethinking the Public Sphere: A Contribution to the Critique of Actually Existing Democracy." In *Habermas and the Public Sphere*, edited by Craig Calhoun, 109–42. Cambridge, MA: The MIT Press, 1992.

Gamson, William A. *Power and Discontent.* Homewood, IL: Dorsey Press, 1968.

Gandhi, Mohandas. "An Appeal to the Nation (17-7-1924)." In *The Collected Works of Mahatma Gandhi.* New Delhi, India: GandhiServe Foundation, 1999.

———. *Constructive Program: Its Meaning and Place.* Ahmedabad, India: Navajivan Publishing House, 1945.

———. "Hind Swaraj." In *Gandhi: 'Hind Swaraj' and Other Writings*, edited by Anthony Parel. 1909. Cambridge, UK: Cambridge University Press, 1997.

———. "My Faith in Nonviolence." In *The Power of Nonviolence: Writings by Advocates of Peace*, 45–46. 1930. Boston: Beacon Press, 2002.

———. "My Notes (30-8-1925)." In *The Collected Works of Mahatma Gandhi.* New Delhi, India: GandhiServe Foundation, 1999.

————. *Non-Violent Resistance (Satyagraha)*. Mineola, NY: Dover, 2001.

————. *Satyagraha in South Africa*. Translated by Valji Govindji Desai. Ahmedabad, India: Navajivan Publishing House, 1954.

————. *The Story of My Experiments with Truth*. 1948. New York: Dover Publications, 1983.

Ghadirian, Abdu'l-Missagh. *Materialism: Moral and Social Consequences*. Oxford, UK: George Ronald, 2010.

Giddens, Anthony. *The Constitution of Society: Outline of the Theory of Structuration*. Cambridge, UK: Polity Press, 1984.

Gliessman, Stephen R., and Eric W. Engles. *Agroecology: The Ecology of Sustainable Food Systems*. 3rd ed. Boca Raton, FL: CRC Press, 2015.

Godfrey-Smith, Peter. *Theory and Reality: An Introduction to the Philosophy of Science*. Chicago: University of Chicago Press, 2003.

Gorski, Philip. "Beyond the Fact-Value Distinction: Ethical Naturalism and the Social Sciences." *Society* 50 (2013): 543–53.

Gottlieb, Roger, ed. *This Sacred Earth: Religion, Nature, Environment*. 2nd ed. New York: Routledge, 2004.

Goulet, Dennis. *Uncertain Promise: Value Conflicts in Technology Transfer*. New York: Apex Press, 1989.

Gramsci, Antonio. *Selections from the Prison Notebooks of Antonio Gramsci*. Edited by Quinton Hoare and Geoffrey N. Smith. New York: International Publishers, 1971.

Gray, John. *Enlightenment's Wake: Politics and Culture at the Close of the Modern Age*. London: Routledge, 1996.

Guptill, Amy E., Denise A. Copelton, and Betsy Lucal. *Food and Society: Principles and Paradoxes*. Cambridge, UK: Polity Press, 2013.

Habermas, Jürgen. *Between Facts and Norms: Contributions to a Discourse Theory of Law and Democracy*. Translated by William Rehg. Cambridge, MA: The MIT Press, 1996.

————. *Communication and the Evolution of Society*. Translated by Thomas McCarthy. Boston: Beacon Press, 1979.

————. *Postmetaphysical Thinking*. Translated by W. M. Hohengarten. Cambridge, MA: The MIT Press, 1992.

————. "Secularism's Crisis of Faith: Notes on Post-Secular Society." *New Perspectives Quarterly* 25 (2008): 17–19.

————. "Some Further Clarifications of the Concept of Communicative Rationality." In *On the Pragmatics of Communication*, edited by Maeve Cooke. Cambridge, MA: The MIT Press, 1998.

————. *The Structural Transformation of the Public Sphere.* Translated by Thomas Burger and Frederick Lawrence. Cambridge, MA: The MIT Press, 1991.

————. *Theory of Communicative Action.* Translated by Thomas McCarthy. Boston: Beacon Press, 1984.

Hanley, Paul. *Eleven.* Victoria, BC, Canada: FriesenPress, 2014.

Harding, Sandra, ed. *The Feminist Standpoint Theory Reader.* New York: Routledge, 2004.

Harrison, Peter. *Narratives of Secularization.* New York: Routledge, 2017.

Hartsock, Nancy. *Money, Sex, and Power: Toward a Feminist Historical Materialism.* New York: Longman, 1983.

————. "Political Change: Two Perspectives on Power." *Quest: A Feminist Quarterly* 1, no. 1 (1974): 10–25.

Headland, Thomas, Kenneth Pike, and Marvin Harris, eds. *Emics and Etics: The Insider/ Outsider Debate.* Newbury Park, CA: SAGE, 1990.

Held, Carsten. "The Meaning of Complementarity." *Studies in History and Philosophy of Science* 25, no. 6 (1994): 871–93.

Hill-Collins, Patricia, and Sirma Bilge. *Intersectionality.* Cambridge, UK: Polity Press, 2016.

Hobbes, Thomas. *Leviathan.* 1651. Oxford, UK: Oxford University Press, 2012.

Holdcroft, Anita. "Gender Bias in Research: How Does It Affect Evidence Based Medicine?" *Journal of the Royal Society of Medicine* 100, no. 1 (2007): 2–3.

Holmes, Robert, and Barry Gan, *Nonviolence in Theory and Practice.* 2nd ed. Long Grove, IL: Waveland Press, 2005.

Honig, Bonnie. *Political Theory and the Displacement of Politics.* Ithaca, NY: Cornell University Press, 1993.

Horkheimer, Max. "The Latest Attack on Metaphysics." Translated by Matthew J. O'Connell. In *Critical Theory: Selected Essays*, 132–87. 1937. New York: Continuum Publishing, 2002.

Huemer, Michael. *Ethical Intuitionism.* New York: Palgrave, 2005.

The International Teaching Centre. *The Five Year Plan 2011–2016: Summary of Achievements and Learning.* Haifa, Isreal: Bahá'í World Centre, 2017.

————. *Insights from the Frontiers of Learning.* Haifa, Israel: Bahá'í World Center, 2013.

Johnson, Monte. *Aristotle on Teleology*. Oxford, UK: Oxford University Press, 2005.

Johnson, Paula A., Therese Fitzgerald, Alina Salganicoff, Susan F. Wood, and Jill M. Goldstein. "Sex-Specific Medical Research: Why Women's Health Can't Wait." Boston: Brigham and Women's Hospital, 2014.

Johnston, Lucas. *Religion and Sustainability: Social Movements and the Politics of Environment*. New York: Routledge, 2014.

Jones, E. Stanley. *Gandhi: Portrayal of a Friend*. Nashville, TN: Abingdon Press, 1948.

Kant, Immanuel. *Groundwork of the Metaphysic of Morals*. Translated by Mary Gregor and Jens Timmermann. 1785. Cambridge, UK: Cambridge University Press, 2012.

Karlberg, Michael. *Beyond the Culture of Contest: From Adversarialism to Mutualism in an Age of Interdependence*. George Ronald Bahá'í Studies Series. Oxford, UK: George Ronald, 2004.

———. "Constructive Resilience: The Bahá'í Response to Oppression." *Peace & Change* 35, no. 2 (2010): 222–57.

———. "The Paradox of Protest in a Culture of Contest." *Peace and Change* 28, no. 3 (2003): 329–51.

———. "The Power of Discourse and the Discourse of Power: Peace as Discourse Intervention." *International Journal of Peace Studies* 10, no. 1 (2005): 1–25.

Karlberg, Michael, and Bita Correa. "Development at Systematic Learning and Capacity Building." In *Education, Learning and the Transformation of Development*, edited by Amy Skinner, Matt Baillie-Smith, Eleanor Brown, and Tobias Troll, 19–35. New York: Routledge, 2016.

Kasser, Tim. *The High Price of Materialism*. Cambridge, MA: The MIT Press, 2002.

Kim, Alison M., Candace M. Tinge, and Teresa K. Woodruff. "Sex Bias in Trials and Treatment Must End." *Nature* 465, no. 7299 (2010): 688–89.

Kindon, Sara, Rachel Pain, and Mike Kesby, eds. *Participatory Action Research Approaches and Methods: Connecting People, Participation and Place*. New York: Routledge, 2007.

Klein, Naomi. *This Changes Everything: Capitalism vs. The Climate*. New York: Simon & Schuster, 2015.

Kniss, Fred, and Gene Burns. "Religious Movements." In *The*

Blackwell Companion to Social Movements, edited by David Snow, Sarah Soule, and Hanspeter Kriesi, 694–715. Oxford, UK: Blackwell Publishing, 2011.

Korsgaard, Christine. *The Sources of Normativity*. Cambridge, MA: Harvard University Press, 1996.

Kuhn, Thomas. *The Structure of Scientific Revolutions*. Chicago: University of Chicago Press, 1970.

Kurlansky, Mark. *Nonviolence: The History of a Dangerous Idea*. New York: Modern Library, 2008.

Laclau, Ernesto, and Chantal Mouffe. *Hegemony and Socialist Strategy*. London: Verso, 1983.

Lakatos, Imre. *The Methodology of Scientific Research Programmes*. Cambridge, UK: Cambridge University Press, 1978.

Lakoff, Robin. *Language and Woman's Place*. New York: Harper & Row, 1975.

Lample, Paul. "In Pursuit of Harmony between Science and Religion." *Journal of Bahá'í Studies* 26, no. 4 (2016): 23–58.

———. *Revelation and Social Reality: Learning to Translate What Is Written into Reality*. West Palm Beach, FL: Palabra Publications, 2009.

Landefeld, C. Seth. "Commercial Support and Bias in Pharmaceutical Research." *The American Journal of Medicine* 117, no. 11 (2004): 876–78.

Lange, Friedrich. *The History of Materialism and a Critique of Its Current Significance*. Translated by Ernest Chester Thomas. 1866. New York: The Humanities Press, 1950.

Lee, Frederic. *A History of Heterodox Economics: Challenging the Mainstream in the Twentieth Century*. New York: Routledge, 2009.

Leslie, Stuart W. *The Cold War and American Science: The Military-Industrial-Academic Complex at MIT and Stanford*. Rev. ed. New York: Columbia University Press, 1993.

Leunissen, Mariska. *Explanation and Teleology in Aristotle's Science of Nature*. Cambridge, UK: Cambridge University Press, 2010.

Lexchin, Joel, Lisa A. Bero, Benjamin Djulbegovic, and Otavio Clark. "Pharmaceutical Industry Sponsorship and Research Outcome and Quality: Systematic Review." *BMJ: British Medical Journal* 326, no. 7400 (2003): 1167–70.

Longino, Helen. *Science as Social Knowledge: Values and Objectivity in Scientific Inquiry*. Princeton, NJ: Princeton University Press, 1990.

Lukes, Steven, ed. *Power.* Readings in Social & Political Theory. New York: New York University Press, 1986.

Lukes, Steven. *Power: A Radical View.* 2nd ed. London: Palgrave, 2005.

MacEoin, Denis. "Baha'ism." In *The New Penguin Handbook of Living Religions,* edited by John Hinnells, 618–43. 2nd ed. New York: Penguin, 2000.

MacIntyre, Alasdair. *After Virtue: A Study in Moral Theory.* 3rd ed. Notre Dame, IN: University of Notre Dame Press, 2007.

Mackie, John. *Ethics: Inventing Right and Wrong.* London: Penguin Books, 1977.

Mantena, Karuna. "Gandhi and the Means-Ends Question in Politics." *Occasional Papers of the School of Social Science, Yale* 46 (2012).

Marglin, Stephen A. *The Dismal Science: How Thinking Like an Economist Undermines Community.* Cambridge, MA: Harvard University Press 2010.

Marsh, Charles. *The Beloved Community: How Faith Shapes Social Justice, from the Civil Rights Movement to Today.* New York: Basic Books, 2004.

Marx, Karl, and Friedrich Engels. *The German Ideology.* Edited by C. J. Arthur, translated by W. Lough, C. Dutt, and C. P. Magill. 1846. London: Lawrence & Wishart, 1967.

Mattaini, Mark. *Stategic Nonviolent Power: The Science of Satyagraha.* Edmonton, AB, Canada: Athabasca University Press, 2013.

Mendieta, Eduardo, and Jonathan VanAntwerpen, eds. *The Power of Religion in the Public Sphere.* New York: Columbia University Press, 2011.

Merton, Thomas. *Gandhi on Non-Violence.* New York: New Directions, 1964.

Miller, Jean Baker. "Colloquium: Women and Power." *Stone Center for Developmental Services and Studies Work in Progress,* no. 882–01 (1982): 1–5.

———. *Toward a New Psychology of Women.* 2nd ed. Boston: Beacon Press, 1976.

Molineaux, Pascal. "Strengthening Local Economies and Community Identity: FUNDAEC's Experience," translated by Paul Hanley. In *The Spirit of Agriculture,* edited by Paul Hanley, 169–80. Oxford, UK: George Ronald, 2005.

Monroe, Kristen. "Biology, Psychology, Ethics, and Politics: An Innate Moral Sense?" In *On Human Nature: Biology, Psychology, Ethics, Politics, and Religion*, edited by Michel Tibayrenc and Francisco J. Ayala. Cambridge, MA: Academic Press, 2017.

———. *Ethics in an Age of Terror and Genocide: Identity and Moral Choice*. Princeton, NJ: Princeton University Press, 2012.

———. *The Hand of Compassion: Portraits of Moral Choice During the Holocaust*. Princeton, NJ: Princeton University Press, 2004.

———. *The Heart of Altruism: Perceptions of a Common Humanity*. Princeton, NJ: Princeton University Press, 1998.

Monroe, Kristen Renwick, Adam Martin, and Priyanka Ghosh. "Politics and an Innate Moral Sense: Scientific Evidence for an Old Theory?" *Political Research Quarterly* 62, no. 3 (2009): 614–34.

Morgan, Kevin, and Jonathan Murdoch. "Organic vs. Conventional Agriculture: Knowledge, Power and Innovation in the Food Chain." *Geoforum* 31, no. 2 (2000): 159–73.

Moser, Paul, ed. *Contemporary Materialism: A Reader*. New York: Routledge, 1995.

Moss, Kary L., ed. *Man-Made Medicine: Women's Health, Public Policy, and Reform*. Durham, NC: Duke University Press, 1996.

Mouffe, Chantal. *Agonistics: Thinking the World Politically*. London: Verso, 2013.

———. *The Democratic Paradox*. New York: Verso, 2000.

———. *The Return of the Political*. New York: Verso, 2005.

Moulton, Janice. "A Paradigm of Philosophy: The Adversary Method." In *Discovering Reality: Feminist Perspectives on Epistemology, Metaphysics, Methodology, and Philosophy of Science*, edited by Sandra Harding and Merrill Hintikka, 149–64. Boston: Kluwer, 1983.

Nagel, Thomas. *Mind and Cosmos: Why the Materialist Neo-Darwinian Conception of Nature Is Almost Certainly False*. Oxford, UK: Oxford University Press, 2012.

———. *The View from Nowhere*. Oxford, UK: Oxford University Press, 1986.

Nongbri, Brent. *Before Religion: A History of a Modern Concept*. New Haven, CT: Yale University Press, 2012.

Nye, David E. *Technology Matters: Questions to Live With*. Cambridge, MA: The MIT Press, 2006.

O'Hanlon, Michael E. *The Science of War*. Princeton, NJ: Princeton University Press, 2009.

Oreskes, Naomi, and John Krige, eds. *Science and Technology in the Global Cold War.* Boston: The MIT Press, 2014.

Palmer, David. "Religion, Spiritual Principles, and Civil Society." In *Religion and Public Discourse in an Age of Transition: Reflections on Bahá'í Thought and Practice,* edited by Geoffrey Cameron and Benjamin Schewel, 37–69. Waterloo, ON: Wilfrid Laurier University Press, 2018.

Parel, Anthony. *Pax Gandhiana: The Political Philosophy of Mahatma Gandhi.* Oxford, UK: Oxford University Press, 2016.

Patel, Raj. *Stuffed and Starved: The Hidden Battle for the World Food System.* New York: Melville House Publishing, 2012.

Pelto, Pertti J. *The Snowmobile Revolution: Technology and Social Change in the Arctic.* Long Grove, IL: Waveland Press, 1987.

Pew Forum on Religion & Public Life. "The Global Religious Landscape: A Report on the Size and Distribution of the World's Major Religious Groups as of 2010." Washington, DC: Pew Research Center, 2012.

Philpott, Daniel. "Has the Study of Global Politics Found Religion?" *Annual Review of Political Science* 12, no. 1 (2009): 183–202.

Philpott, Daniel, and Gerard Powers, eds. *Strategies of Peace: Transforming Conflict in a Violent World.* Oxford, UK: Oxford University Press, 2010.

Piketty, Thomas. *The Economics of Inequality.* Cambridge, MA: Harvard University Press, 2015.

Plato. *Republic.* Translated by Robin Waterfield. Oxford, UK: Oxford University Press, 1993.

Poland, Jeffrey. *Physicalism: The Philosophical Foundations.* Oxford, UK: Clarendon, 1994.

Polanyi, Karl. *The Great Transformation: The Political and Economic Origins of Our Time.* 2nd ed. Boston: Beacon Press, 2001.

Popper, Karl. *The Logic of Scientific Discovery.* London: Hutchinson, 1975.

Putnam, Hilary. *The Collapse of the Fact/Value Dichotomy.* Cambridge, MA: Harvard University Press, 2002.

———. *Ethics without Ontology.* Cambridge, MA: Harvard University Press, 2004.

Queen, Christopher. *Engaged Buddhism: Buddhist Liberation Movements in Asia.* Albany, NY: State University of New York Press, 1996.

Ratti, Manav. *The Postsecular Imagination: Postcolonialism, Religion, and Literature.* New York: Taylor & Francis, 2013.

Rawls, John. *A Theory of Justice*. 2nd ed. Cambridge, MA: Harvard University Press, 1999.

Razavi, Shahriar. "Bahá'í Participation in Public Discourse: Some Considerations Related to History, Concepts, and Approaches." In *Religion and Public Discourse in an Age of Transition: Reflections on Bahá'í Thought and Practice*, edited by Geoffrey Cameron and Benjamin Schewel, 163–90. Waterloo, ON: Wilfrid Laurier University Press, 2018.

Reardon, Betty. *Women and Peace: Feminist Visions of Global Security*. New York: State University of New York Press, 1993.

Reverby, Susan M. *Examining Tuskegee: The Infamous Syphilis Study and Its Legacy*. Chapel Hill, NC: University of North Carolina Press, 2009.

Rieger, Joerg, and Kwok Pui-lan. *Occupy Religion: Theology of the Multitude*. New York: Rowman & Littlefield, 2012.

Rorty, Richard. *Consequences of Pragmatism*. Minneapolis, MN: University of Minnesota Press, 1982.

Rowbotham, Sheila. "The Women's Movement and Organizing for Socialism." In *Beyond the Fragments: Feminism and the Making of Socialism*, edited by Sheila Rowbotham, Lynne Segal, and Hilary Wainwright, 21–155. London: Merlin Press, 1979.

The Ruhi Institute. *Learning About Growth*. Cali, Colombia: The Ruhi Institute, 1991.

Salvatore, Armando. *The Public Sphere: Liberal Modernism, Catholicism, Islam*. New York: Palgrave, 2007.

Salverda, Wiemer, Brian Nolan, and Timothy M. Smeeding, eds. *The Oxford Handbook of Economic Inequality*. Oxford, UK: Oxford University Press, 2009.

Sayer, Andrew. *Why Things Matter to People: Social Science, Values and Ethical Life*. Cambridge, UK: Cambridge University Press, 2011.

Schaik, Carol P. van. "Social Learning and Culture in Animals." In *Animal Behaviour: Evolution and Mechanisms*, edited by Peter Kappeler, 623–54. Berlin: Springer, 2010.

Schewel, Benjamin. *Seven Ways of Looking at Religion: The Major Narratives*. New Haven, CT: Yale University Press, 2017.

Schmitt, Carl. *The Concept of the Political*. Translated by George Schwab. 1932. Chicago: University of Chicago Press, 2007.

Schock, Kurt. *Civil Resistance Today*. Cambridge, UK: Polity Press, 2015.

Sen, Amartya. *The Idea of Justice*. Cambridge, MA: Harvard University Press, 2009.

Seung, T. K. *Intuition and Construction: The Foundation of Normative Theory.* New Haven, CT: Yale University Press, 1993.

Shah, Timothy, Alfred Stepan, and Monica Duffy Toft, eds. *Rethinking Religion and World Affairs.* Oxford, UK: Oxford University Press, 2012.

Shahvar, Soli. *The Forgotten Schools: The Bahá'ís and Modern Education in Iran, 1899–1934.* London: Tauris Academic Studies, 2009.

Sharp, Gene. *The Politics of Nonviolent Action.* Boston: Extending Horizons Books, 1973.

———. *Waging Nonviolent Struggle: 20th Century Practice and 21st Century Potential.* Boston: Porter Sargent Publishers, 2005.

Sharp, Lauriston. "Steel Axes for Stone-Age Australians." *Human Organization* 11, no. 2 (1952): 17–22.

Shiva, Vandana. *Staying Alive: Women, Ecology, and Development.* Berkeley, CA: North Atlantic Books, 2016.

———. *The Violence of the Green Revolution: Third World Agriculture, Ecology, and Politics.* New York: Zed Books, 2000.

Shoghi Effendi. *Arohanui: Letters to New Zealand.* 1946. Fiji Islands: Bahá'í Publishing Trust of Suva, 1982.

———. Statement to the Special United Nations Committee on Palestine, 1947.

———. *The World Order of Bahá'u'lláh.* Wilmette, IL: US Bahá'í Publishing Trust, 1938.

Shrader-Frechette, Kristin, and Laura Westra, eds. *Technology and Values.* New York: Rowman & Littlefield, 1997.

Shue, Henry. *Climate Justice: Vulnerability and Protection.* Oxford, UK: Oxford University Press, 2014.

Slessarev-Jamir, Helene. *Prophetic Activism: Progressive Religious Justice Movements in Contemporary America.* New York: New York University Press, 2011.

Smith, Christian. *Disruptive Religion: The Force of Faith in Social Movement Activism.* New York: Routledge, 1996.

———. *The Emergence of Liberation Theology: Radical Religion and Social Movement Theory.* Chicago: University of Chicago Press, 1991.

———. *To Flourish or Destruct: A Personalist Theory of Human Goods, Motivations, Failure, and Evil.* Chicago: University of Chicago Press, 2015.

———. *What Is a Person?: Rethinking Humanity, Social Life, and the Moral Good from the Person Up.* Chicago: University of Chicago Press, 2010.

Smith, Merritt Roe, and Leo Marx, eds. *Does Technology Drive History?: The Dilemma of Technological Determinism.* Boston: The MIT Press, 1994.

Smith, Richard. *The Trouble with Medical Journals.* London: Royal Society of Medicine Press, 2006.

Smith, Todd. "The Relativity of Social Construction: Towards a Consultative Approach to Understanding Health, Illness, and Disease." PhD diss., University of Toronto, 1997.

Smith, Todd, and Michael Karlberg. "Articulating a Consultative Epistemology: Toward a Reconciliation of Truth and Relativism." *Journal of Bahá'í Studies* 19 no. 1 (2009): 59–99.

Snarr, Melissa. *All You That Labor: Religion and Ethics in the Living Wage Movement.* New York: New York University Press, 2011.

Sørensen, Majken Jul. "Constructive Resistance: Conceptualising and Mapping the Terrain." *Journal of Resistance Studies* 2, no. 1 (2016): 49–78.

Stiglitz, Joseph E. *The Price of Inequality: How Today's Divided Society Endangers Our Future.* New York: W. W. Norton & Company, 2013.

Stoljar, Daniel. *Physicalism.* New York: Routledge, 2010.

Stratton-Lake, Philip, ed. *Ethical Intuitionism: Re-Evaluations.* Oxford, UK: Oxford University Press, 2002.

Taylor, Charles. *A Secular Age.* Cambridge, MA: Harvard University Press, 2007.

Temple, Brian. *Philadelphia Quakers and the Antislavery Movement.* Jefferson, NC: McFarland, 2014.

Tenner, Edward. *Why Things Bite Back: Technology and the Revenge of Unintended Consequences.* New York: Vintage Books, 1996.

Turner, Bryan. *Regulating Bodies: Essays in Medical Sociology.* London: Routledge, 1992.

The Universal House of Justice. *The Institution of the Counsellors.* Haifa, Israel: Bahá'í World Centre, 2001.

———. Letter to the Bahá'í Students Deprived of Access to Higher Education in Iran, September 9, 2007.

———. Letter to the Bahá'ís of Iran, March 2, 2013.

———. Letter to the Bahá'ís of the World, January 17, 2003.

———. Letter to the Bahá'ís of the World, November 9, 2018.

———. Letter to the Believers in the Cradle of the Faith, March 21, 2011.

———. Letter to the Conference of the Continental Boards of

Counsellors, December 27, 2005.

———. Letter to an Individual Bahá'í in the United States, February 4, 2018.

———. Letter to the World's Religious Leaders, 2002.

———. Ridván Message to the Bahá'ís of the World, 1996.

———. Ridván Message to the Bahá'ís of the World, 2008.

———. Ridván Message to the Bahá'ís of the World, 2010.

Vinthagen, Stellan. *A Theory of Nonviolent Action: How Civil Resistance Works*. London: Zed Books, 2015.

Vitzthum, Richard. *Materialism: An Affirmative History and Definition*. Amherst, NY: Prometheus Books, 1995.

Warner, Michael, Jonathan VanAntwerpen, and Craig Calhoun, eds. *Varieties of Secularism in a Secular Age*. Cambridge, MA: Harvard University Press, 2010.

Warner, Rob. *Secularization and Its Discontents*. London: Continuum Books.

Wartenberg, Thomas E. *The Forms of Power: From Domination to Transformation*. Philadelphia, PA: Temple University Press, 1990.

Wasserstrom, Steven M. "Islamicate History of Religions?" *History of Religions* 27, no. 4 (1988): 405–11.

Weber, Max. "Domination by Economic Power and by Authority." In *Power*, edited by Steven Lukes, 28–36. New York: New York University Press, 1986.

Weindling, Paul. *Victims and Survivors of Nazi Human Experiments: Science and Suffering in the Holocaust*. New York: Bloomsbury Academic, 2015.

Whyte, William Foote, ed. *Participatory Action Research*. London: SAGE, 1991.

Wilson, James. *The Moral Sense*. New York: Free Press, 1993.

"Worldwide Adherents of All Religions by Six Continental Areas, Mid-2002." *Encyclopædia Britannica*, 2003. Encyclopedia Britannica Premium Service, accessed July 16, 2003, http:// www.britannica.com/eb/article?eu=420485.

Wrong, Dennis H. *Power: Its Forms, Bases, and Uses*. New Brunswick, NJ: Transaction Publishers, 1997.

Yaphea, John, Richard Edmanb, Barry Knishkowyc, and Joseph Hermand. "The Association between Funding by Commercial Interests and Study Outcome in Randomized Controlled Drug Trials." *Family Practice* 18, no. 6 (2001): 565–68.

Ziarek, Ewa Plonowska. *An Ethic of Dissensus: Postmodernity, Feminism, and the Politics of Radical Democracy.* Stanford, CA: Stanford University Press, 2001.

Zucker, Irving, and Annaliese K. Beery. "Males Still Dominate Animal Studies." *Nature 465* 465, no. 7299 (2010): 690.

Index

'Abdu'l-Bahá, IX, 82–85, 91
    on evolution, 164–65
    on latency, 102, 165
    on science, 85
    on the harmony of science and religion, 165
    on the oneness of humanity, 83
    on the soul, 165–166
    on the unity of religions, 83–84
Abizadeh, Arash, 147–48
Adorno, Theodor, 175
agency, X, 32–35, 41–42, 44–45, 47, 54, 65–66, 100–03, 145, 163, 191
    as constructing social phenomena. *See* social construction
    collective, 32, 41–42, 66, 102, 120, 177, 186
    of marginalized groups, 49
agonism, 115–116, 139, 143–47
    agonistic pluralism, 151, 212
    existential antagonism, 146
    maximalist theories of, 143–45
    minimalist theories of, 143
altruism, 47, 61–63, 126, 149–50, 170–71
antagonism, 144
Appiah, Kwame, 48
Arbab, Farzam, VII, IX, 66–68
Arendt, Hannah, 143
Aristotle, 17, 53–55, 154, 160
Association for Bahá'í Studies, 96
    conference, VII, 96
attunement, 2, 13, 18–33, 40, 42, 44–45, 62–63, 65, 75, 78, 81, 86, 115, 130, 174
    anomalous attunement, 197

fabricated attunement, 197
general attunement, 197
specified attunement, 196

Bahá'í community, IX, 5, 81–82, 86–87, 91, 96–97, 100–11, 113
    accompaniment, 99, 109–10
    assemblies, 111
    Bahá'í youth, 108
    capacity building, 92, 94, 96, 102, 110, 112
    community building, 93, 96–99
    conceptual framework, 96–97
    culture of learning, 82, 85, 91–94, 100–03, 105
    discourse on power, 86, 109, 111
    discourse on religion, 86–89, 92, 95
    experience of, IX, 12, 87, 91, 100, 113, 115–16, 150, 187, 190
    participation in public discourse, 90–91, 95, 98
    social justice efforts, 96, 100, 102, 109, 185
    training institutes, 92–94, 98–99, 107
    translation of Bahá'í teachings into reality, IX, 89, 93–94, 110
    unity in diversity, 113, 150, 173
    universal reconstruction, 113
Bahá'í Faith, IX, 81, 85, 91, 105, 107, 108
    foundational texts, IX, 82–83, 102, 105
    spiritual principles, 3, 66, 107, 203
Bahá'í International Community, 95
Bahá'í teachings, 88, 165
    on achievement of unity, 105
    on divine civilization, 172
    on environmental stewardship, 203
    on evolution, 164–65
    on gender equality, 87, 96
    on harmony of science and religion, 85, 163, 165
    on justice, 112
    on oneness of humankind, 82–84, 88, 89, 102, 150, 172, 180
    on racial equality, 87
    on religious violence, 73, 77
    on repression, 188
    on social order, 188
    on the soul, 164–66

on unity of religions, 83, 84
Bahá'í World Center, 94
    Office of Public Discourse, 95
    Office of Social and Economic Development (Bahá'í International
    Development Agency), 94
Bahá'u'lláh, IX, 82, 90, 101–02, 106, 110–11, 115, 165
    on justice, 115
    on latency, 165
    on social order, VII
    on the oneness of humanity, 90
    on unity of religions, 84
Benhabib, Seyla, 138
Bernstein, Richard, 128
Bhaskar, Roy, 154
Boggs, Carl, 185
Boulding, Kenneth, 57–58

capitalism, 51, 136, 186
Carnap, Rudolf, 130
Chalmers, Alan, 26, 30
climate change, 9, 17, 49. *See also* environment: ecological crises
colonialism, 39, 51, 56, 83, 135–36
communism, 51, 144
Connolly, William, 146
consciousness. *See* subjectivity (consciousness)
constructive programs, 185–87
constructive resilience, 188
consultative epistemology. *See* epistemology
Continental Board of Counsellors, 93
Cooke, Maeve, 140, 141, 142, 176
    socio-cultural learning, 140–43
cosmopolitanism, 148
critical theory, 136, 137, 175–76
critique
    immanent, 139
    transcendent, 139
culture of contest, VIII, 146–49, 186
cynicism, VIII, 55, 188, 190
Darwin, Charles, 161, 164

democracy, 143–45, 184–85
Descartes, René, 130–31
Dewey, John, 128, 131–32
dualism (fact/value), 128, 131–36, 154, 160, 175

economics, 2, 49, 52, 54, 149, 175
    economic determinism, 51
egoism, 63, 109, 126
Einstein, Albert, 17, 19, 23, 26, 61, 122, 125
environment, 72
    climate change. *See* climate change
    ecological crises, X, 11, 14, 139, 180
    stewardship of, 38, 72
epistemology, IX, 4, 11, 15–18, 33, 91, 130
    Bahá'í-inspired, IX
    consultative epistemology, 18, 20, 24, 28, 30, 34, 86, 107, 196–97
    epistemological foundationalism, 129
    epistemological premises, 4–6
    epistemological relativism, 4, 115, 152, 188
    epistemological tensions, VIII, 2
    horizontal epistemologies. *See* knowledge: horizontal approaches to
    social epistemology, 174
    vertical epistemologies. *See* knowledge: vertical approaches to
equality, 47, 59–60, 69, 145
    gender equity, 10, 15, 87
    inequality, 49, 135
    power equality, 59–60
    racial equality, 87
error theory, 124–125
eugenics, 50, 74–76, 118
evolution, 33, 149, 160–70, 172
    as omnidirectional, 168
    social evolution, 51–53, 161, 163, 172

falsification, 70
Feyerabend, Paul, 12
Foucault, Michel, 49, 56, 196

Frankfurt School, 136, 175
Freud, Sigmund, 175
FUNDAEC, 95
Gandhi, Mohandas, 181–88
Giddens, Anthony, 56–57
global warming. *See* climate change
Godfrey-Smith, Peter, 26, 30
Grameen Bank, 178
gravity, 16–20, 23, 117, 126, 159

Habermas, Jürgen, 48, 136–43, 156, 176
    communicative action, 137
    strategic action, 137
Hartsock, Nancy, 57
historiography, 49
Hobbes, Thomas, 56, 146
Holocaust, 16, 70, 74, 75, 77, 118
Horkheimer, Max, 175
human nature, VIII, 57, 68, 97, 171
human rights, 10, 25, 38, 91
    and children, 10
    and minorities, 10
    global discourse on, 10
    protection of, 10
    Universal Declaration of Human Rights, 38
humanities, 9, 49–52, 175
Hume, David, 132

identity politics, 143, 144, 146–50
Institute for Studies in Global Prosperity, 96, 108
interfaith movement, 86–87, 90
International Teaching Center, 93, 94
intersubjective, 39, 42–44, 133–34, 138, 156, 158, 175
intuition, X, 6, 26, 40, 42–43, 62–64, 91, 100, 103, 154–56
    intuitionism, 155
Junior Youth Spiritual Empowerment Program, 95, 109–11
justice, 6, 25, 38–42, 45, 47–50, 55, 61–66, 71, 73, 76–77, 89, 103–
    04, 110, 112, 126, 154–59, 158, 175–77, 180–81, 186, 189

Kant, Immanuel, 63
Karlberg, Michael, 4, 16–17, 19, 23, 25, 34, 60
King, Martin Luther, 188
knowledge, VII, 13, 57, 130, 139, 170
    and power, VII, VIII, 2, 44, 49–50, 59, 71, 81, 107–08, 115–17,
    178, 188
    conceptualizing, VII, 2, 50–55
    episteme, 53, 140
    epistemology. *See* epistemology
    foundational knowledge, 16
    generation of, 1–2, 5–7, 33–34, 40–42, 49–50, 55, 61, 63, 66–67,
    69, 100–05, 116, 131, 174–79, 186
    horizontal approaches to, 11–12, 14
    learning, IX, 1, 41, 54–55, 69–71, 100, 103, 106, 131, 137, 140
    locally contextualized, 178
    normative dimension of, I, 5
    of social phenomena, 9
    phronesis, 53
    prescriptive, 1
    relationship to truth, 53
    sharing economy, 61
    subjective, 53
    systems of, VIII
    techné, 53
    vertical approaches to, 11–12, 14–15
Korsgaard, Christine, 48
Kuhn, Thomas, 70–71, 196

Laclau, Ernesto, 143
Lample, Paul, IX, 38, 66, 91
latency, 34–36, 101–02, 113, 117, 165–80
learning, 42
logic, 26, 42–43, 63, 131, 134
    deductive, 26
    inductive, 26–27
logical positivism. *See* positivism
Lukes, Steven, 56

MacIntyre, Alasdair, 48

Marx, Karl, 56, 117, 175
Marxism, 66
material reality, 22
materialism, 6–7, 69, 88, 117–18, 124, 128–29, 137, 139, 158 160–63, 166–67, 169, 173, 188
Miller, Jean Baker, 57
Monroe, Kristen, 149–50
Mouffe, Chantal, 143–47, 150, 151

Nagel, Thomas, 48, 119–24, 127, 134, 150, 153, 159–63, 166, 170, 172
    view from nowhere, 119, 120
Nazism, 66, 140
neoliberalism, 54, 59
Neurath, Otto, 129–30
Newton, Isaac, 17–19, 23, 26, 45, 61, 119, 122, 125
nihilism, 2, 158, 161, 190, 191
normative, 3
    arguments, 6
    definition of, 3
    standards, 69–71, 73–74, 76, 111, 113, 135, 139–41
normative discernment, 45, 63–64, 159
normative foundationalism. See realism: normative realism
normative relativism. *See* relativity
normativity, 119, 122–24, 126, 134, 139, 159

objectivity, 119–26, 133–134, 160–61, 172, 174
    objective inquiry, 120–21, 134
ontology, 3, 130, 134–36, 153–154, 179
    ontological foundationalism, 3, 115, 129–30, 190
    ontological premises, 3–5, 27
    social ontology, 153–54, 164, 174

Palmer, David, 202–03
participatory action research, 177–79
physicalism, 115–22, 142
Plato, 134, 154, 156–58
    Platonic Forms, 154, 156–58
pluralism, 70, 144–46, 151

Popper, Karl, 70
positivism, 124, 132–33, 154, 158, 159, 175–76, 197
post-secularism, 72, 78
power, 4–5, 8–9, 14, 35, 46, 49, 54, 76, 117, 143–44, 150, 173, 175, 184
    adversarialism, 59–60, 104–05, 201
    and gender, 62–63
    as capacity, 57
    as corrupting knowledge, 49, 50, 58–59, 67, 104, 117, 189
    balance of power relations, 59–61
    conceptualizing, 55–61, 65, 67, 71, 108
    expanded analysis of, 60, 104
    generating oppressive or emancipatory structures of knowledge, 105
    mutualism, 57–63, 76, 104, 112, 186
    power against, 58
    power over, 55–56, 59–64, 76, 104–05
    power to, 57–58, 60
    power with, 58
pragmatism, 115–16, 127–36
prefiguration, 185–86
privilege, 2, 10, 41, 57, 75–77, 185
    and moral responsibility, 10
    and social construction, 5
    and survival, 10
    and technological development, 47
    as corrupting knowledge, 8–9, 35, 50, 115, 186
proceduralism, 115–16, 136, 137, 143, 155
    epistemic proceduralism, 137
progress, 137, 147, 159, 188
    collective, 137
    GDP as measure of, 51
    human capacity as measure of. See normative discernment
    materialist ideologies of, 66
    non-linearity of, 147
    problem solving as measure of, 118
    technology as measure of, 51
public policy, 51
Putnam, Hilary, 48, 128, 132–36, 153

Rawls, John, 48, 63, 155–56
realism, 3, 12, 64
  anti-realism, 12, 124, 127, 164
  critical realism, 154
  normative realism, 13, 123, 127, 137, 153–54, 176
  ontological realism, 154
reality, VIII, 6–7, 15–35, 39, 46–50, 58–73, 75, 81–84, 88, 93–94,
  97, 101–02, 105–06, 115, 118–36, 138, 141, 143, 150–51, 154–61,
  165–67, 172–74, 177–78, 181, 188
  and human cognition, 20
  enabling and constraining features, 6, 19, 20, 25, 27, 28–32, 35–
  37, 40, 67, 86, 160, 174
  independent of human cognition, 11, 36
  material reality, 28, 37–38, 41, 46, 84, 86, 104, 106, 119–20
  social reality, 1–4, 23, 26, 28, 31, 35–39, 42, 44, 46, 48–50, 53, 56,
  60, 63, 71–72, 79, 86, 93, 104, 107, 112–113, 117, 147, 158–59, 162,
  172, 174–76, 178, 185, 187, 189
  spiritual reality, 166, 180
relative attunement. See attunement
relativism, 12
relativity, 50, 102, 133
  and human rights, 15
  and truth, VIII, 1–2, 15, 19, 20, 23–26, 31–32, 30, 45, 48, 50, 102,
  180–81, 189
  normative relativism, 115, 133, 176
  relative embodiment of truth. *See* truth
religion, 65–70, 77, 79, 81, 84, 92, 116, 177
  and social movements, 77–78
  as social construct, 72, 83, 116
  fanaticism, 40, 67–68, 73, 100, 113, 118
  manipulation of spiritual truths, X, 78, 93
  normative discourse on, 71–80, 82–85, 92, 95, 120
  reconciling science with, 73
  reconciling with science, 5, 71, 73–75, 78–79, 89, 90–91, 94, 107,
  117, 172, 177–78, 188
  religious belief, VIII, 72, 76, 81, 86
  religious violence, 68, 72–73, 76, 88, 113
  sectarianism, 72, 75
  Western, 77

resilience. *See* constructive resilience
revelation, VIII, 73, 95, 101
Rorty, Richard, 11, 128
Ruhi Institute, 92, 108

Salt March (Dandi Satyagraha), 182
satyagraha, 181–84
Schewel, Benjamin, 78–79
Schmitt, Carl, 143, 146
science, 22, 27, 29, 32–35, 46, 48, 56, 58–59, 73–76, 81, 84–85, 116,
    126–28, 134–35, 158, 177
  advancement of, 26–30, 134
  and conceptual frameworks, 27, 40, 75
  applied sciences, 28, 31, 41, 77, 135
  as a social enterprise, 29–30, 41
  as social construct, 32–33
  climate science, 9
  ethics of, 70, 81
  funding of, 29–30, 70, 76, 82, 133
  history of, 27–28, 48, 71
  natural sciences, 2–7, 18, 21, 25–26, 31, 33, 40–43, 50–53, 54, 65,
    100, 103, 121, 174
  neuroscience, 170
  normative discourse on, 69–71, 74–75, 81
  philosophy of, 18, 26, 35, 124, 175
  scientific method, 27, 70, 90
  social sciences, 2, 21, 49–50, 82, 147, 153, 174–79
secularism, 118
secularization theory, 72, 78, 118
Sen, Amartya, 48
Seung, Thomas, 154–60
Sharp, Gene, 183, 188
Shoghi Effendi, 5, 82, 91
  on science, 85–86
  on the oneness of humanity, 83
slavery, 38, 43–44, 49, 135
Smith, Todd, IX, 12–14, 18–20, 195, 196, 197
social change, VIII, 1, 5, 40–44, 70, 72, 142, 153, 180–83
  activism, 181, 183, 190

movements for, 49, 52, 72, 77, 183, 186
non-adversarial approaches to, VIII, 150, 178, 186–87
ontological basis for, 3–4
participatory processes of, 5, 115
social construction, 4–5, 12, 17, 33–42, 47, 66, 72, 100, 155–56, 160, 177, 196, 197
and horizontal approaches to knowledge, 11
social constructivism, 155
social constructs, 4–5, 10, 32–40, 44–47, 53, 72, 100, 102, 115, 124, 131, 140, 159
social Darwinism, 10, 50, 74
social engineering, 5, 41
social order, VII, 145–47, 189
Bahá'í, 97, 105, 113
constructing a new, VIII, 1–4, 49, 55, 63, 70–71, 117–18, 133, 137, 146, 150, 159, 184, 185, 188–89
current, VII, X, 137, 182, 185
Western, 4–5, 61, 118, 147, 188
spiritual principles, 10, 71, 72, 97, 101, 104, 113–15, 158, 178
spiritualism, 158
standpoint theory, 21
subaltern, VIII–IX, 116
subjectivity, 117, 120–24, 126, 137
subjectivity (consciousness), 14, 79, 83, 90, 101, 117, 121–23, 127, 132, 149, 158, 161–63, 168–74, 179–80
collective consciousness, 132, 158, 172
superstition, X, 68–72, 77, 84, 85, 113

tangibility, 13–15, 32, 37
Taylor, Charles, 48, 142
technology, 10, 38–40, 44, 46, 50–52, 56–57, 67, 147, 158, 173, 188
and privilege. *See* privilege
technological determinism, 51–52
teleology, 160–68, 172, 173
terrorism, 75, 76, 88
truth, 17, 20–22, 57
analytic truths, 21
circumstantial truths. *See* truth: contingent truths
contingent truths, 21–22

foundational truths, 10, 20–23, 28, 30–31, 36, 40, 58, 71, 93, 106, 130, See also truth: normative truths
independent of human cognition, 38
material truths, 31, 40, 45, 49–50, 58, 69, 71, 73, 86, 91
normative truths, 6–12, 14–15, 20, 28, 31, 34–59, 68–69, 71, 73, 77, 79, 82, 86, 91, 97, 104, 106–07, 116–17, 125–28, 132, 135–38, 140–44, 150, 153–59, 172, 174–79, 181, 188–89
ontological truths, 4, 17, 129–30, 159
relative embodiment of, 39–40, 39, 41–52, 58, 68, 71, 79, 82, 86, 91, 97, 104, 106, 132, 159, 172, 174–75, 181
relative embodiment of truth in social constructs, 39
synthetic truths, 197
transcendent truths. See truth: normative truths
truth claim, 4, 17–26, 27–28, 32–33, 52–55, 63, 68, 71, 76, 84, 89, 125, 129, 130–33
assessing truth claims about a complex multifaceted phenomenon, 22
empirical, 124
epistemological, 17, 130
normative, 8, 15, 20, 138
relationship to truth, 23–26, 27–28
relatively attuned, 22
Tuskegee Study, 74

United Nations, 87, 95, 100, 178
United Nations Development Programme (UNDP), 178
United Nations Educational, Scientific and Cultural Organization (UNESCO), 178
Universal House of Justice, IX, 82, 87, 91–94, 106, 112, 172
on cooperation, 106
on power, 106
on the oneness of humankind, 107
utilitarianism. See pragmatism

value realism. See realism: normative realism
virtue, 29, 62, 73, 157–59, 163, 180

Wartenberg, Thomas, 55
Weber, Max, 56

wisdom, 53
World War II, 51

Yunus, Muhammad, 178

CPSIA information can be obtained
at www.ICGtesting.com
Printed in the USA
LVHW050253100523
746528LV00001B/34

9 7809